THE
STORY
OF

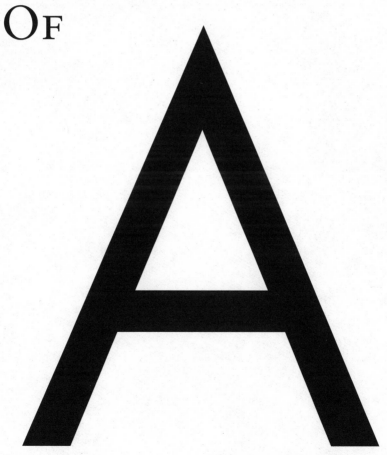

A B C D E
F G H I J K
L M N O P
Q R S T U
V W X Y Z

THE STORY OF

A

The Alphabetization of America
from *The New England Primer*
to *The Scarlet Letter*

PATRICIA CRAIN

STANFORD UNIVERSITY PRESS
STANFORD, CALIFORNIA

Stanford University Press
Stanford, California

© 2000 by the Board of Trustees of the
Leland Stanford Junior University

Printed in the United States of America

Library of Congress Cataloging-in-Publication Data

Crain, Patricia.
    The story of A : the alphabetization of America from
    The New England primer to The scarlet letter / Patricia Crain.
        p.   cm.
    Based on the author's thesis (Ph.D.)—Columbia University.
    Includes bibliographical references (p.) and index.
    ISBN 0-8047-3174-8 (cloth: alk. paper)
    ISBN 0-8047-3175-6 (pbk.: alk. paper)
    1. English language—Alphabet—Study and teaching—
United States.   2. Hawthorne, Nathaniel, 1804–1864.
Scarlet letter.   3. Alphabetizing—United States—History.
4. Literacy—United States—History.   5. Language arts—
United States.   6. United States—Civilization.
7. New England primer.   I. Title.

PE2818 .C73   2000
302.2'244'0973—dc21   00-055705

Original printing 2000
Last figure below indicates the year of this printing:
09   08   07   06   05   04   03   02

Designed by James P. Brommer
Typeset in 9.5/14.5 Sabon and Futura

In Memoriam

Margaret Mary O'Malley
Mary Cooper Robb

ACKNOWLEDGMENTS

I am deeply grateful to the many people who sustained, advised, and challenged me while I wrote this book. First, to my teachers at Columbia University, where I began this project. Andrew Delbanco must accept the blame for getting me into this racket to begin with and for being my ideal of a dissertation advisor. Ann Douglas's brilliance as a reader of nineteenth-century culture is a continuing revelation, and her support of this project has been a boon. Dorothea von Mücke generously combines the intellectual virtues of rigor and theoretical innovation with sisterly warmth and kindness. At my dissertation defense, Robert Ferguson and Ellen Condeliffe Lageman offered attentive and careful readings. Jonathan Arac has been a model teacher and kind counselor from the very beginning of this project.

For specific interventions, bibliographic assists, and an assortment of other kindnesses, I thank Peter Balaam, Daniel Cohen, Allison Giffen, David Mazella, Steven Nissenbaum, Robert O'Meally, Thea Potakis, Emily Sloat Shaw, Wings White, Ron Zboray, and The Reading Group, especially Judy Cohn and Carola Marte. I am grateful to Jennifer Monaghan, who very generously critiqued the first two chapters. I wish to thank Ruth M. Meyler for kind permission to use her photograph of the misericord in Beverly Minister. Matthew Fink, Pat Skantze, and Pamela Wilkinson all supplied crucial encouragement and criticism, and indispensable camaraderie, when I was first imagining this book. I am grateful to Lisa Gitelman for her brilliant readings of media and to Patrick Horrigan for his innovative writing, and to both for their warm interest in this project. I thank my colleagues at Princeton for their interest in this book—most especially Martin Harries for treating me to wonderful alphabetic references, and all the participants in the English Department's Works-in-Progress series, to whom I presented a version of Chapter 4. I am very grateful for the sustaining friendship and critical intelligence of Laura Agustín, Michael Kaufmann, Lucy Rinehart, and Maria Russo, who have all been with me from first to last, reading pages, staring at images, advising and collaborating. For her friendship, her scholarship, and her generosity, I wish especially to thank Carol McGuirk. Years before I imagined this book, my niece Jessie Crain and I tried out all the "posturemaster" positions; I am grateful to her and to the rest of my family —John Crain, K. C. Crain III, Jane Larkin, Charles Crain, as well as Sophie and Hildy Johnson, for their warm support.

I wish to acknowledge with gratitude the institutions that gave me financial and research support: the American Antiquarian Society, the American Society for Eighteenth-Century Studies, Columbia University, the Library Company of Philadelphia, Princeton University, the Mellon Foundation, the Spencer Foundation, and the Mrs. Giles Whiting Foundation. I thank Princeton University's Committee for Research in the Humanities for funding some of my research and most of the images reproduced in this book. Like so many other Americanists, I feel an especially deep debt to everyone on the staff of the American Antiquarian Society, and wish especially to acknowledge Georgia Barnhill, Joanne Chaisson, Alan Degutis, John Hench, Tom Knowles, Marie Lamoureux, Caroline Sloat, Caroline Stoffel, and Laura Wasowisz. Connie King at the Philadelphia Free Library has been an ongoing help and I thank her for many references and for introducing me to the great cache of the Rosenbach Collection. The book was finished at the Newberry Library, where I held a Spencer Foundation Fellowship in the History of Education, and I owe a great debt to the staff there, especially Paul Gehl, and to all of my colleagues from the splendid 1998–1999 fellowship year.

I am grateful to my readers at Stanford University Press, Robert Gross, Paul Gutjahr, and Karen Sanchez-Eppler; to my editor, Helen Tartar, for her enthusiasm, her patience, and her support; and to the editorial team of Nathan MacBrien, Kate Warne, and Anne Canright for their calm expertise.

CONTENTS

FIGURES

"You think me foolish to call instruction a torment, but if you had been as much used as myself to hear poor little children first learning their letters and then learning to spell, if you had ever seen how stupid they can be for a whole morning together, and how tired my poor mother is at the end of it, as I am in the habit of seeing almost every day of my life at home, you would allow that to torment *and to* instruct *might sometimes be used as synonimous words."*

"Very probably. But historians are not accountable for the difficulty of learning to read; and even you yourself, who do not altogether seem particularly friendly to very severe, very intense application, may perhaps be brought to acknowledge that it is very well worth while to be tormented for two or three years of one's life, for the sake of being able to read all the rest of it. Consider—if reading had not been taught, Mrs. Radcliffe would have written in vain—or perhaps might not have written at all."

—Jane Austen, Northanger Abbey

Le plus grand chef-d'oeuvre de la literature n'est jamais qu'un alphabet en désordre.

    —Jean Cocteau

By the meaningless sign linked to the meaningless sound we have built the shape and meaning of western man.

    —Marshall McLuhan

The aspects of things that are most important to us are hidden because of their simplicity and familiarity.

    —Ludwig Wittgenstein

PROLOGUE

n an allegory of humanist learning in Gregorius
Reisch's *Margarita Philosophica* (1504), the learned
Nicostrata holds out the hornbook, emblazoned with
the letters of the alphabet, in her right hand; in her left,
she holds the key to the tower of learning (Fig. 1). By these means, the
young scholar begins his initiation into a system of learning; he will then
progress through the trivium and quadrivium, finally achieving the scholastic heights of theology. Until he knows the alphabet the child is on the
outside of the tower. While the hornbook is his key to entry, it is only a
key: rhetoric and logic constitute the young scholar's real work.

By the nineteenth century in the United States, the ascent to knowledge has been newly imagined (Fig. 2). In a playful but telling picture
from a children's alphabet book, the architectural space of the tower,
associated with closeted study and scholarly community, has become
a staircase in the open air, rather like a monument in a public plaza.

Figure 1 Grammatica. *Margarita Philosophica* by Gregorius Reisch (1504).
(Courtesy of the Newberry Library, Chicago)

The Story of [A]

Elevated to the pinnacle, the woman has been transformed into Fame, bearing, as her only marks of learning, some lingering traces of Minerva. Leading up to her and the laurels she holds out are steps of gold, marked with the letters of the alphabet. Her spectators appear to be a family, small and seemingly awestruck—or starstruck—not so much, perhaps, by the task of climbing those steep steps up to A as by the reward that awaits them there.

These two images emphatically illustrate a shift in the status of alphabetic learning, from a preliminary and initiatory position in rhetorical culture to an elaborated and elevated one during the founding decades of the alphabetized culture of the United States. In the emblem of Grammatica, the alphabet represents a first step in a highly organized and institution-

Figure 2 The Alphabet Ladder. From *The Alphabet Ladder, or Gift for the Nursery* (New York: Solomon King, c. 1823). (Courtesy of the American Antiquarian Society)

alized system of knowledge, sponsored by Christianity.[1] *The Alphabet Ladder*'s letters, by contrast, while seeming to bypass the learning of anything in particular, constitute *all* the steps to the acquisition of celebrity. If the first image limns the shape of humanist learning, the second describes pedagogy's place in the formation of mass culture.

This book is about the alphabetization of American culture. By alphabetization I mean the array of individual, social, and institutional practices surrounding the internalization of the alphabet, the first step in literacy training. Important conversations in colonial through antebellum American studies during the last decade reveal a historical competition among three communications technologies—rhetoric, manuscript, and print. These categories are often deployed as descriptors of specific and distinct "cultures." The traditional notion of print's hegemony has been challenged by findings of the persistence and centrality of oral practices (Cmiel, Fliegelman, Looby) and of manuscript circulation (Hedrick, Shields). Print has been newly positioned as a cultural formation, like others, rather than as an unchanging determinant of culture (Warner). Reading and literacy are conceived not only as complex social practices (Gilmore, Hall) but also as significant economic ones (Zboray). This book joins in these revisions by turning to the site of the alphabetic text. This location is central not only as an intersection for the entire array of communications technologies. Of equal importance is the alphabet's intimate relationship with childhood and children. The alphabet is the technology with which American culture has long spoken to its children and within which it has symbolically represented and formed them.

I take as my starting point the transformation in the organization and transmission of knowledge during the period spanning the colonial to antebellum years in America from primarily rhetorical to primarily print or alphabetic modes. Some current comparatist work has focused on the general collapse of rhetoric around 1800.[2] What has been lacking is attention to what replaced it. Emerging from the materials of, at first, Reformation, then Enlightenment, and finally Romantic pedagogy, alphabetization, fueled by an explosive print marketplace, creates the readers, writers, and consumers of print. Beginning with Petrus Ramus in the sixteenth century, reformers progressively stripped rhetoric down from its traditional five parts to four, three, and sometimes two. It might be argued that once rhetoric ceded the memory art, its demise was guaranteed, for it had lost its purchase on interiority. By the beginning of the nineteenth century, alphabetization supplants rhetorical training, not only as a mode of communication but as a primary structuring of subjectivity.[3] Rhetoric generates our entire critical vocabulary, and this has perhaps blinded us to the force of alphabetization, which has consequently seemed transparent, as though we had internalized the propaganda of the nursery: "As easy as ABC."

Pedagogy has often been treated as an informative "context" or "background" to literary studies, if sometimes with transforming results.[4] But such context or background describes materials of culture as somehow separate from writers writing and readers reading, and as being imported into literary texts or reflected by them. This book regards the materials of literacy, historically considered, as having a central and essential, not a neighboring or antiquarian, place in literary studies. As an object of study, the artifact of the alphabet offers access to a broad range of cultural formations, including the contours of ideology, as they have developed over time. As a social practice, alphabetization is not separate from literary texts, nor is it only a recurrent theme or motif (though it is this too); rather, alphabetization in the modern period establishes the very possibilities of authorship and readership, permeating the formation of both persons and texts. The project of understanding alphabetic learning reveals the shape, the motives, and the functions of postrhetorical literature, especially the literature of alphabetization in the United States.

Print and widespread literacy produce new genres of literature, both high and low. "Of all the major genres only the novel is younger than writing and the book," writes Mikhail Bakhtin, and the novel "alone is organically receptive to new forms of mute perception, that is, to reading" (*Dialogic*, 3). The pages that follow focus not only on the novel but also on the "low" genres that transmit the "new forms of mute perception" through representations of the alphabet between 1650 and 1850 in America. The two texts with which I begin and end the book speak to each other across genres and decades. *The New England Primer*, originating in the culture of anonymous primers and meant to be a transparent tool for both literacy and piety, survives for 150 years as the essential literacy manual of Anglo-America. This primer and its successors contribute to the formation of a literacy on which *The Scarlet Letter* must rely and with which its very composition grapples. *The Scarlet Letter* too is a primer of sorts, initiating into advanced literacy generations of American children and adolescents.

My object of study is a particular cultural artifact, the alphabet, and my focus is mainly on one kind of alphabet: the letters as they are transmitted through elementary reading instruction texts and practices. These representations of the alphabet have particular textual, tropic, and cultural characteristics. They are made in a certain way; that is, they have a poetics. These poetics reveal discursive patterns that allow us to eavesdrop, so to speak, on the conversation American culture has with itself about literacy in its formative decades, and that reveal the cultural origins of strongly held beliefs about the value of reading and books.

The term *alphabetization* derives from the romance-language verb— to alphabetize, to be alphabetized—for the getting and giving of literacy. English lacks an equivalent term. I find it useful in a number of ways: it allows us to think of literacy as an action—derived from a transitive verb—rather than a state or quality. It also goes a small way toward defamiliarizing literacy and keeping in the forefront the importance of the alphabet to the kind of literacy I mean. *Alphabetization* has become current in scholarship to describe the spread of print and literacy acquisition between the sixteenth and nineteenth centuries in Europe.[5] I sometimes use the word with an additional, more local inflection, referring specifically to the individual's process of becoming literate. I mean, then, by alphabetization, the constellation of activities and practices—often amounting to rites and rituals, both individual and institutional—that surrounds the learning and teaching of the alphabet. Alphabetization is the process of internalizing the technology of the alphabet; it is what is required of individuals and, collectively, societies, in order to become literate. It, like the alphabet, has a history, and while the stated goals of literacy programs may look similar over time, alphabetization is a historically specific phenomenon.

I am examining an artifact that has properly been claimed by an array of disciplines: anthropology, art history, communications, education, graphic arts, history, linguistics, literacy studies, literature, media studies, rhetoric, semiotics, typography. At one point or another, I draw on scholarship from most of these fields to help me to examine the alphabet. If what follows seems to be more about images than about text, that is because learning to read means first and foremost learning how to look. In addition, the alphabet easily slips out of focus as an object of study. The alphabet functions best when it dissolves, disappearing into text; only then does it become fully legible. But I've had to keep an eye on it, and so I've brought it back continually into a realm where its operations are visible. As an object of representation, the alphabet is an androgyne, moving back and forth between text and image. Images often convey material that strongly contrasts with the verbal messages of the text, and I read them as ways in which the culture pictures to itself the complexities of its formation of literacy.

The alphabet, of course, has an ancient history, but its function changes dramatically when it is deployed in America in the complex project of widespread literacy. In the first three chapters of this book, I analyze the ways in which the alphabet is represented to beginners, through primers and ABC books, in colonial through antebellum America. The texts I discuss are long lived: *The New England Primer* is in use for the entire period, and alphabet texts first published in 1750 reappear in new guises in 1850. The remaining chapters pursue the alphabet into the realm of the novel at the beginning of an era that F. O. Matthiessen called the "American Renaissance." Here the alphabet goes undercover, only to emerge as a figure newly embedded in and underwriting the very conditions of narrative.

This book charts the development of alphabetization in America as a crucial location of acculturation, socialization, and ideology. Chapter 1 considers three examples of ABCs printed to train newcomers in the "art of reading," a discipline that between 1650 and 1800 increasingly permeates American life. Here I introduce ways of thinking about the alphabet, first as a genre of text, with a historical development, and second in relation to the visual and verbal tropes with which the alphabet becomes associated. This chapter describes the alphabet's linkage to belief systems that attempt to infuse meaningless letters, arbitrarily arrayed in time-honored sequence, with significance. The juxtapositions and the rituals that orthodoxies provide in conjunction with the alphabet create the generic conventions of the alphabetic text and its associated images. Three examples of the early modern alphabet—the Christ's Cross Row, Comenius's *Orbis Pictus* alphabet, and the image-alphabet of *The New England Primer*—chart the alphabet's gradual change of venue from church to marketplace.

Chapter 2 maps out a historical territory encompassed by "The Republic of ABC," the lowly counterpart to the high-culture discourse of the Enlightenment's Republic of Letters. Children are newly prized in the late eighteenth and early nineteenth centuries, but in a paradoxical way. While as the "rising generation" they are repositories of hopes for the future, they also conserve festive behaviors that deviate from adult middle-class propriety, and as such are vehicles for cultural memory. If these positions seem incommensurable, they nonetheless meld in the canny marketing strategies of printers addressing the new child reader. The eighteenth century sees an explosion of the market for ABC books, chapbooks, and reading primers. The pedagogical alphabet as a genre accrues to it increasingly complex elements of textuality. At the same time, the alphabetic image becomes antic and expressive. The ABC book has never received literary consideration (or much in the way of bibliographical consideration, for that matter). To provide tools for assessing this material, I offer a morphology of the alphabetic text, grounded in the alphabet's inherent functions. Manipulated by the compilers of primers and ABC books, these alphabetic functions are the foundation of the innovations in alphabetic images and texts of the eighteenth and nineteenth centuries. These new—now long-familiar— expressions articulate both elementary literacy's new status and the ways in which alphabetization in a market-driven culture indelibly links acts of reading to acts of acquisition, conjoining subjectivity and consumption.

A primer rhyme from the 1840s asks, "Without my book, what should I do?" This is the anthem of the early nineteenth century, for by this time literacy had become a constituent part of middle-class subjectivity. Chapter 3 investigates the emergence of women as the primary medium by which the alphabet is transmitted. Through readings of several pedagogical texts I show how mothers are meant to counter the atomizing potential of alphabetization by asserting a connection between the alphabet, things in the world, and the mother's voice—and ultimately the mother's body. Domestic ideology's sentimental alphabetization refers every word to mother and home, imagining the scene of instruction tangled up in mother's skirts. If earlier forms of alphabetization were shaped by a combination of the state, the public sphere, and the commercial space of the print shop, the new alphabetization of the nineteenth century is formed by emergent spaces and ideals: domesticity, the home, maternal femininity, the schoolroom. Particular kinds of narrative, as well as gendered fictive plots, result from this structure of alphabetization. While the discourse of femininity accommodates itself to and contributes to the new, intensely internalizing models of literacy, a resistant masculine plot arises as well.

In Chapters 4 and 5 I turn to rival novels of 1850, *The Scarlet Letter* and *The Wide, Wide World*. At the center of each, the relationship of a girl and her mother is forged in the heat of alphabetization. What draws readers to these texts, then as now, is their mobilization of particular modes of and expectations for the reading experience, which are manifest in the very shape of their narratives, not only at the level of the plot but at the level of the sentence as well. One novel has endured, and the other, long in eclipse, has been recently revived: *The Wide, Wide World* has become legible again as new demands are made on reading and readers in a transforming media environment. As a genre, the novel of alphabetization sends the alphabet out into the wide world, with feeling. The realism of the novel amplifies the mission and the method of the reading primer by assuring its consumer that reading is itself a way of being in the world—indeed, that it is *the* way of being in the world.

In Susan Warner's *The Wide, Wide World*, which I consider in Chapter 4, a narrative of alphabetic realism constitutes well over half of the text, though the novel is remembered as the story of Ellen Montgomery's spiritual journey. The tension between these two discursive practices—in which narrative elaborates, describes, and rolls outward on the one hand, and focuses heatedly on the interior alphabetization of a little girl on the other—captures the shape of midcentury literacy.

In the closing chapter, I turn to the most frequently taught American novel, *The Scarlet Letter*. What are the conditions of possibility for a novel whose central character is the first letter of the alphabet? What alphabet is Hawthorne reading—or for that matter, writing with—in *The Scarlet Letter*? Hawthorne finds in the alphabet an artifact that resonates with his sense of how people move through and are shaped by what he calls "the world's artificial system." He feels the alphabet, like a mote in the eye that can't be removed; somewhat painfully it both shapes and distorts perception. His scarlet letter's résumé might look like this: it unfolds to reveal a narrative; it takes on human form; it has a rich Puritan as well as an Elizabethan heritage; it is created by a woman's art, but is a disciplining tool of the bureaucracy; it can be found in nature; it can represent many things to many people, but it is also an object of representation; it ranges freely between the satanic and the sacred; it is intimately involved in forming children. *The Scarlet Letter*'s allegory of alphabetization plays itself out through this red letter, whose behavior so carefully replicates that of the pedagogical alphabet. In *The Scarlet Letter*, Hawthorne reimagines and reconfigures his own early literacy, and identifies his own authorship with the public disciplines of prison and scaffold. Hawthorne's easy relation with the institutions of publishing and of pedagogy over a century and a half are due, I argue, to his capturing and contributing to the structure of alphabetization that has long maintained in American culture.

In the Epilogue, I reflect on current alphabetic representations, bringing the conversation up to the present with speculations about the status of letters in postmodernity. Three instances—a painting that incorporates a letter, the operation of letter grades in schools, and the animated letters of *Sesame Street*—manifest a profound transformation in the relation of the alphabet to the human that current literacy debates have yet fully to take account of. Alphabets and alphabetization are deeply implicated not only in our relation to language but also in our relation to children and in our discourses about children and childhood. During modernity the history of the child and the history of the alphabet have proceeded hand in hand; to attend to one is to uncover news about the other. To be attuned to the ways in which we think and write the alphabet is to witness the small change of cultural capital at work.

When they are in their original order they are inert. Scatter them,
sow them, let them multiply, distribute them in different combinations,
and they will become alive, active and aggressive. If you do not
believe me, consider the mutual slaughter wrought on each other
to this day by men of letters.

> —*Erasmus*

Chapter One

Alphabetical Order:

The Genre of the Alphabet from

the Christ-Cross Row

to *The New England Primer*

"I n Adam's fall / We sinned all." The opening lines of *The New England Primer*'s image-and-rhyme alphabet associate first man, first sin, and first letter of the alphabet (Figs. 3–5). The doctrine of Original Sin has rarely been so vividly or poignantly expressed. Belated readers of *The New England Primer* have long used this rhyme as a touchstone for thinking about Puritan New England: in fallen language, the benighted child of Puritanism is implicated in the fall of man. But theology is only part of the mise-en-scène that renders these words legible to us or to their original readers, and doctrine alone cannot explain the book's success. *The New England Primer* is the central elementary reading book for several generations of Anglo-Americans. Historians have estimated that as many as six million copies were printed between the end of the seventeenth century and the mid–nineteenth century.[1] To put these figures in perspective, one might recall that the population of the

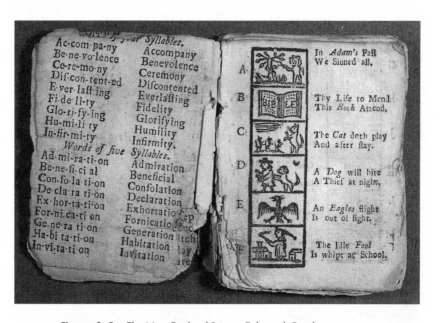

Figures 3–5 *The New England Primer, Enlarged. For the more easy attaining the true reading of English. To which is added, the Assembly of Divines Catechism. Figure 3 (above), A through F; Figure 4 (top, right), G through S; Figure 5 (bottom, right), T through Z.* These images are from one of two extant *New England Primers* from 1727, the earliest editions so far recovered. While millions were printed between 1690 and 1850, only a few hundred have been found. This alphabet combines emblematic, biblical, and commercial imagery, which were not in the seventeenth century entirely distinguished from one another. (Courtesy of the American Antiquarian Society)

United States did not break three million until 1800. One of the longest-lived and most successful literacy manuals in history, *The New England Primer* inaugurates American alphabetization.

The New England Primer's "In Adam's fall" contrasts strikingly with later secular conventions for alphabetization. The familiar alpha-

G — As runs the *Glafs*,
Mans life doth pafs.

H — My *Book* and *Heart*
Shall never part.

J — *Job* feels the Rod
Yet bleffes GOD.

K — Our *KING* the
good
No man of blood.

L — The *Lion* bold
The *Lamb* doth hold.

M — The *Moon* gives light
In time of night.

N — *Nightingales* fing
In Time of Spring.

O — The *Royal Oak*
it was the Tree
That fav'd His
Royal Majeftie.

P — *Peter* denies
His Lord and cries.

Q — Queen *Efther* comes
in Royal State
To Save the JEWS
from difmal Fate.

R — *Rachel* doth mourn
For her firft born.

S — *Samuel* anoints
Whom God appoints.

T — *Time* cuts down all
Both great and fmall.

U — *Uriah's* beauteous Wife
Made *David* feek his
Life.

W — *Whales* in the Sea
God's Voice obey.

X — *Xerxes* the great did
die,
And fo muft you & I.

Y — *Youth* forward flips,
Death fooneft nips.

Z — *Zacheus* he
Did climb the Tree
His Lord to fee.

Now the Child being entred in his
Letters and Spelling, let him
learn thefe and fuch like Sentences by Heart, whereby he will
be both inftructed in his Duty,
and encouraged in his Learning.

The Dutiful Child's Promifes.

I Will fear GOD, and honour the KING.
I will honour my Father & Mother.
I will Obey my Superiours.
I will Submit to my Elders.
I will Love my Friends.
I will hate no Man.
I will forgive my Enemies, and pray to
God for them.
I will as much as in me lies keep all God's
Holy Commandments.

bet catchphrase "A is for apple," for example, seems almost to proclaim ideological neutrality. Meaning is nonetheless embedded within it, not only in the resonant "apple," but in the very structure of the alphabetic statement.[2] What the *Primer*'s image-rhyme combination and the synecdoche of its heir's secular version have in common is a purposeful turn away from the alphabet's inherent meaninglessness. The verbal and visual tropes that surround the alphabet cloak the fact that the unit of textual meaning—the letter—lacks meaning itself. The alphabet's semantic vacuum represents a threat to orthodoxy, for into this space competing meaning systems may rush. Orthodoxies defend themselves by effacing the alphabet's meaninglessness in a variety of ways. Alphabetic characters in pedagogical alphabets are arrayed in certain configurations, in conjunction with other signs, with images, and with texts. These accessories give the meaning-free alphabet a mask of sense. The features of the alphabet's mask change over time, drawn as they are from a cultural moment's fund of meaningfulness. Where a culture goes to make sense of itself is where the alphabet too scavenges. While one might be used to thinking in an archeological fashion about excavating layers of meaning, the student of the alphabetic text digs down only to reveal a null. It is the content of those layers that yields interest.

The alphabet is a technology that, in the early modern period, is transmitted through a genre of text. And although the generic conventions of the alphabetic text arise in response to historically specific cultural demands, these responses outlive the moment that engendered them. Genre is a repository of "undying elements of the *archaic*"; although a genre "lives in the present . . . it always *remembers* the past, its beginnings" (Bakhtin, *Problems*, 106). The elements of the archaic embedded in the alphabetic text contribute both to the genre of the alphabet and to the very experience of alphabetization.

Icon and Ritual in the Crossrow:
The Way of the Alphabet

Texts that teach the alphabet cross national and linguistic boundaries and span generations. Primers were first used in the fourteenth century as guides to daily prayer and church services; by the sixteenth century they regularly included the alphabet, becoming all-purpose first books. Only gradually did children become the primer's explicit audience, and only gradually did reading instruction per se overtake prayer as the primer's central purpose.[3] The hornbook originated in the fifteenth century and, with scant change, remained in use into the nineteenth. Similarly, the first picture book for children, Comenius's *Orbis Sensualium Pictus* (1658), was, more than a century after its European debut, praised by Goethe and read by Wordsworth;[4] the Comenian alphabet filled the opening pages of primers published in Philadelphia in the early nineteenth century. In early America, *The New England Primer* taught some five generations of Anglo-Americans how to read.

The alphabet traditionally was first presented to the student in other media and material than, strictly speaking, books. Erasmus suggests baking letter-shaped cookies and carving letters of ivory (*De recta*, 400, 597–598).[5] Like the later inventions of alphabet blocks in the nursery and alphabet posters in the schoolroom, these devices communicate the strictly graphic aspect of letters, in isolation from any phonetic or semantic association. This external or material alphabet functions as a sensual—visual and tactile—cue to the oral performance of recognizing and naming the individual letters. From the Renaissance until well into the nineteenth century, the primary tool for inspiring this alphabetical ritual was the hornbook or battledore—a small paddle, usually made of wood, sometimes backed with leather, inscribed with an alphabet and, usually, numerals and the Lord's Prayer, then covered with a transpar-

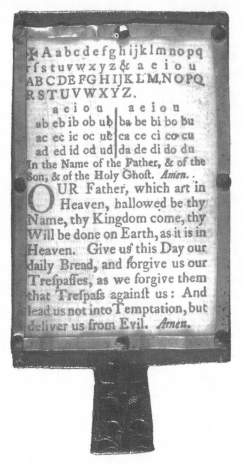

Figure 6 A characteristic hornbook. This example is backed in leather. (Courtesy of the Newberry Library, Chicago)

ent piece of flattened ox-horn (Fig. 6).[6] Hornbooks were peculiarly personal and often formed part of a child's wardrobe, being attached by a string or thong to a belt. The hornbook's physical intimacy both mirrors and promotes the child's internalization of the alphabet.

In its early print manifestations, the pedagogical alphabet is headed not by the letter A but by the "Christ's Cross": (Fig. 7).[7] From at least the fifteenth until well into the nineteenth century, the alphabet's English nickname was the "Christ-Cross Row," shortened to "criss-cross row" and "crossrow."[8] Because the alphabet is associated with Catholic iconography, as if the two sets of signs were really part of one semiological system, one of the struggles of the Reformation would be to wrest the alphabet away from the Church.

Today, ✠ represents the imprimatur of the Catholic Church on copyright pages. In its connection to the early modern alphabet as well, this cross carries an imprimatur or licensing effect; this "let it be printed," however, is directed not to the artisan printer but to the mind and memory of the young scholar. In essence, ✠ combines "let it be

Figure 7 The Christ-cross row, or criss-cross row, or crossrow. Note the pattée cross, which serves to open the alphabet and to punctuate the text. (From Tuer, facing 182)

printed" with "let it be imprinted on the memory." The cross is meant to function like Aristotle's signet ring, both impressing itself on the memory and marking out a "place" in a memory system in which to store the items that are ranged with it.[9] Like modern copyright, the cross authorizes the existence of the alphabet and associates the letters with sacred authorship, especially since another long-lived function of ✠ in liturgical missals is to mark gospel passages. This symbol both conveys information and generates ritual behavior. Catholic folklore has it that the gesture cued by this cross, in which, with the index finger crossed behind the thumb, one etches small crosses in succession on the forehead, the lips, and the breast, is accompanied by the silent

Figure 8 The alphabet in the form of the Latin cross. (From Tuer, 54; courtesy of the Newberry Library, Chicago)

mnemonic "in my mind, on my lips, in my heart." This ancient formula appears as well in early reading primers.[10] These gestures, both physical and mental, associated with benediction and with the name of God, are transferred to the alphabet.[11] As Anne Ferry puts it, "*Crossrow* denoted a row of signs named especially for its nonalphabetic mark, which corresponded to a physical ritual [making the sign of the cross] signifying an invisible grace" (19).[12] Ferry underscores the alphabet's link to the supernatural and the occult, but the cross also secures the alphabet's place in institutional power, helping to embody its regimes in the child through repetitive physical gestures.[13]

In an even more emphatic representation, the alphabet appears, according to Andrew Tuer (54), in the form of a Latin cross (Fig. 8). In this calligram, a magico-religious border corrals the letters, binding them to the most sacred icon of the Church. As a consequence of this pedagogical crusade, the alphabet is made to seem as natural or familiar as the cross, yet at the same time the cross tends to inhibit or even prohibit the use of the alphabet outside the sacred realm, of which the cross is the boundary marker. This cross thus becomes a kind of plus sign, appending the alphabet like a string of colonies to the empire of Catholic icons.

The pedagogy of the crossrow draws upon the Church's institutional roles as a visual memory theater and as a site of oral rituals. First, the full alphabet functions in these examples as a monolithic visual image, preceding the sense of the alphabet as a series of discrete graphic or phonic elements. One is reluctant to break the Latin cross alphabet into elements, lest one sacrifice in the process the wholeness of this holy icon.[14] But the crossrow manifests the alphabet-as-image as well; preceding the alphabet, ✠ signals, by association, a distinctly nonelemental, nonlinear, holistic reading.[15] The hornbook's alphabet is often accompanied by the Lord's Prayer and the sign of the cross ("In the name of the father," etc.), prayers that, like nursery rhyme, are impermeable to reading, with reading's linearity and duration. The fact is that they don't *have* to be read: they are known without reading. Like the response portions of the liturgy, these are utterances first, and only secondarily are they what we think of as texts. Even the recitation of the letters is scant preparation for reading, since these sounds are in most cases not the same as the phonic value of the letters. In the oral realm in which prayer originates, the visual and the aural share the kind of all-at-once-ness that elementary reading instruction partakes of. But while oral prayers and visual icons carry specific meanings that one might be able to articulate, this is not true of the alphabet-as-a-whole, which seems to represent an abstract "Literacy." Literacy in operation requires that the alphabet be broken into elements and recombined to make sense: B, Ba, Bat. But this alphabet-all-at-once, accompanied by prayers already gotten by heart, exemplifies alphabetization: aurally or visually, the alphabet and the prayers are taken in, internalized.

Pedagogically, these Catholic alphabets diverge from the classical models on which so much else in the scholastic tradition depends. The classical alphabet is elemental. In Greek, *stoicheia*, and in Latin, *elementi*, *literae*, or *litteratura* convey a sense of discrete, if powerful, units.[16] By contrast, the Catholic alphabet follows a liturgical paradigm sharing a family resemblance with the Way of the Cross, combining visual cues with oral performance. The fourteen Stations of the Way of the Cross are visual images arrayed along the sides of a church; they may be as stark as a cross or as detailed and elaborated as the plastic arts can make them. At each station, prayers are repeated; the image is an aide-mémoire for a meditation. The stations, which are always there along the walls of the church silently accompanying the business that passes before them, recede into the general sacred decor until they are activated by ritual. The elements then contribute to a full sacred narrative; each element performs an act in the longer drama, but the wholeness of the passion is always primary.[17]

The alphabet, too, generates ritual, not only in the recitation of the names of the letters, but in a prayer signaled by the seemingly inarticulate, if highly charged, ✠:

> Christes Crosse be my speede in all vertue to proceede, A, b, c, d, e, f, g, h, i, k, l, m, n, o, p, q, r, s, &. t, double w, v, x with y, ezod, &. per se, con per se, tittle tittle est, Amen. When you haue done begin againe, begin againe.[18]

The prefacing formula "Christ's Cross me spede" is known in English by the early fifteenth century, according to the *OED*. This apotropaism or benediction perhaps originated to depose the other possibilities for the alphabet, namely the maledictions, heresies, and apostasies of alchemy and cabala. Similarly, the closing formula—"est, Amen"—typically follows the alphabet in sixteenth-century reading primers securing sacred ritual closure.[19]

Here at the beginning of modern literacy are aspects of alphabetical learning that will prove lasting.[20] The alphabetic ritual designed to generate infinite repetitions of the names of the letters binds the alphabet to a cyclical pattern. The frame for this naming is worth noting; a folkloric verbal playfulness in rhyme and rhythm combines with a sober message affixing literacy to virtue. In the early modern period, the alphabet, which in our era has become emblematic of the secular, shares a border with sacred iconography. Christology as a system has this in common with the alphabet as a system: its meaning manifests itself only by its repetition, and without repetition it has no meaning at all. One of the characteristics of the sacral is its reproducibility, its repeatability. Mircea Eliade describes participation in ritual as a way of partaking of sacred time, which "always remains equal to itself, it neither changes nor is exhausted" (69). At the center of Christian ritual is the infinite repetition of the Eucharist. Like the elements of the Eucharist, which if they were never again to be activated would lie dormant in history or archeology's great deadening display case, letters have no meaning at all unless they are reproduced, copied, used.

But while these systems are analogous, the mission of religious pedagogy has always been to make them seem homologous. The central Christian sacrament of the Eucharist refers to and repeats one sacred event. This is, of course, not the case with the alphabet; there is no originary moment to which the alphabet always refers. Like christology, the alphabet never exhausts itself, never gets used up; by contrast to christology, it exists in profane time, not in sacred time. The Christian canon lacks an originating myth for the alphabet. In cabalistic tradition it is Abraham who invents the alphabet, and elsewhere Adam is said to have received the alphabet from the angel Raphael.[21] While canonical scripture tells no creation story for the alphabet, the linking of ✠ and alphabet sidesteps the question of originating myth. As though by a process of subliminal seduction, ✠ *suggests* a relationship that does not in fact exist between the alphabet, sacred iconography, and sacred

ritual. This suggestion glides into near-sacramental status as generations of infant scholars enact the pedagogic ritual.

The Comenian Alphabet:
What the Animals Said to Adam

Reformation literacy campaigns, motivated by a desire for unmediated
(if carefully guided) access to Bible reading by the devout, transformed
the status of both the child and the alphabet during the seventeenth
century. When the alphabet came wrapped in a bound book in the
primers of the sixteenth century, it looked much like the hornbook alphabet. The genre of the alphabetic text is revolutionized in the seventeenth century in the most sustained fashion by the Bohemian humanist educator Johann Amos Comenius (1592–1670). Exiled during the
Reformation diaspora, Comenius was well known as both pedagogue
and philosopher in England, where he was befriended by the influential
educator Samuel Hartlib, as well as on the Continent, where he lived in
Sweden and in the Netherlands. The Netherlands provided Comenius
with the Reform intellectual and publishing network that allowed him
to become one of the best-known educational theorists of the time; indeed, he was invited, according to Mather's *Magnalia*, to become the
president of Harvard College, where his Latin text *Januarum Linguarum Reserata* (1647) may have been required reading.[22] Comenius's
pacifist, universal brotherhood philosophy, "pansophia," with its concomitant search for a universal language, shaped his notions of language teaching. Although he was committed to vernacular education,
exile required him to write in the scholarly lingua franca, Latin.[23]

In both the English petty school and its New England counterpart,
the curriculum was founded on Latin grammar, and grammar texts had
been a staple of the print shop since Gutenberg.[24] Comenius envisioned
a graded curriculum, responsive to the changing needs of children of

different ages, and planned a set of progressive texts titled with architectural metaphors—vestibule, doorway, courtyard, palace, treasury (Bowen, 20)—of which he completed the first two in his lifetime. The notion of the book as architectural space was not unique to Comenius but is, rather, an inheritance of the rhetorical art of memory, which used architecture as a mnemonics. The dropping down into childhood, however, of aspects of the memory art is characteristic of the first books designed specifically for children, and lingers within them long after the art has vanished entirely from the teaching of rhetoric.

Comenius's most important schoolbook is a preliminary text, representing not an architectural space bearing a relationship to the "palace of learning" but the very ground of all learning in the Comenian scheme, the world itself. This book, *Orbis Sensualium Pictus*, or *The Visible World*, is known as the first picture book for children and contains one of the first picture alphabets for children. Enormously popular, the book went into 244 editions between 1658 and 1964.[25] The Comenian alphabet survives into the nineteenth century in the *Orbis Pictus* itself and in James Greenwood's *London and Paris Vocabulary*, as well as in various more popular venues. While originating from notions of universal language and Adamic language theory, the Comenian alphabet follows a typical downscaled trajectory in the marketplace, ending up embedded in at least two American mass market children's books published around the turn of the century.[26]

The *Orbis Pictus* depends for its efficacy on its use of the medium of print, on the implications of the illustrated alphabet, and on the way in which the reader is regarded by the text.[27] A schoolbook designed to teach Latin along with (depending on the edition) one or more vernacular languages, the *Orbis Pictus* does not presume elementary literacy and therefore was used not only in school but almost certainly also at home, as a nursery book.[28] Comenius expects it to be so used and urges in his preface, "Let it be given to children into their hands to delight themselves withall as they please, with the sight of the Pictures, and making them as familiar to themselves as may be, and that even at home, before they be put to School" (A5v).[29]

Formally, the *Orbis Pictus* draws on a rich tradition of encyclopedias and illustrated books,[30] including earlier Catholic and contemporary Counter-Reformation texts. It shares with them a supplementarity of text and image. Catholicism had long used pictures as both a substitute for and an accompaniment to literacy; the emphatically iconic, symbolic, and emblematic nature of much that Catholicism transmits flows easily over the boundaries between the pictorial and the verbal. By contrast, for Comenius the supplementarity of picture and text functions to engage the reader with the "visible world" rather than with the symbolic or supernatural or invisible world. Along the way, an underlying but unstated mission is effected as the *Orbis Pictus* draws the child-scholar securely into the realm of print. The encyclopedism that Comenius promotes derives from the Greek ideal of *enkyklios paideia*—the circle of education, the foundation of classical humanism.[31] With encyclopedism, this capacious ideal shifts from people to books, as though by the end of the Renaissance the world had simply become too wide to be incorporated in persons. But while the book is thus becoming a central fixture, it does so in disguise: the new organization of knowledge that the *Orbis Pictus* supports is meant to be found not in the memory, nor in the commonplaces of rhetorical or logical *inventio*, nor in books, but in the world itself.

In the *Orbis Pictus*, the child-reader is figured as an active participant, via his surrogate in the text. Master and student, as collaborators in the progress toward Comenius's ideal of universal brotherhood through universal language, constitute the narrative frame. The opening invitation sets a genial, distinctly nonagonistic tone ("Come, Boy! Learn to be

Figure 9 "Come, Boy! Learn to be Wise." The "Invitation" from the *Orbis Pictus*. (Courtesy of the Newberry Library, Chicago)

wise!"; Fig. 9); the last page prints the same image, accompanied by a cheery "Farewell" from the master, who sends the boy on to "read other good books diligently, and thou shalt become learned, wise, and Godly" (309). In Comenius's system, "the proper acquisition of language must logically lead to the conversion of the world" (Cohen, 20). The Comenian-bred pupil is sent off to help bring about this happy event.

The *Orbis Pictus* carries two epigraphs, which mutually define its project: Aristotle's "Nihil est in intellectu, quod non prius fuit in sensu" (Nothing is in the understanding which was not first in the senses) and Genesis 2:19–20, in which Adam names the animals. Both the sense experience of the child and the creatures over whom man has dominion have a share in this pedagogy. In his preface Comenius calls his book "our *little Encyclopadia* [*sic*] of things subject to the senses" (x). Each page has a picture and a short narrative keyed to the numbered elements in the picture. The child-reader is invited, then, into the wide world, in which print shops and bookbinderies, stage plays and fencing schools, sea fish and shellfish, are illustrated in detail. Comenian iconology is explicitly representational and its object of mimesis is the visible world. The windows or frames through which the reader views these representations perform a taxonomic function; each plate is a kind of pre-Linnean ark, drawing like next to like.

The tormenting of Malefactors.

Supplicia Maleficorum.

Figure 10 "The Tormenting of Malefactors" from the *Orbis Pictus*. (Courtesy of the Newberry Library, Chicago)

The Comenian child still lives in a Renaissance sensorium, to use Walter Ong's term, and in this world it is proper to invite the child to scrutinize "Deformed and Monstrous People" and "The Tormenting of Malefactors" (Fig. 10). In addition, for all of Comenius's emphasis on the visible, in the same worldly vitrine as waterfowl and singing birds are emblems for "God's Providence," "Temperance," "Diligence," "Prudence," "Arts belonging to Speech," and so on (Figs. 11 and 12). The Comenian world is thus one in which abstract qualities are as accessible to pictorial representation and logical categories as natural phenomena or trades. Along with the "visible world" of the title, Comenius portrays as well "things invisible," which, as in the emblem tradition, are "reduced after their fashion" to visible things (A4v). Hence, this encyclopedia offers visual representations of God (Fig. 13) as well as "The Soul of Man." The *Orbis Pictus* looks both backward and forward, so that medieval and Renaissance iconography share the same visual field with a scientific rationality. In the wild cattle section, along with the roe, the boar, and the hare, the unicorn is blandly pictured, who "hath but one [horn], but that a precious one" (61). And yet many other creatures, even those, like ant and pelican, with blinding iconographic traditions, are presented with the cool taxonomic ethic of encyclopedism.

The Master intro-
duces the Comenian
alphabet (Fig. 14) in
his "Invitation":

> Before all things,
> thou oughteth to
> learn the plain
> sounds, of which
> mans speech con-
> sisteth; which living
> Creatures know
> how to make, and
> thy tongue know-
> eth how to imitate,
> and thy hand can
> picture out.
>
> Afterwards wee
> will go into the
> world, and we will
> view all things. (3)

While it is merely a
practical matter to in-
troduce the alphabet
at the beginning of a
reading text, Comen-
ius gives the alphabet
a universal priority.
His scene of instruc-
tion echoes Genesis in
its "Before all things"

CXII.

Temperantia.

Temperance.

Tem-

Figure 11 "Temperance" from the *Orbis Pictus*. (Courtesy of the Newberry Library, Chicago)

and its reference to Adam's "living Creatures" ("and whatsoever Adam
called every living creature, that was the name thereof," Gen. 2:19).

(202)

XCIX.

Arts belonging
to the Speech.

Artes Sermonis.

Grammar, 1.	*Grammatica* 1.
is converſant	verſatur
about Letters, 2.	circa *Literas*, 2.
of which it maketh	ex quibus componit
words 3.	*Voces* (*verba* 3.
& teacheth how to utter,	eaſq;docet rectè eloqui
write, 4.	ſcribere, 4.
put together,	conſtruere,
and part them rightly.	diſtinguere [interpun-
Rhetorick, 5.	*Rhetorica* 5. (gere.]
both as it were	
paint 6.	pingit 6. quaſi
a rude ſſozm 7.	rudem *formam* 7.
of Speech with Oratory	Sermonis *Oratoriis*
	Flou

Figure 12 "Arts Belonging to the Speech" from the *Orbis Pictus*. (Courtesy of the Newberry Library, Chicago)

Knowledge itself has been redeemed. Rather than resulting in
eviction from Eden, to learn the
letters is to be equipped for an
outing: "Afterwards wee will go
into the world." Only after the
tongue and hand have mastered
the alphabet will the world be
available for viewing; alphabetization renders not merely texts
but the world itself legible. In
order to view the world properly, the pre-Babel language of
Adam must be recovered. Comenius asserts, for the first time

Figure 13   "God" from the *Orbis Pictus*.
(Courtesy of the Newberry Library, Chicago)

within the history of the pedagogical alphabet, that learning the alphabet must precede perceiving the world, a notion that will undergird
later alphabetization.

Comenius supports this alphabetic revolution with two further innovations. First, this picture alphabet extends and exploits the possibilities of the visual field for the pedagogical alphabet, establishing both
the image and the printed page as central constituents of alphabetization. And second, Comenius tries to make sense of the alphabet,
stripped as it is in his system of explicitly religious meaning. The Comenian alphabet is a phonology (Cohen, 19); that is, of the three aspects of the alphabet—graphic representation, phonic value, and the
names of the letters—Comenius emphasizes sound. The naming of the
letters is subordinated to the imitating of the sound of the "living creature" with the tongue, and the "pictur[ing] out" of the shape of the letter with the hand. In common with other seventeenth-century theorists,

Cornix cornicatur.　　　*á á* A a
The Crow cryeth.

Agnus balat.　　　*be e e* B b
The Lamb blaiteth.

Cicáda strider.　　　*ci ci* C c
The Grashopper chirpeth.

Upupa dicit.　　　*du du* D d
The Whooppoo saith.

Infans éjulat.　　　*é é é* E e
The Infant cryeth.

Ventus flat.　　　*fi fi* F f
The wind bloweth.

Anser gingrit.　　　*ga ga* G g
The Goose gaggleth.

Os halat.　　　*háh háh* H h
The Mouth breatheth out.

Mus mintrit.　　　*í í í* I i
The Mouse chirpeth.

Anas tetrinnit.　　　*kha kha* K k
The Duck quacketh.

Lupus ululat.　　　*lu ulu* L l
The Woolf howleth.

Ursus murmurat. *mum mum* M m
The Bear grumbleth.

Figure 14 The alphabet phonology from the *Orbis Pictus*. (Courtesy of the Newberry Library, Chicago)

(5)

Felis clamat   *nau nau* V v
𝕿𝖍𝖊 𝕮𝖆𝖙 𝖈𝖗𝖞𝖊𝖙𝖍.

Auriga clamat.   ó ó ó O o
𝕿𝖍𝖊 𝕮𝖆𝖗𝖙𝖊𝖗 𝖈𝖗𝖞𝖊𝖙𝖍.

Pullus pipit.   *pi pi* P p
𝕿𝖍𝖊 𝕮𝖍𝖎𝖈𝖐𝖊𝖓 𝖕𝖊𝖊𝖕𝖊𝖙𝖍.

Cúculus cúculat.   *kuk ku* Q q
𝕿𝖍𝖊 𝕮𝖚𝖈𝖐𝖔𝖜 𝖘𝖎𝖓𝖌𝖊𝖙𝖍
   𝖈𝖚𝖈𝖐𝖔𝖜.

Canis ringitur.   *err* R r
𝕿𝖍𝖊 𝕯𝖔𝖌 𝖌𝖗𝖎𝖓𝖓𝖊𝖙𝖍.

Serpens ſibilat.   ſ S s
𝕿𝖍𝖊 𝕾𝖊𝖗𝖕𝖊𝖓𝖙 𝖍𝖎ſſ𝖊𝖙𝖍.

Graculus clamat.   *tac tac* T t
𝕿𝖍𝖊 𝕵𝖆𝖞 𝖈𝖗𝖞𝖊𝖙𝖍.

Bubo ululat.   *u u* U u
𝕿𝖍𝖊 𝕺𝖜𝖑 𝖍𝖔𝖔𝖙𝖊𝖙𝖍.

Lepus vagit.   *va* W w
𝕿𝖍𝖊 𝕳𝖆𝖗𝖊 ſ𝖖𝖚𝖊𝖆𝖐𝖊𝖙𝖍.

Rana coaxat.   *coax* X x
𝕿𝖍𝖊 𝕱𝖗𝖔𝖌 𝖈𝖗𝖔ɑ𝖐𝖊𝖙𝖍.

Aſinus rudit.   *y y y* Y y
𝕿𝖍𝖊 𝕬ſſ𝖊 𝖇𝖗𝖆𝖞𝖊𝖙𝖍.

Tabanus dicit.   *ds ds* Z z
𝕿𝖍𝖊 𝖂𝖗𝖊𝖊𝖟𝖊 𝖔𝖗 𝕳𝖔𝖗ſ𝖊-
   𝖋𝖑𝖎𝖊 ſ𝖆𝖎𝖙𝖍.   B 3

5

Comenius attempts to connect letters to the natural world.[32] In the Comenian Eden, while Adam was naming the animals, they, presumably, were giving him back the alphabet. These letters are phonic representations of animals' own natural cries. The *Orbis Pictus* accomplishes an aural version of the grapes of Zeuxis, the Greek painting so realistic, so goes the legend, that birds pecked it.[33] Comenius hopes for a similar kind of transparency for his alphabet images: from these sound images we could attract the animals themselves.

The naturalness, or transparency, of the letters is not limited, however, to the cries of animals; E is a human baby's sound, H is the human mouth breathing out, and O is the cry of the carter. This suggests that there are two kinds of utterances: a natural, irresistible, autonomic kind, which we share with the animals—an exhale, the cry of a baby, the communication between working man and working beast; and an artificial, learned kind—that of alphabetic, educated speech, which we draw from the animals, but which distinguishes us from them. The difference, in this scheme, between nature and artifice, between what the animals do and what people do, is taxonomic; Comenian man organizes nature. Adam's task, naming the animals, really amounted to putting them in their place; in the Comenian Eden this amounts to ranging the creatures in alphabetical as well as generic order.

The *Orbis Pictus* offers this story about the alphabet: its home is in the natural world, accessible to the senses of sight and hearing and capable of representation by images; the mouths of the unwitting animals emit the alphabetic sounds, which man, in his dominion, knows how to harvest. The implicit narrative of the *Orbis Pictus* alphabet is constructed of predicates: "The Crow cryeth á á"; "The Chicken peepeth pi pi." The accretion of these predicates creates a world that is naturally alphabetized; such a world would be one in which the alphabet is both easy to learn and virtually impossible to avoid.

While the Comenian alphabet relies on the sound of the individual letters to flood the alphabet with Edenic meaning, on the printed page the phonic value of the letters is subordinated to the visual images. As a Ramist, Comenius perceives that the memory will take in the letters and everything else, not only because they are properly arranged and organized, but also because their visual presentation favors remembering:[34] "For the yong [sic] A b c Scholar will easily remember the force of every Character *by the very looking upon the Creature*, till the imagination being strengthened by use can readily afford all things" (ix; my emphasis).

Even though it depends on images, the Comenian alphabet and picture book emerge in an atmosphere of Reformation iconoclasm. Although some contemporaries complained that Comenius used too many pictures and that he should have pictured only items hard to come by in the ordinary schoolroom (Keatinge, 79), the point of the Comenian picture is precisely that it redeems images for Reformation pedagogy. For Comenius, images of the world aren't tainted with iconicity. The *Orbis Pictus*'s emphasis on "things in the world" channels the energies of the image into its representational rather than symbolic or emblematic aspects. That is, when the crow cries, he is not, for example, Aesop's crow, for he has no story of his own to tell, neither allegory nor moral lesson to convey. Comenius wants us to hear the crow's cry anew, a purposeful cry from the orderly Comenian world in which natural chaos is banished equally with the chaos of Catholic and fabulist superstition. In addition, the images in the *Orbis Pictus* rely on an aspect of iconicity well known to Catholicism but never before exploited in the interests of transmitting the alphabet: the sheer pleasure of looking.[35]

The advent of the image in pedagogy invests the student's attention in books and the printed page, drawing him away from oral ritual. This is the beginning of a bond between book and child, which exceeds or even bypasses the master-student relationship. The association of the alphabet with visual images functions to naturalize the sign, to make it seem not arbitrary but necessary. The alphabet hence acquires some of the characteristics of the visual image. By associating words with pictures, the Comenian system is using the time-honored methods of the rhetorical memory art's *imagines agentes*, the striking images meant to impress themselves upon the mind.[36] Indeed, so successful was the *Orbis Pictus* in the institutionalization of alphabetic learning that we now think it second nature to relate animal sounds to the nursery (what does the cow say?, etc.).

Letter/Image/Text in The New England Primer

The most notorious and long-lived alphabet in the American tradition inherits the linking of image and alphabetic text from Comenius. Fully committed to vernacular literacy, *The New England Primer* emerges and circulates within the new American print marketplace supported by one of the most successful literacy campaigns in history.[37] In the *Primer* the alphabet takes on configurations that will prove massively successful in America. *The New England Primer* draws upon the hornbook and primer traditions of early print culture as well as the Comenian picture book for children. But the *Orbis Pictus* is essentially a cosmopolitan, ecumenical-reform, humanist production, developing out of and contributing to a rational encyclopedism with roots in Latin-school culture and rhetorical tradition. *The New England Primer*, by contrast, is, as a whole, distinctly provincial, doctrinaire, evangelical. The literacy encouraged by the *Orbis Pictus* is an adjunct to rhetoric, depending on the taxonomies of the commonplaces and traces of the memory art. That book's long life can be attributed to the continuing, if continually declining, vitality of rhetoric in pedagogy into the nineteenth century. While doubtless many children who learned their letters from the

Primer went on to rhetorical training at Boston Latin or to careers in ministry and the law, *The New England Primer* transmits literacy independent of rhetoric, intended rather for generations of shopkeepers and goodwives.

The *Primer*'s mission diverges from that of the *Orbis Pictus* not merely in its relation to rhetoric, but in its relation to the very foundation of language. The *Primer* stands as a reminder of what else happened in Eden besides Adam's creaturely salon. In a sense, the *Orbis Pictus* and the *Primer* are teaching two different languages. In practical terms, the *Orbis Pictus* is devoted to teaching Latin along with the vernacular; philosophically, Comenius's project is to renew language, and mankind thereby, by recovering the alphabet's God-given natural source. But the monolingual *Primer* is resigned to doing what it can with fallen language. Like the rest of American Puritan teaching, the *Primer* seems to take an any-means-necessary approach to its task. The *Primer*, in contrast to the *Orbis Pictus*, is less the product of a theory than of a situation. It is this that marks it as an invention of a modern orthodoxy, which, like an adapting organism, suits itself to its medium of capitalist enterprise.

The New England Primer's early success can be attributed both to the timing of its introduction to America and to the entrepreneurial ethic of its compiler. It owes its staying power to the promise of constant surveillance in its religious message and the use that it makes of traditional cultural images. As for timing, in New England the arrival of the *Primer* may have seemed a special providence; for when the printer Benjamin Harris began publishing it there, arguably in about 1690,[38] the spiritual fate of the colonists, especially the young, was a growing concern. The *Primer* might be seen as the ideal reader for the Halfway Covenant, a kind of surrogate parent to keep an eye on errant children and raise them up into the fold.[39]

While the Comenian primer exploited print technology and distribution networks, in many ways Comenius belongs to rhetorical rather than print culture. The first publisher of *The New England Primer* was, by contrast, an ink-stained wretch: one of the first newspapermen. A long and vivid career in London, including a stint in the pillory, preceded Harris's immigration to Boston in 1689. Like most other printers of the day, he published a range of popular genres in addition to his newspapers.[40] Among his other productions were broadsides, such as "An Excellent New Ballad, / To the Tune of How Unhappy is Phillis in Love" (London, 1681) and "The Leacherous Anabaptist: or, the Dipper Dipt. A New Protestant Ballad" (1681); a deck of cards containing "an History of all the Popish plots that have been in England"; a gift pamphlet called "A new yeares gift for Protestants, or a looking glasse displaying the sweet face of Popery" (1682). He advertised the job-printing of "Bills, Bonds, and Indentures &c." in his 1692 almanac, along with a tonic, for sale in his London Coffee-House in Boston, "*against all manner of Gripings*, called aqua anti torminalis . . . *cures the Griping of the guts and the wind cholick. . . .* "[41] But Harris was not only a journalist, coffeehouse proprietor, and sometime snake-oil salesman; he was also the official printer of the laws of Massachusetts for 1692 and 1693, and printer as well of several works by Cotton and Increase Mather. As journalist, printer, and entrepreneur, Harris operates in a world of nascent mass-market sensationalism and of the exigencies and odd bedfellows of the marketplace. It is from this marketplace that many of the images of his *Primer* emerge.

The New England Primer, even more emphatically than the *Orbis Pictus*, cannily uses the resources of orality to draw its readers into the world of print. The conventional view of the *Primer* focuses sensibly on its religious content, taking for granted the medium of transmission and the context in which this medium develops. This oversight is evidence of the lasting success of its format and, more generally, of the lasting success of print, like other communications technologies, to efface or mask its aspect as technology, to naturalize itself, through a process of importing imagery from previous, related technologies.

The goal of the *Primer*, according to its title page, is to further "the more easy attaining of the true reading of English." To this end, the book is loosely divided into three sections:[42] alphabetical instruction, including three or more alphabets and a syllabarium; reading practice in the form of hymns, verses, and moral sentences ("An Alphabet of Lessons for Youth"), along with some general knowledge (books of the Bible, days, months, counting time, etc.); and catechisms. Either or both the Westminster Assembly's catechism and John Cotton's "Spiritual Milk" are always included, as is the martyrdom of John Rogers, a piece of Puritan hagiography from Foxe's *Book of Martyrs*, which always appears with a woodcut of Rogers being burned at the stake, wife and children looking on. Sometimes the book ends with "A Dialogue between Christ, Youth, and the Devil." The *Primer*, then, offers, in a somewhat amplified and elaborated form, the traditional contents of the primer, as constituted since the mid–sixteenth century. The additions and repetitions—the alphabet in several versions, more than one catechism, in conjunction with a catechetical dialogue—lend to print the copiousness of oral performance. Through repetition print replicates recitation, imitating aural echoes.

Crucial to understanding the primers of this period is a recognition of what such books mean by the "art of reading," referred to on many *Primer* title pages. The term "art" distinguishes this mode of reading as a technique, a skill. An "art of reading" requires something other than ordinary "reading," which through the sixteenth century still centrally meant "advice or counsel" in the substantive and "to advise or explain" in the verb (Ferry, 10). The *art* of reading was the technique of transferring the skills of analphabetic reading—comprehending the world—to alphabetic reading, and consisted in learning how to look at and comprehend print; learning how to look at pictures in books; and, along the way, learning what books are good for.

The Roman alphabet has been a stable entity for only about two hundred years. The alphabet of *The New England Primer* includes "&" as its final character, contains the long *s* (*ſ*), and many editions present ligatures as though they are extra characters. The alphabet varies between twenty-four and twenty-six letters, sometimes within the same edition (the image-alphabet, for instance, is always twenty-four letters). Many editions of *The New England Primer* and of other primers through the nineteenth century contain alphabets in roman, italic, and the black-letter Gothic or so-called English types. The variety of fonts and types is a reminder that the primer was introducing the alphabet into a nonalphabetized culture and to a nonprint audience. The *Primer*'s opening pages offer the alphabet as elements in a series, A B C, divided by category into vowels and consonants and into typographical uppercase and lowercase, or, in the contemporary phrasing, great and little letters: Aa Bb Cc. The alphabet is often presented out of order as well, following the ancient practice of requiring students to recite the alphabet backward and from the middle to each end.

Each alphabet serves a distinct function. The typographical alphabet introduces the elements of print and the order of the letters. At the same time, it announces the project of the pages that follow. This monolithic alphabet takes on the iconic aspects of the Christ's Cross: the alphabet preceding the text establishes the virtue and raison d'être of that text. In Puritan America, literacy is sufficiently established as a pious goal, linked to Bible reading. Following the typographical alphabet and the syllabarium, the icon-alphabet is the first section of the *Primer* to make sense. That is, the alphabet and syllabarium build up to isolated words, sometimes very complex ones. But these are exercises in pronunciation, quite separate from meaning.

The most-quoted couplet of *The New England Primer*—"In Adam's fall / We sinned all"—is, as I suggested at the beginning of this chapter, often cited to convey the book's orthodox piety. But the rest of the alphabet seems to belong to a separate cultural project, since almost two-thirds of its image-rhymes are more or less secular.[43] This introductory couplet, like the cross at the beginning of the criss-cross row, and like the Comenian crow, functions to establish an attitude toward the alphabet and to anchor it to a universe of sense. More like the crossrow than the *Orbis Pictus*, *The New England Primer* opens with an A that is postlapsarian and not yet regenerate, capturing the situation of language in the Puritan world. The Comenian alphabet conveyed an urbane, cosmopolitan view of nature, in which a carter's cries are the equivalent of a crow's and in which the natural world is ordered conveniently for the use of man-the-humanist. But *The New England Primer* alphabet is savvy and slangy, more urban than urbane, purveying not so much words of wisdom as words to the wise. In this literacy project, the carter is no longer an object, but a subject: I read, you read, he reads, all we sinners read. Rather than an ABC of orthodoxy, the alphabet that follows is a spirited ABC of a fallen world, in which "In Adam's fall / We sinned all" constitutes less a warning than a sign, as if to say, "We're all sinners, and here's an inventory of our sin-filled world": A stands equally for advertisement and advisement. If the Comenian alphabet imagines a world in which animals cry out the sounds of the letters, the *Primer*'s alphabet is no less ambient. In the world of the *Primer* nature has retreated from the precincts of Comenius's humanist natural history into a world of the merely signifying, the world, that is, of Puritan typology. For this reason the *Primer* doesn't pull nature's tail to get it to cry "A"; instead, it relies on a world of signs that already exists in the rough-and-tumble realm of commerce from which the book emerges.

The Comenian alphabet's identification of the letter with the articulation of God's creatures is an expression of a philosophy and a theology; the criss-cross row, too, anchors the alphabet in a system. In the *Primer*, the alphabet itself becomes an occasion for display, for narrative, for showing pictures. The consequence is an increase in the prestige and visibility of the alphabet. While most of the image-rhyme pairs of the *Primer* alphabet lack the striking ideological content of the opening example, they nonetheless suffuse the alphabet with meaning. The syntax of the rhymes' alphabetic assertions gives priority to the content of their mininarratives, rather than to the letter of the alphabet with which each is associated. (Out of context, it's hard to know what letter "My Book and Heart" or "The Royal Oak / It was the Tree" is peddling.) Although the presumed goal of the *Primer* image-alphabet is to teach the letters, these letters play a supporting role and are subordinated to both image and text; so constrained is the letter by this schema that in some editions it is suppressed altogether.

Formally drawing upon the structure of the Renaissance emblem, *The New England Primer*'s alphabet (see Figs. 3–5) has three parts: the letter, the image, the rhymed text. Like the emblem, this alphabet offers an image (for A, the icon of Adam, sometimes Adam and Eve, sometimes complete with the Tree of Knowledge and the serpent), an *explicatio* (the rhyme), and a motto (from *mot*, here not a word but a letter).[44] What do these emblems teach? The layout seems to encourage the eye to escape the disciplined movements required to read text and to rove about looking at the pictures. Similarly, the rhyming of the mottoes accompanying the images and letters discourages the slow discipline of reading. A few repetitions and even the "idle fool" would probably have the little verses "by heart." Without great effort, then, with familiar means of pleasurable looking and nursery-rhyme repetition, reading begins. All that's missing is reading itself. But the looking and repetition are the reading of traditional culture, and the *Primer* scavenges from such visual artifacts as tavern signs and such oral/aural artifacts as folk rhymes, rhyming slang, and popular broadsides the materials of literacy.

The opening combination marks out the kind of alphabet this is, associating it with the ongoing nature of the Fall. The second image introduces the Good Book, making it continuous with the book in the reader's hand. From A to B, the *Primer* alphabet offers this small narrative: Adam disobeyed, and his legacy is sin; the Bible can help redeem us if we will just take it and read. But then comes C: "The Cat doth play / And after slay." One might find a doctrinal message in these words— that fallen nature is untrustworthy, or that God has a plan for every creature—but, like the other references to animals in this alphabet, this rhyme is simply proverbial. Indeed, only a proverbial reading can take account of that sly picture of a fiddle-playing cat and three dancing mice.[45] The folk motif of the heigh-diddle-diddle cat appears in print in its more familiar Mother Goose incarnation in the mid–eighteenth century (Fig. 15).[46] The image is much older, having appeared in manuscript in a fifteenth-century book of hours (Fig. 16), as well as in the decor of that vast compendium of artisanal folklore, the cathedral. Cats have been fiddling now for as long as six centuries on misericords in Hereford, Wells, Beverley Minster, and other English cathedrals (Fig. 17).[47] The *Primer* audience, however, was not likely to be familiar with these clerical cats; they more likely knew the conceit from oral transmission and from another medium, one much more apposite to the task of the *Primer*: the tavern sign.

The Cat and Fiddle is noted as an inn sign from as early as 1589, and there was a pub by that name in London's Fleet Street in 1638.[48] The

SONG BOOK. 41

CAT AND A FIDDLE.

HIGH Diddle, Diddle,
A Cat and a Fiddle;
The Cow jump'd over the Moon:
The little Dog laugh'd
For to fee the Sport,
And the Difh ran after the Spoon.

G I G A.

Figure 15 Cat and Fiddle from Nurse Lovechild's *Tom Thumb's Song Book* (1788). (Courtesy of the American Antiquarian Society)

Figure 16 *(above)* Cat and Fiddle, from a fifteenth-century Book of Hours. (From Harleian MS. 6563, British Library; in Sillar and Meyler, pl. 47) (By permission of the British Library)

Figure 17 *(left)* Cat and Fiddle, Beverley Minster misericord. Sillar and Meyler read this cat's audience as kittens, not mice. (In Sillar and Meyler, pl. 30) (By permission of Ruth M. Meyler)

precise origin of the images or the expression is uncertain, but scholars' speculations reveal at least this: the phrase emerges from a world of slang and cant—the realm of oral tradition—that moves freely between spoken and "signed" articulation.[49] Both "cat" and "fiddle" have a host of secondary meanings pertaining to sex, theft, cash, and vomit, among other vividly carnivalesque topics.[50] The adoption of this heigh-diddle-diddle cat by the nursery happens late, in its ninth life, and like much nursery lore, it originates in street and yard. As for the less roistering images of the *Primer* alphabet, even the seemingly pious ones moonlight on the street as well, as tavern, inn, and shop signs: Adam (Fig. 18), the Bible, the Royal Oak (Fig. 19), Bible and Heart, the Eagle, the Moon, the Hour-Glass, the King's Head, the Lion and Lamb.[51] The Whale was surely a common trade or inn sign in Boston, Salem, Sag Harbor, Manhattan, and Nantucket. Like the alphabet images, tavern signs were sometimes captioned by rhymes.[52]

If writing originates, as many scholars now believe, in the "reckoning technologies" and token systems of early trade economies,[53] it should not be surprising that a successful literacy manual expresses the commercial environment that produces and circulates it.[54] Furthermore, analysis of the modern advertising image has resonance for these early American precursors. In "The Rhetoric of the Image," Roland Barthes defines the mass-culture image, specifically the advertising image. But his observations illuminate the early modern versions of these images as well, and remind us of their origins in the materials of mass literacy. He notes that a characteristic of images is their polysemy, a kind of semantic flexibility or fickleness. The image, by its very nature, "implies . . . a 'floating chain' of signifieds" (28). Societies then develop "techniques . . . to *fix* the floating chain of signifieds, to combat the terror of uncertain signs." Barthes suggests that "the linguistic message is one of these techniques," anchoring, in an advertising caption or voice-over, the inherently dangerous image to a set of meanings. In the advertising image as well as in more self-consciously ideological image-text situations, the text

> is really the creator's (and hence the society's) right-of-inspection of the image: anchoring is a means of control . . . confronting the projective power of the figures, as to the use of the message; in relation to the freedom of the image's signifieds, the text has a *repressive* value, and we can see that a society's ideology and morality are principally invested on this level. (29)

In representations of the alphabet, it is the alphabet that must be anchored, the

ADAM AND EVE.

Figure 18 The sign of Adam. (From Larwood and Hotten, pl. X, facing 224; courtesy of the Newberry Library, Chicago)

image that does the anchoring. The anchoring image is in turn a recognizable member of a family of images: in the crossrow, Catholic iconography; in the *Orbis*, Edenic essentialism. Characteristically, the alphabet here straddles a boundary; not only does the alphabet constitute the threshold between oral and literate modes, but it is also a nexus between image and text.

As for the *Primer*'s text, its rhymes draw on earlier rhyming alphabets, designed for newly literate adults and to be read aloud.[55] The *Primer* clearly echoes one such alphabet, "Finch His Alphabet" (London, 1630), which opens with an Adam quatrain, followed by a verse whose sentiment is akin to "Thy Life to Mend, / This Book Attend."[56] This alphabet also pairs Xerxes (who "for his beastliness . . . had great blame") with Youth in the final two quatrains, just as the *Primer* does, though to a different purpose. While these patterns suggest that the Finch alphabet may have had some influence on the *Primer*'s image-alphabet, in general the pious dicta of Finch's alphabet, like the alphabetical material found in writing manuals of the seventeenth century,[57] are models not for the *Primer*'s rhyming alphabet but for its "Alphabet of Lessons for Youth."

The success of the image-rhyme alphabet depends precisely on its heteroglossia and the impression it gives of having been assembled in the workaday space of the print shop.[58] Indeed, the consistency of the final ten verses—all beginning with the letter they represent (only J and N do in the earlier verses), and all, but for two memento mori, biblical—suggests that they were drawn from a different source than the earlier letters. The first fourteen letters range across themes of social life. Two are explicitly political—O, "the Royal Oak," and K, "Our King the good / No man of blood."[59] Some are proverbial or derive from animal fables (C, D, E, F, L, M, N). Several of the images are memento mori borrowed, like the structure of their display, from the emblem tradition and gravestone art (B, G, H, T, Y). Narrative themes emerge in these rhymes only to be submerged again. The verses are loosely linked by motifs—of discipline, for example (A, C, D, F, J, T)—and by rhetorical figures, such as antithesis, and, of course, by rhythm and rhyme. To insist on this alphabet's moral consistency is to misapprehend the ideology most in operation within it.[60] In the end, what these rhymes convey is commensurate with their origins: from everywhere and nowhere, they come together in a miniature market-day for the letters.

The image-rhyme alphabet of the *Primer* is in the nature of what the Russian folklorist Vladimir Propp called a "hybrid formation." Describing the mingling of folktale motifs, Propp notes that "folklore formations arise not as a direct reflection of life . . . , but out of the clash of two ages or of two systems and their ideologies. The old and the new can exist not only in a state of unresolved contradictions; they may also enter into hybrid formations" (11). The image-alphabet of *The New England Primer* marks this text as a boundary genre: a folk literacy primer, whose success owes something to its function as a kind of balance wheel for "unresolved contra-

ROYAL OAK.

Figure 19 The sign of the Royal Oak, into which King Charles II escaped at Boscopel (from the Roxburghe Ballads, 1660, as printed in Larwood and Hotten, pl. VI, facing 96; courtesy of the Newberry Library, Chicago)

dictions." To note a few of these contradictions: literate versus oral/folk ways of looking at and living in the world; the pressure of the Halfway Covenant on both the converted and the unregenerate; the tension between a forceful ethic of fifth-commandment piety with the new, non-aristocratic, iconoclastic, and in some ways antiauthoritarian ethic of Puritanism; and the beginnings of the consumer revolution that would transform the Atlantic economy in the eighteenth century.

The ubiquity of these images, their unavoidability, is what Comenius wanted for his alphabet; but his restricted audience of Latin learners, his own position of exile, and his soon-antiquated theory of Adamic language limited his influence, especially in America. The "naturalness" of the Comenian menagerie is strictly theoretical. But *The New England Primer* increases the alphabet's range by linking it to what already constitutes reading in oral culture: that is, negotiating by landmarks and signs. While writing manuals, addressed to the next stage of literacy, and to older and sometimes more elite readers, incorporate literacy into the body by engaging the hand,[61] the *Primer* alphabet begins to engage the whole body. A British pamphlet of 1775 urges that one attach spiritual notions to street signs in order to be able to walk through London constantly reminded of one's godly duty, which would amount to a kind of walking version of the *Primer*.[62] The melding of the ancient memory art with commercial signs, of spirituality with symbols of capital, the slippage of folk culture into an incipient mass culture: these are some of the accomplishments of *The New England Primer*. The iconoclast Comenius, in order to free the alphabet from Catholic iconicity, established the link between images and the alphabet. Similarly, *The New England Primer*, manual of piety as well as of literacy for nearly two centuries, while seeming to bind the alphabet to orthodoxy, in fact bound it firmly to the traffic of daily life.

The Education of youth is, in all governments, an object of first consequence. The impressions received in early life, usually form the character of individuals, a union of which forms the general character of a nation.

　　　　—*Noah Webster*

Chapter Two

THE REPUBLIC OF ABC:

ALPHABETIZING AMERICANS,

1750–1850

R epublican discourse encouraged what Thomas Jefferson called the "More General Diffusion of Knowledge," in the interests of creating a citizenry that would be informed and rational, able to govern, ready to be governed.[1] Articulating a sentiment that would become nearly proverbial during the following decades, in 1787 Noah Webster called for systematic public education, whose imagined infant scholar would embody national memory: "As soon as he opens his lips, he should rehearse the history of his own country; he should lisp the praise of liberty and of those illustrious heroes and statesmen who have wrought a revolution in her favor" ("On the Education of Youth," 65). The child becomes a ventriloquist of revolutionary history and hagiography and an encyclopedia of patriotic narrative. Beyond the nursery, the eighteenth-century alphabet functioned to organize knowledge as it became a large-scale ordering tool, structuring encyclopedic, bureaucratic, and cultural projects of the Enlightenment. At the same time, the alphabet became a means for the emerging book trade to pursue its newly prominent child-consumer. To circulate and reproduce itself among this "rising genera-tion," the Enlightenment Republic of Letters relied on its lowly coun-terpart, the Republic of ABC, for the work of transmitting elementary literacy.

Alphabet books, primer alphabets, and alphabet narratives talk out of both sides of their mouths. They depend on and refer to high-culture literacy discourses, but they share the press with almanacs, broadsides, chapbooks, job-printing ephemera, and newspapers. The social spaces of the print shop, as well as of the schoolroom and the nursery, help to shape the alphabet's discursive space. While the alphabet generates and perpetuates discourses of Christian and republican literacy, it often does so with a festive or satiric laugh, which taps traditional culture's carni-vals, fairs, festivals, and ballads, as well as the literary, political, and so-cial life of the day. This laugh started with *The New England Primer*'s "The Cat doth play/And after slay," and gains force in the alphabeti-cal images and narratives of the eighteenth century.

With the aid of these images and narratives the alphabet masquer-ades as a discourse. By this I mean that narrative and tropic devices ac-crue to the alphabet and increase its range and power as an essential component of acculturation and socialization in early America. The shift in the cultural position and significance of the alphabet goes hand in hand with transformations in the image of the child and of child-hood. If the alphabet is the medium through which the child newly be-comes acculturated, the child is similarly the medium through which the alphabet permeates the culture; this partnering, in turn, claims trans-parency for the symbolic form of the child and implies an organicism for the alphabet.

In this chapter, I will begin by addressing the revolutions in the sta-

tus of children and in the status of images in pedagogic texts in the
eighteenth century that provide the conditions for the emergence of
new forms of elementary literacy—the subject of the rest of the chapter.
To observe the alphabet at work, I then offer a morphology of alphabetic texts. And finally, I will propose a cultural poetics for the alphabet, based on an analysis of the tropes encountered in alphabet texts.

Children and Images

The efficacy of images in the rearing and education of children has a
long provenance.[2] But Reformation iconoclasm tries to overturn this
tradition, affiliated with Catholicism, by suppressing the visual image.
While Comenius went some distance toward reviving images for Protestant pedagogy, the *Orbis Pictus* was sometimes criticized for overusing
pictures. For eighteenth-century Americans, authorities as diverse as
John Locke, Cotton Mather, Jonathan Edwards, Isaac Watts, François
Fénelon, and Jean-Jacques Rousseau, while advancing the cause of the
child, advance the cause of the image, whether they intend to or not,
and further erode Puritan and evangelical iconoclasm.

For Cotton Mather, children have the "image of God . . . renewed
upon them" through the process of catechizing; lacking the discipline
of the catechism, they "will Retain the *Image* of *Satan* on them" ("On
Catechising," 266). Drawn on Mather's knowing child, God's image effaces that of Satan, with which the child is born. Mather figures the
mind as a habitat for images; it is alternately a substance on which images may be drawn or imprinted and an architectural space in which
images can be positioned: "By *Catechizing* your *Children* you Enrich
their Minds, with incomparable *Treasures*" (266). Trained in rhetoric
at Harvard in the 1670s, Mather relies on ancient tropes of how mind
and memory work; the mind is a treasure-house, a *thesaurus*, an architectural space, in which images are arrayed. The power of images, how-

ever, is not restricted to the mental world; or rather, the mental world is not restricted to mind. For Mather, images engage the entire physical being of the child. "How *lovely* a Spectacle" dutiful children are, Mather writes in *Corderius Americanus*, and "How *odious* a Spectacle" are the "*Children of Satan*" (17). The pedagogic ritual of the catechism's question and response, according to Mather's scheme, transmits images; any spectator will see within the seemingly transparent child the images that have formed him.

Jonathan Edwards's theory of images has similar consequences. Edwards aligns Lockean psychology with his own typology such that the "facts of experience became . . . the 'shadows,' the very 'images' of divinity. . . . The thing could then appear as concept and the concept as thing" (P. Miller, "Introduction," 19–20). For Edwards the image offers a language of unmediated, divinely formed and organized signs, in the shape of the very things of the world.

The doctrine of transparency implicit in Mather's and Edwards's theories of images applies to men and women as well as to children, but it is most powerful as it affects the most susceptible, that is, women and children. The power of images had long been noted in regard to pregnant women, and this was still forcefully argued scientifically into the nineteenth century, before descending into folklore. James Burgh, for example, believed, as did many others, that the "tabula rasa could be written upon before birth" and that "the sight of uncouth objects" by a pregnant woman could "produce a monster."[3]

The power of images in child-rearing takes on a new meaning with the spread of cheap books for children[4] and the increasing acceptance of sensationalist psychology, especially through Locke's *Some Thoughts Concerning Education* (1693), one of the most influential books in the colonies.[5] For the Abbé Fénelon, also a widely read authority in America, it is the "softness" of the child's brain that makes everything "easily impressed on it" (10) and "renders very vivid the images of all objects which are perceived" (15).[6] The child must be attended to at once and with great care, while still susceptible:

> So we must hasten to write on their brains while the characters can be easily formed there. But we must be careful in choosing the images which should be inscribed, for we should store up in a receptacle so small and so precious only the choicest things. . . . The first images inscribed on the brain while it is still soft and where nothing as yet has been written are the most deeply impressed. (15)

The Lockean Nonconformist minister Isaac Watts, among the most influential eighteenth-century writers for children, notes in terms similar to Mather's and Fénelon's that it

> is owing to observation that our *mind is furnished with the first, simple and complex ideas* . . . we take the impressions of [things] on our minds from the original objects themselves, which give a clearer and stronger conception of things. . . . Whereas what knowledge we derive from *lectures, reading,* and *conversation,* is but the copy of other men's ideas, that is, the picture of a picture; and is one remove further from the original. ("Improvement of the Mind," 20; emphasis in original)

Ideas and images for Watts, as for Locke, are indistinguishable: "An *idea* is generally defined a *representation of a thing in the mind*; it is a representation of something that we have seen, felt, heard, &c. or been conscious of. That notion or form of a horse, a tree, or a man, which is in the mind is called the *idea of* a *horse,* a *tree,* or a *man*" ("Logic," 316; emphasis in original).

Under the sway of these theorists, Satan's image is gradually erased from conceptions of the infant mind. But for Mather, as for many others in the eighteenth century, the lingering influences of the doctrine of innate depravity, of Reformation iconophobia, of the image's power for evil, mean that images are to be tolerated warily, and cautiously framed, rather than wholeheartedly embraced. In response to this perceived power of images, some compilers of *The New England Primer* "evangelized" its icon-alphabet in the midcentury.[7] Many printers jettisoned the folk images and replaced them with a set of biblical images—even a "Christ Crucified," unimaginable for an earlier Puritan iconoclasm.[8] One edition, which mistakenly printed the old rhymes against the new images, scandalized a minister: "What! Are the children to be told that the death of their Redeemer is of no more importance than the death of a mouse!" He felt "obliged to disfigure the picture with my pen, as much as if it was a Graven Image."[9] In the eighteenth century as now, images can still carry a power that, for some, can only be countered by disfigurement.[10] Far from being neutral, an image can directly cause the breaking of God's law, for the offended divine refers to the locus classicus of Judeo-Christian iconoclasm, the second commandment: "Thou shalt not make unto thee any graven image" (Exodus 20). This particular iconoclast, however, has somewhat outlived his epoch, for the long and the short of it is that by the middle of the eighteenth century, pictures in books are too well established a fact of life for the forces of iconoclasm, much weakened in any case, to combat. For the pious, the point now is to choose which images to transmit as a flood of children's books pours onto the market.[11]

Children as Images

Until the 1750s, *The New England Primer* and the hornbook are the sole domestically produced media carrying the letters of the alphabet to colonial New England children. In the first decades of the eighteenth century, other books appear from American presses for the express use of children: James Janeway's *A Token for Children* (Boston, 1700), Thomas White's *A Little Book for Little Children* (Boston, 1702), *The School of Good Manners* (New London, 1715), Dr. Watts's *Divine*

Songs Attempted in Easy Language for the Use of Children (Boston, between 1715 and 1730), Benjamin Harris's *The Holy Bible in Verse*
(1717).[12] The short titles give the impression that the children addressed
inhabit the familiar, pastoral childhood realm of modernity. But Janeway's "token" means something like "teaching aid," and his title continues: *Being an Exact Account of the Conversion, Holy and Exemplary
Lives, and Joyful Deaths of Several Young Children.*[13] Both their dark
content and the very existence of these books signal shifts in the way
children are regarded. For the first time it becomes possible for a child's
life and death to be "exemplary"—to have meaning, that is, separate
from the meaning of the adult life it might have lived.[14] In "the lovely
spectacle of the dutiful child,"[15] Cotton Mather, and other late Puritan
as well as evangelical writers, transform children into visual aids.

Philippe Ariès notes two aspects of this changed status in the newly
recognized "special nature" of the child (129). On the one hand, children may be petted and coddled as delightful and amusing objects; on
the other, they may be disciplined and shaped as "fragile creatures of
God who needed to be both safeguarded and reformed" (133). Ariès
sees these two tendencies combining with a third—"concern about hygiene and physical health" (133)—in the eighteenth-century family.[16]
Locke's *Thoughts Concerning Education* opens, in fact, with highly detailed advice on the care of the child's body.[17] The physician Benjamin
Rush, a signer of the Declaration of Independence and a promoter of
education, connects pedagogy with a physical regimen, not so much for
the sake of health per se as for discipline: "To assist in rendering religious, moral and political instruction more effectual upon the minds of
our youth, it will be necessary to subject their bodies to physical discipline," by which he means that "they should live upon a temperate
diet," including "the black broth of Sparta, and the barley broth of
Scotland" (*Plan*, 23).

Interest in the child's physical health is accompanied by a concern for the deportment of the child's body—how it stands, sits, places its hands, moves its facial features, and so on.[18] The sociologist Pierre Bourdieu argues that

> if all societies . . . that seek to produce a new man through a process of "deculturation" and "reculturation" set such store on the seemingly most insignificant details of *dress, bearing,* physical and verbal *manners,* the reason is that, treating the body as a memory, they entrust to it in abbreviated and practical, i.e., mnemonic, form the fundamental principles of the arbitrary content of the culture. (*Outline,* 94)

In effect, children become in the eighteenth century the *imagines agentes* of Western culture, and books are enlisted to help structure their minds and bodies. The memory art, the first of the five parts of rhetoric to drop almost entirely away from rhetorical training by the eighteenth century, hasn't vanished; it has fallen into the nursery, joining forces with the nursery rhyme, the fairy tale, and the folktale to help form the new genres of children's literature.[19]

The new status of the child highlights the child's innocent charm, the child's body, and the child's soul. While we might consider this last to be a private and invisible attribute, the state of the soul was of public interest to the Puritan community, as well as to the developing Christian republican community. All three of these aspects of the child regard him or her from the outside. William Ivins notes that "visual images, unlike verbal descriptions, address themselves immediately to the same sense organs through which we gather our visual information about the objects they symbolize" (59). Hence the importance of visual signals in educating the child, and the importance of images in transmitting lessons to a being so imagelike itself.

The foremost "exemplary child" of eighteenth-century America is arguably not a small Puritan martyr, but Rousseau's fictional Emile.[20]

Emile honors the special nature of childhood: "Love childhood; promote its games, its pleasures, its amiable instinct" (79). More than this, Rousseau treats childhood, virtually, as a unique *place*, of which *Emile* will provide the map: "Childhood is unknown. Starting from the false idea one has of it, the farther one goes, the more one loses one's way" (33). Childhood is a foreign country, and domesticating its child inhabitant requires great care.

The narrator of *Emile* is an iconophobe, at least as regards the education of the very young child: "In general, never substitute the sign for the thing except when it is impossible for you to show the latter, for the sign absorbs the child's attention and makes him forget the thing represented" (170); "Things, things!" are what is wanted rather than "babbling education" (180). Both signs and images, including those found on the pages of books, are withheld from Emile; only things, objects in the world, are permitted. Things, allied with the rhetorical category of *res*, are inherently philosophical or true, while *written* words are decadent, mere signs, mere images.[21]

For Rousseau, things oppose the mere signs of things.[22] But the one book permitted to Emile somewhat complicates these distinctions; it is what literary history identifies as among the earliest novels: *Robinson Crusoe*. Emile is allowed to model himself on this fictional narrator precisely because of Crusoe's Emile-like isolation from society, his engagement with things rather than signs and images. The fact that Robinson is himself a figment tips the narrator-tutor's hand: Emile's whole environment is a spectacle created and manipulated by his tutor. Emile's seemingly immediate experiences are consequences of his tutor's constant mediation. This manipulation has turned Emile's world of things into a world of signs. Notably, however, they are signs that stand only for themselves; they are nontypological, elemental signs. Things for Rousseau do not represent other, better, spiritual matters. The tutor is the deity of Emile's universe, but it is a universe in which, by contrast with Puritan typology, "things as they are" suffice. *Crusoe* and *Emile* are fictional narratives. The clay of Emile's flesh is formed of Rousseau's need for an example, just as Plato's Republic is a creation of dialectic, an illustration of an idea. What both *Emile*, paradoxically and against Rousseau's will, and *Crusoe* do is create an environment for images of things, an environment for illustrations, for pictures.[23]

Combined with a welcoming cultural environment for the distribution of images, the deference of adults to the new status of the child has consequences for the production and marketing of books. Early books for children respond to, cater to, and attempt to engage one, sometimes all three, of the newly central aspects of the child—that is, its charm and capacity to entertain and be entertained; its soul; its body. The audience of adults who purchased "small books" from the book peddler had already perceived the utility of books for self-education and entertainment.[24] While American children's books before 1750 tended to interest themselves in the child's soul, the 1729 English translation of Perrault's *Histories, or Tales of Past Time* doubtless made its way into some households as well. By the 1740s in England, Mary Cooper and John Newbery began printing children's storybooks, many of which were first imported and then pirated by booksellers and printers in the colonies.[25] Among the earliest American imprints of these imports were primerlike books, containing alphabets, catechisms, prayers, moral dicta, and both fairy tales and moral tales. Within these books, and in the simple ABC book that appears at about the same time, the alphabet develops as a genre, as a commodity, and as a discourse.

Telling the Alphabet

From 1750 on, the alphabet was dressed up and decked out, animated, ornamented, narrated, and consumed. Accompanying the elevation of images in alphabetic learning are enriched narrative and poetic strategies, which, like images, amplify the letters. In Chapter 1, I referred to the implicit stories that the image-letter-text sets tell in narratives structured by accretion, whose "plots" are prior to them and constitute their ground of existence. Beginning with the alphabets of the eighteenth century, these implicit plots yield to conscious storytelling as the fixative by which the letters are bound.[26] Indeed, to recite the alphabet is sometimes to "tell" it.[27] A chapbook riddle puts the telling in the mouth of the alphabet: "Although we cannot speak a word, / We tell what others do."[28] At the same time, the stories written expressly for children—a new genre of literature that rises with the novel and is, in some cases, indistinguishable from it—begin to import the alphabet as a plot element.

One of the first American editions of an educational children's book on the peddler rather than the Puritan model is the 1750 *Child's New Play-Thing*, containing (among prayers, a catechism, and fables) the first American printing of the two long-lived alphabet rhymes "A Apple Pye" and "A was an Archer" (Figs. 20 and 21).[29] In these alphabets words do not supplement a visual image, as they do in *The New England Primer*. Rather, the text functions to embody and animate the letter. "A Apple Pye" puts the letters on top, both syntactically and narratively, as subjects of predicates, agents of action: "B bit it / C cut it / D divided it."[30] Here is an overt story, generated by aggressive verbs, characters for a child-reader to identify with, and the presence of a vivid, yearning narrative voice: "I wish I had a piece of it now in my hand." As it comes to the surface, narrative makes manifest or brings into existence other elements of the alphabetical environment, among them hunger and strife, comedy and satire. Narrative thus permits the alphabet to express as well as to contain and regulate the passions.

In "A was an Archer, and shot at a Frog," "Apple Pye"'s companion

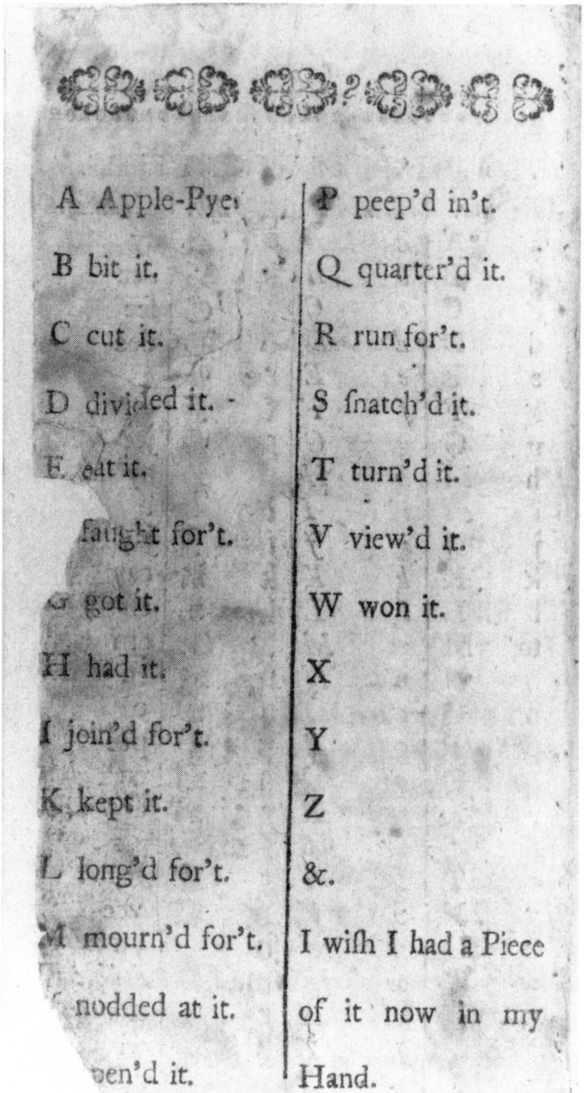

A Apple-Pye.

B bit it.

C cut it.

D divided it.

E eat it.

faught for't.

G got it.

H had it.

I join'd for't.

K kept it.

L long'd for't.

M mourn'd for't.

nodded at it.

pen'd it.

P peep'd in't.

Q quarter'd it.

R run for't.

S ſnatch'd it.

T turn'd it.

V view'd it.

W won it.

X

Y

Z

&c.

I wiſh I had a Piece of it now in my Hand.

Figure 20 "A Apple-Pye" from *The Child's New Play-Thing* (1750). (Courtesy of Rare Books Division, the New York Public Library, Astor, Lenox, and Tilden Foundations)

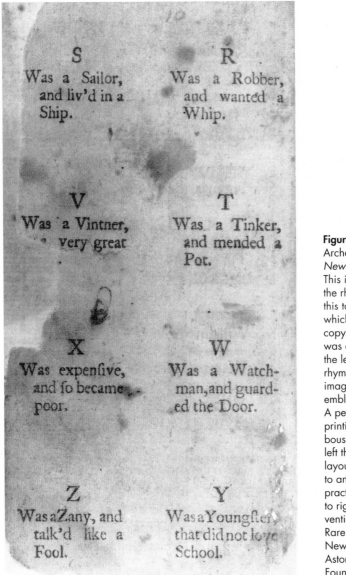

S
Was a Sailor,
and liv'd in a
Ship.

R
Was a Robber,
and wanted a
Whip.

V
Was a Vintner,
very great

T
Was a Tinker,
and mended a
Pot.

X
Was expenſive,
and ſo became
poor.

W
Was a Watch-
man, and guard-
ed the Door.

Z
Was a Zany, and
talk'd like a
Fool.

Y
Was a Youngſter
that did not love
School.

Figure 21 "A was an Archer" from *The Child's New Play-Thing* (1750). This is the sole page of the rhyme remaining in this tattered edition, which is the only extant copy. The layout of "A was an Archer" situates the letter above the rhyme, in the place the image holds in the emblem tradition. A peculiarity of this printing is also its semi-boustrophedon, right-to-left then left-to-right, layout, an odd reference to ancient reading practices before left to right became conventional. (Courtesy of Rare Books Division, the New York Public Library, Astor, Lenox, and Tilden Foundations)

piece in its first print appearance, the letters are similarly represented as people doing things. But rather than the minidrama of "Apple Pye," powered by desire and centered on consumption, this alphabet presents a republic of ABCs whose citizen-letters are identified and categorized according to trade ("B was a Butcher), state ("D was a Drunkard," "X was expensive"), or station ("K was a King," "N was a Nobleman"). The letter, meantime, usurps both the place—at the top of the sequence, as in an emblem book—and the visual force of the image. Some of the memorably absurd rhymes shake up, or shake down, conventional hierarchies: not only does an archer shoot at a frog, but "K was a King, and he govern'd a Mouse." In "A Apple Pye" the letters come to life for the sake of consuming the pie, for the sake of the action (Figs. 22–25). But in "A was an archer" the action is secondary to the array of types, of roles, of persons, as though drawn from a dramatis personae or a masquerade catalog:[31] queen, sailor, oysterwench, captain, tinker (Figs. 26 and 27).

The next extant printing of both "A Apple Pye" and "A was an Archer," in *Tom Thumb's Play-Book* (1764),[32] reprinted at least eight times in the eighteenth century, inaugurates the lasting association of the primer and alphabet book with the folktale. This association continues the trajectory established in *The New England Primer* that links elementary literacy with traditional, oral culture. Both the full title—*Tom Thumb's Play-Book: To teach children their letters as soon as they can speak. Being a new and pleasant method to allure little ones in the first principles of learning*—and the contents (alphabet, alphabet rhymes, syllabary, catechism, prayers), like those of most of the cheerily instructive books of the period, are somewhat paradoxical. The playful pseudonym, the entertaining alphabet rhymes, and a two-page syllabic interlude of "Ab eb ib ob ub" precede the rather gentle Anglican "Scripture Catechism":

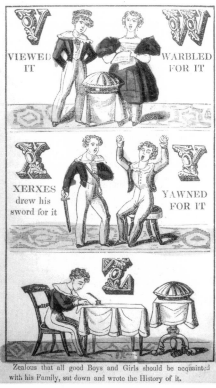

Figures 22–23 From *Dunigan's History of an Apple Pie* (New York, 1843–1848). *Figure 22 (left)*, A through C; *Figure 23 (right)*, V through Z. By the 1840s, the alphabet and its implied child-reader are thoroughly gentrified, far removed from this alphabet's original "festive banquet." Thoroughly rationalized, fully clothed, and bled of their earlier cannibal natures, these letters can safely inhabit the drawing room, as well as the schoolroom and nursery. This alphabet replaces festive values with family values, emphasizing domestic interiors, tidy manners, and the linear continuity of Z's new historiography. (Courtesy of the American Antiquarian Society)

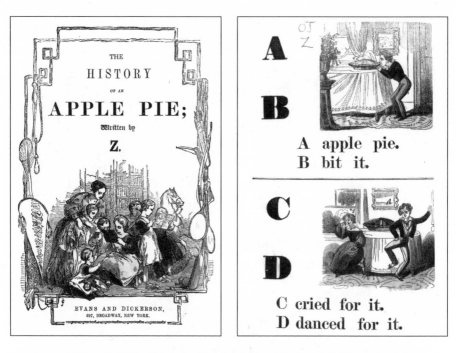

Figures 24–25 Title page (*Fig. 24, left*) and A through D (*Fig. 25, right*) from *The History of an Apple Pie* (New York, 1850s). In this large-format (6" x 8") pamphlet, hand-colored by the publisher, appetite is entirely effaced: you can have your pie, but apparently nobody will any longer admit to wanting to eat it too; they'd rather read about it, together with other preternaturally placid children. Though framed by the equipment of active games and sports, these are emphatically indoor children. This copy of *The History* is notable as well for its inscription: "Aunt Phoebe's little Girl/Died 1860—5 yrs old." Thus this little book, saved as a relic of a child's life, functions somewhat as the Bible does, to record and commemorate a death. (Courtesy of the Rare Book Department, The Free Library of Philadelphia)

Quest. My good child, tell
     me who made thee?
Ans. God.
  Q. Who redeemed you?
  A. Jesus Christ.
  Q. Who sanctifies and
     preserves you?
  A. The Holy Ghost.
    (20)

The playful tone, enlisted to "allure little ones," contrasts, to the point almost of absurdity or parody, with the pious elements of the text. The consequence is that lowliness overwhelms holiness.

Figure 26 The 1824 *Men among the Letters*, using the by-now familiar "A was an Archer" rhyme, follows the "tableau" illustration convention. (Courtesy of the American Antiquarian Society)

As it happens, Tom Thumb is an appropriate guide to the alphabet, for according to his lore, he shares some attributes often assigned to the alphabet, that is, smallness, insubstantiality, mutability, and supernatural origin. In the tale of Tom Thumb, as it first appeared in print in 1621, Tom's tininess both empowers him and puts him at risk.[33] Most important, his size is the defining characteristic from which the narrative flows. Because of his size, he gets eaten by a cow; his size is his salvation as he exits naturally in a cow flop. His size means that Tom requires almost no nourishment; he ends up at the court of the king because of his size. But not only is there no trace of Tom's sometimes scatological adventures in the *Play-Book*, there is no trace of the figure of Tom or of his story at all. "Tom Thumb," a catchphrase by the mid–eighteenth century, has entered fully into the publishing marketplace and become a kind of brand-name.[34]

Tom's smallness translates lowliness into prodigy; this is all that re-

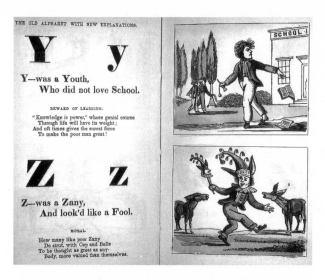

Y   y

Y---was a Youth,
Who did not love School.

REWARD OF LEARNING.

"Knowledge is power," whose genial course
Through life will have its weight;
And oft times gives the surest force
To make the poor man great!

Z   Z

Z---was a Zany,
And look'd like a Fool.

MORAL.

How many like poor Zany
Do strut, with Cap and Bells
To be thought as great as any-
Body, more valued than themselves.

Figure 27 *"A was an archer and shot at a frog"! The old alphabet with new explanations, for the Tommy Thumbs of Yankeedom (1846). This alphabet evinces anxiety over this archer rhyme's festive nonsense: it requires "New Explanations." A title-page rhyme suggests uses for the alphabet in writing to "Creditor or Debtor," to "absent friends," or for a literary audience. By the 1840s "old alphabets" were objects of nostalgic and patriotic interest, while still actively in use as nursery and school texts. (Courtesy of the American Antiquarian Society)*

mains of the original tale in Tom's new function as a brand-name. Tom echoes the situation of the eighteenth-century child and of the small books marketed to this child, as well as the alphabet they often contain. Seemingly insignificant and insubstantial, the alphabet is the basis of the new republican literacy.

The Alphabet on Top

Benjamin Rush and Noah Webster are the two strongest voices for an American paideia in the early republic. Both conceive literacy as part of a larger cultural reformation. In Rush's view, "Mothers and school-masters plant the seeds of nearly all the good and evil which exist in our world. Its reformation must therefore be begun in nurseries and in schools" ("Thoughts upon Amusements," 6–7). Learning to read is critical, for a "free government can only exist in an equal diffusion of literature" (*Plan*, 3). For Rush the association between schools and prisons is explicit and inverse: "Every member of the community is interested in the propagation of virtue and knowledge in the state. . . . it will be true oeconomy in individuals to support public schools." The "batchelor," he continues, can "sleep with fewer bolts and locks to his doors" (*Plan*, 8). Better schools will lead to "fewer pillories and whipping posts, and smaller jails, with their usual expenses and taxes." The costs of "confining, trying and executing criminals amount every year, in most of the counties, to more money than would be sufficient to maintain all the schools that would be necessary in each county" (*Plan*, 9). Webster, too, considers that a "good system of education should be the first article in the code of political regulations, for it is much easier to introduce and establish an effectual system for preserving morals than to correct by penal statutes the ill effects of a bad system" ("On the Education of Youth," 64).

As we have seen, the eighteenth century regards the child as a new kind of person. While recognizing the special nature of the child, theorists like Rush and Webster evince an anxiety that will mark American pedagogy during the nineteenth century. Anticipating the child's entry into the community, Rush advises: "Let our pupil be taught that he does not belong to himself, but that he is public property" (*Plan*, 19). In keeping with this anxiety, Rush also issues one of the era's most emphatic calls for discipline and order:

> I consider it as possible to convert men into republican machines. This must be done, if we expect them to perform their parts properly, in the great machine of the government of the state. . . . [Government must] revolve upon the wills of the people, and these must be fitted to each other by means of education before they can be made to produce regularity and unison in government. (*Plan*, 27)

Rush mixes his mechanistic republicanism with the new, seductive, nonagonistic romantic pedagogy. He critiques the contemporary schoolmaster as "the only despot now known in free countries" and proposes a new kind of teaching, without corporal punishment, which would require instructors to gain the "confidence" of their pupils ("Thoughts

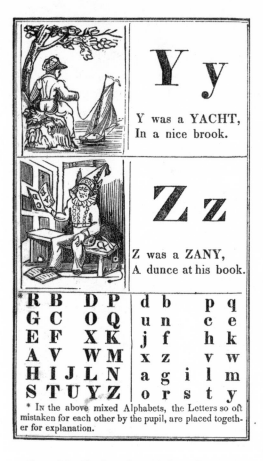

Y was a YACHT,
In a nice brook.

Z was a ZANY,
A dunce at his book.

R	B	D	P	d	b		p	q
G	C	O	Q	u	n		c	e
E	F	X	K	j	f		h	k
A	V	W	M	x	z		v	w
H	I	J	L	N	a	g	i	l	m
S	T	U	Y	Z	o	r	s	t	y

* In the above mixed Alphabets, the Letters so oft mistaken for each other by the pupil, are placed together for explanation.

Figure 28 The Zany from *Mother's Own Primer* (1840). (Courtesy of the Rare Book Department, The Free Library of Philadelphia)

upon Amusements," 12).[35] Rush is the spokesman for what many in this period dream of: in essence, an American paideia, homogeneous, regulated, disciplined, Christian, and republican. It is within this environment, in which the alphabet is becoming the key to republican literacy and the internalized disciplines of romantic pedagogy, that the alphabet kicks up its heels.

The secular alphabets of the early republic charm—"allure," "entertain," "amuse," are favorite blurb-verbs of their publishers— through association with images and narratives positioned at the same level in the cultural hierarchy as the genre of the primer or alphabet book. Which is to say, low down. The "lowness" of the alphabet as a genre, of the "crude woodcut" as visual art, of the child as human being, of the chapbook as printed object, of the nursery and the school as social spaces, of women as teachers[36]—this shared lowliness is posed against the increasing centrality of widespread literacy to high culture.[37]

As low genres, primers and alphabet books become conservators of the low. Elements from traditional culture that were rapidly being excised by a new middle-class gentility now drop down into the nursery and the schoolroom. Alphabet books and primers regularly display both a tension between low and high culture and a melding of the two. Popular motifs and their genteel revisions—a laughing, raucous, and bawdy mischievousness, on the one hand, and a recognizably modern educational ethic, either informational or moralizing, on the other—share the same book, the same page, sometimes the same sentence. To the extent that early American culture turned children into mnemonic devices, festivity is retained in children while it is also being beaten out of them.

The consistent pairing of two figures, the Youth and the Zany, exemplifies this mode of festive discipline, beginning with the *Child's New Play-Thing* (1750): "Y was a Youngster, that did not love School. / Z was a Zany, and talk'd like a Fool" (Figs. 28–30).[38] The Youngster (or, as he appears in other versions and other texts, the

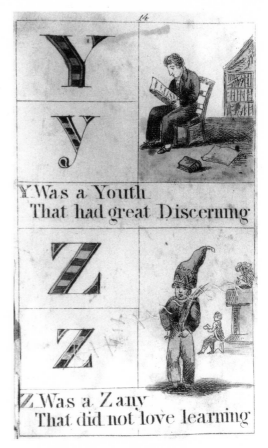

Figure 29 Youth and Zany from *The Alphabet Ladder* (1822). Here the association between youth and the zany is a more intimate one—both are pictured in a study or a school setting. The zany is really a dunce here, holding the means of his own punishment, the ferule, in place of the fool's staff. The zany is simply youth gone wrong and, presumably, a transient role, or at least one susceptible of conversion. (Courtesy of the American Antiquarian Society)

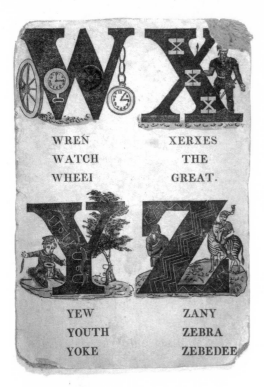

WREN
WATCH
WHEEl

XERXES
THE
GREAT.

YEW
YOUTH
YOKE

ZANY
ZEBRA
ZEBEDEE

Figure 30 Youth and Zany from children's story cards. (Courtesy of the American Antiquarian Society)

Youth) rubs elbows with robbers, vintners, kings; a category defined by age is placed alongside categories defined by trade, condition, and social rank. The role of Youth has discernible attributes; the reluctant student had long been a stock character in school satires. Sharing the page with this newly prominent youngster, the zany descends from the commedia dell'arte *zanni*, the artful, scheming, and bumbling clown; parodies of scholars and pedagogues are mainstays of commedia tradition (Fig. 31).[39]

Not only the zany, but also the dunce, the Merry Andrew, the fool, the quack-doctor jostle against images of objects, animals, tradesmen, and so on (Figs. 32–38). The Merry Andrew is the comical sidekick of the carnival mountebank or the quack-doctor—familiar figures in the rural marketplace or country fair, the original of the "snake-oil salesmen." The dunce begins life as a parody of the fastidious scholiast Duns Scotus and gradually descends into the elementary schoolroom as a figure of ridicule; the "idle fool" of *The New England Primer* is usually pictured with a dunce cap. The festive and the theatrical, then as now, had long drawn on traditions of scholastic satire as a treasury of humor, and in the eighteenth century they were joined by the work-for-hire satire of Grub Street hacks.[40]

Figure 31   Harlequin teaches his son, from "Maternità di Arlecchino,"
pl. IX from *The Marvellous Malady of Harlequin*, an eighteenth-century
illustrated Dutch commedia dell'arte scenario designed by G. J. Zavery.
This scenario describes "the illness, pregnancy, and marvellous
confinement of Harlequin as well as the education of his young son."
In true festive and Rabelaisian tradition, after vomiting and mooning
the audience when he gets an "injection" from the doctor, Harlequin
gives birth to sons. The one babe that survives is breast-fed, rocked,
deloused, whipped, and finally, as this plate illustrates, taught to read,
in a comprehensive parody edition of traditional commonplaces of
child-rearing and education. Harlequin begins life as a member of the
ranks of commedia *zanni*, from which the ABC books' zanies descend.
Note the ubiquitous ferule attached to the writing desk. (Reprinted from
Duchartre, following 55; courtesy of the Newberry Library, Chicago)

W stands for Whale, for Waggon, and Wing.

X stands for Xerxes, the great Persian King.

Y stands for Yew Tree, for Youth, and for Yellow.

Z stands for Zany, a foolish Young Fellow

15

Figure 32 *(right)* Like many nineteenth-century alphabets, "Miss Lovechild"'s *Ladder to Learning* (c. 1851) echoes earlier alphabets, especially *The New England Primer*, with its Whale and Xerxes. Here, too, the Zany is shown with a typical accompaniment: books. (Courtesy of the American Antiquarian Society)

Figures 33–34 *(opposite)* The Quack Doctor and the Zany from *A Little Lottery Book for Children* (Worcester, 1788). *Fig. 33 (top)*, Q; *Fig. 34 (bottom)*, Z. Taking up the Lockean prescription to make learning pleasurable, this chapbook turns the alphabet into a game. On the reverse of every letter is a picture: "As soon as the child can speak, let it stick a pin through the side of the leaf where the pictures are" (8) until it hits the letter. (Instructors and readers often used pins as miniature pointers in reading books, and occasionally one comes upon pages with the pin pricks still visible.) The book is prefaced with an elaborate apologia for the gambling device, to be played for "apples, oranges, almonds, raisins, gingerbread or nuts" (7). The cuts for the Merry-Andrew and the Quack Doctor originate in Thomas's *Lilliputian Masquerade* (attributed to Giles Jones), another Newbery-pirated chapbook, which explicitly draws on an urban carnival tradition. The mix of images—animals, objects, roles, as well as emblems (V is "Vanity")—is typical of the genre. (Courtesy of the American Antiquarian Society)

60 Queen LX

70 Quackdoctor LXX

Queen.

Quack-doc-tor.

1900 Zebra MDCCCC

2000 Zany MM

Ze-bra.

Za-ny.

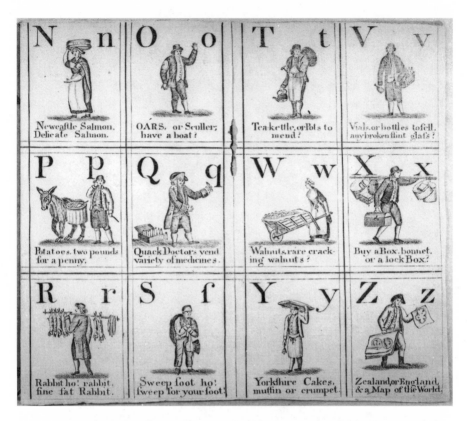

Figure 35 *The Uncle's Present, a New Battledoor* (Philadelphia, 1809), a cardboard hornbook, depicts peddlers' cries, which draw on both an urban tradition and country market and fair imagery. A popular print genre since the sixteenth century (see Shesgreen, 12–22), the "book of cries" adapts to the nursery beginning in the first decade of the nineteenth century with *The Cries of London* (Hartford, 1807; see Rosenbach, 131). The association of the alphabet with street cries is consistent with the orality and, by the turn of the century, the consumerism in the iconography of the ABCs. The Quack Doctor pictured here for Q is the familiar fair character. (Courtesy of the American Antiquarian Society)

Was an Angler, and fifh'd with a Hook.

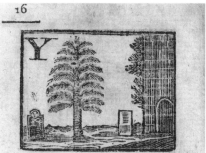

Was a Yew-tree, and grew near a Church.

Was a Blockhead, and ne'er learn'd his Book.

A poor Zany, was left in the Lurch.

Figures 36–37 From *The Royal Alphabet; or, Child's Best Instructor* (Worcester, 1787). *Figure 36 (left)*, A and B; *Figure 34 (right)*, Y and Z. Note that the alphabet itself is figured as the instructor of the title. The blockhead (Fig. 36) here appears as a jester or zany, carrying the fool's staff. Like fools and zanies, the blockhead's main qualification for his role in the ABC dramatis personae is that he "ne'er learn'd his book." He becomes a familiar figure in the literature of ABC, with the common rhyme "Who never learns his ABC, / forever will a blockhead be." Also appearing in this alphabet is Xanthippe, Socrates' wife, who emerges from the tradition of scholar-parody. The zany (Fig. 37) here pictured in stocks, illustrates, more emphatically than most, the intimacy between the festive and the disciplinary. (Courtesy of the American Antiquarian Society)

N, Never were such Times! said
Nicholas Hotch-Potch, as Muley Hassan, Mufti
of Moldavia, put on his Barnacles to see little
Tweedle gobble them up, when Kia Khan Kreuse
transmogrified them into Pippins, because Snip's
wife cried, Illikipilliky, lass a-day! 'tis too bad to
titter at a body, when Hamet el Mammet, the bot-
tle-nosed Barber of Balsora, laughed ha! ha! ha!
on beholding the Elephant spout mud over the 'Prentice, who pricked his trunk with a needle, while
Dicky Snip the Taylor read the Proclamation of
Chrononhotonthologos, offering a thousand sequins
for taking Bombardinian, Bashaw of three tails,
who killed Aldiborontiphoskyphorniostikos.

Figure 38 In R. Stennett's *Aldiborontiphoskyphorniostikos, a Round Game for Merry Parties* (New York, 1829), carnival is incorporated into the parlor in a game that limits the festive activity to tongue-twisting. This round game requires players to repeat a cumulative narrative, full of polysyllabic, mock-Latin names (in alphabetical order), and theatrical intrigue, drawn from a variety of sources, including Henry Carey's 1743 satire *Chrononhotonthologos* (in turn based on Fielding's *Tom Thumb*). *Aldiborontiphoskyphorniostikos* includes an episode of alphabetic cannibalism: letters are turned into pippins and eaten. (Courtesy of the American Antiquarian Society)

Alphabet books, and playful alphabets within primers, are miniature text-image festivals, in which slyness and subversion frolic on authority's turf. Like a pontiff opening a medieval festival, the monolithic alphabet that appears as a frontispiece on many of these books replaces the face of authority and authorship with the sanctioned version of the ABCs, unchanged (with the important exception of the Protestant excision of the cross) over centuries.

"The Alphabet Turn'd Posture-Master": A Morphology of Alphabet Texts

The most important and most characteristic attribute of letters in the new pedagogical alphabet that emerges in the 1750s and develops over the next century is that they *do* things. Letters, for example, settle disputes and incite wars. In *The History of Little Goody Two-Shoes*, the heroine, who becomes the Mistress of ABC College, tenders the solace of letters to bickering spouses: "You must solemnly agree that if one speak an angry word, the other will not answer till he or she has distinctly called over all the letters in the alphabet" (21).[41] If letters soothe the savage conjugal breast, they also exhort to battle: "There was once such a disturbance in the state of Literature, that great A, who presides over the commonwealth of letters was obliged to summon all the members to prepare for war."[42]

In its association with the image, the alphabet exploits the visual field, which is its natural habitat, while the alphabet narrative emphasizes the alphabet's attribute of consistent sequencing. The image intensifies the materiality of the alphabetic sign by association with things in the world, and the alphabet seems, increasingly, *of* the world, not merely a sign but rather a thing of material substance. In the alphabets I discussed in Chapter 1, the letters were passive and inert, acted upon or associated with narrative action, but not themselves agents (e.g.,

"The Crow cryeth á á" and "In Adam's fall / We sinned all"). This changes with alphabets like "A Apple Pye" and "A was an Archer."

In his *Morphology of the Folktale*, Vladimir Propp sets out to study "the folktale according to the functions of its dramatis personae" (20). The alphabet's dramatis personae, by contrast to the folktale's, is constant. As for its functions—its actions or behaviors—the dramatis personae of the alphabet might be said to have only one, and that is somehow to combine into meaningful, readable units. But reading doesn't really qualify as an *inherent* function of the alphabet.[43] The *components* of reading, and of alphabetic learning, however, do: ordering, internalization, representation. That these three functions are present in every alphabetic text is not itself very remarkable. The ABCs come in a conventional order; the student has to take them in, to memorize them to learn to read; the alphabet is transmitted via graphic representation. What is remarkable is the way in which the alphabetic functions appear to extend themselves, draw meaning to themselves, and create the powerful motifs that characterize alphabetic texts.

In the eighteenth century and into the nineteenth, the pedagogical alphabet appears in a number of physical formats and with a variety of formal characteristics. The physical formats range from an updated version of the hornbook—a folded sheet of cardboard with an icon-alphabet—to a few pages in a primer, to an entire book devoted to the letters of the alphabet, in either chapbook or accordion format.[44] Sometimes the pedagogical alphabet makes an appearance inside another kind of text—in the novellas of *Goody Two-Shoes*, for example, and in *Giles Gingerbread*. More rarely, the pedagogical alphabet forms the basis of an entire narrative.[45] Formally, the letters may appear in combination, as a monolith; or they may appear separately, in association with pictures or icons, *as* images or icons themselves, and in alphabet rhymes or narratives.

In the period 1750–1850, three main types of alphabet emerge, based fundamentally on the three functions described above, that is, internalization, representation, and ordering. I describe them here in the chronological order of their rise to prominence, although all three have currency across the entire period under discussion.

Swallow alphabets, from the function of internalization, appear to be the most prominent alphabets before 1800. I borrow this name from the "swallowing" folk motif, in which a protagonist gets eaten (Tom Thumb, Jack the Giant Killer, Red Riding Hood).[46] The folktale nomenclature suits these alphabets, which are among the earliest and most clearly and closely linked to folk motifs. These alphabets display tropes of consumption—letters eating other letters, letters being eaten by children, letters in the mouths of animals, letters pictured with, or as, food. "A Apple Pye" is one model of the swallow alphabet, but the motif is a frequent one. Plainly put, there's a lot of eating in these books, as there is in fairy tales, for some of the same reasons.[47] Letters are sometimes eaten by persons or by other letters within a narrative, but they are consumed also as a commodity on the market.[48]

These alphabets offer leftovers from what Mikhail Bakhtin calls the festive banquet, which he describes as being "intimately connected with speech, with wise conversation and gay truth." In the festive banquet, "man tastes the world, introduces it into his body, makes it part of himself" (*Rabelais*, 281). The Catholic alphabet, headed by the cross and accompanied by oral ritual, implied sacramental consumption. Now the magical food is quite separate from the church, but bears some marks of a folk-centered feast. "A Apple Pye," for example, can seemingly provide vast quantities of food: all twenty-four letters engage with the pie, more than one makes off with the whole thing, and several of them battle for it.[49] Bakhtin notes the transfer, in the Romantic period, beginning with the late eighteenth century, of "the concrete (one might say bodily)

O RARE Harry Parry!
When will you marry?
When Apples and Pears are ripe;
I'll come to your Wedding,
Without any Bidding,
And lie with your Bride all Night.
SONG

A B C D E F G
H I K L M N O
P Q R S T U
V W X Y Z &

SING a Song of Six Pence,
A Bag full of Rye:
Four and twenty naughty Boys,
Baked in a Pye.
And when the Pye was open'd,
The Birds began to sing;
Was not this a dainty Dish,
To set before the King?
LIAR

Figure 39 "Four and twenty blackbirds" from Nurse Lovechild's *Tommy Thumb's Song Book, for all little masters and misses, to be sung to them by their nurses, until they can sing themselves. To which is added, a letter from a lady on nursing* (Worcester: Isaiah Thomas, 1788). Here's Tom Thumb again, performing only as a brand-name. This alphabet pie is in its natural habitat, surrounded by bawdy and festive folk imagery. According to the Opies (*Oxford Dictionary of Nursery Rhymes*, 394–395), the four-and-twenty Blackbirds of the more familiar rhyme had already been at least partially transformed to "naughty boys" in Mary Cooper's 1744 *Tommy Thumb's Pretty Song Book*. They dismiss any originary link between the twenty-four blackbirds and the letters of the alphabet, though clearly this printer imagines such a link. (Courtesy of the American Antiquarian Society)

experience of the one, inexhaustible being, as it was in the Middle Ages and the Renaissance" to an "individual carnival, marked by a vivid sense of isolation" (*Rabelais*, 37). In the literature of alphabetical learning, "the one, inexhaustible being" inheres in the inexhaustible, infinitely consumable alphabet. During the eighteenth century, while reading instruction is entirely oral and reading is not yet an exclusively silent and isolated activity, the alphabet becomes bound to festivity (Figs. 39 and 40).

Alphabet narratives thematize festive and commercial consumption. For example, eating is a central plot device in *The Entertaining History of Tommy Gingerbread: A Little Boy, Who Lived upon Learning* (New York, 1796):

"You must know, Tommy, that all the words in the world are spelt, or made up, of these twenty-four marks or letters," pulling out of his pocket an alphabet cut in pieces, which he had made of gingerbread, for he was by trade a gingerbread baker[;] these he placed in this manner:

a b c d e f g h i k l m

n o p q r s t v w x y z

All the words in the world, says Tommy laughing. (17)

The similar *Giles Gingerbread* opens with an image of the peddler "Old Gaffer Ginger-bread" (Fig. 41):

Old Gingerbread, with wisdom sound,
Sells useful knowledge by the pound,
And feeds the little folks who're good
At once with learning and with food,
What say you, Friends . . . Shall we go buy?
Aye, Aye!—Who's first then, you or I?

Figure 40 "Christmas Pye" from *A Little Pretty Pocket-Book* (1787). (Courtesy of the John M. Wing Foundation, the Newberry Library, Chicago)

In both *Tommy Gingerbread* and *Giles Gingerbread*, the little consumers are meant both to purchase and eat the alphabetic offering, pleasurably internalizing the alphabet:

Heyday, *Giles*, says he, what do you love your Learning so well, as to eat up your book? Why Father, says *Giles*, I am not the only Boy who has eat his Words. No boy loves his Book better than I do, but I always learn it before I eat it. (22–23)

Consumption in these texts amounts to a topos, with three aspects. First, in the marketplace, consumption begins with the buying of the book. As in the passage cited above, many books are preening and self-conscious about this process, containing advertisements blended into the narrative.[50] Second, the text is internalized by the reader, consumed with the eyes, to encourage an intensely visual, internal form of reading.

Figure 41 "Old Gaffer Gingerbread" from *The Renowned History of Giles Gingerbread.* (Courtesy of the American Antiquarian Society)

The internalizing of the alphabet, a task that by the late eighteenth century the vast majority of New England children and adults were mastering, and the newly perceived necessity of reading were part and parcel of what in this period becomes a new aspect of personality.[51] Third, remnants of the ancient sacred orality of the Church meet up with the rhetorical orality of school, and a festive, folk orality of traditional culture.

Body alphabets, which begin to appear in the 1780s, develop from the alphabet's function of representation, especially in its classical mimetic sense as imitation of human action. In these anthropomorphizing images and texts, letters are agents of physical action (Figs. 42 and 43). The emphasis is not on the act of the consumption of the alphabet, but on the *result* of this internalization. These alphabets, like powerful manna, induce physical configurations. In *The Comical Hotch-Potch, or the Alphabet Turn'd Posture-Master*, a "Comic Set / Of fellows form the Alphabet."[52] In this schoolboy satire, the alphabet is conceived as "posture-master," a hybrid eighteenth-century figure, who has a place in the schoolroom, as

The alphabet illustration contains the following letter captions:

A — He first finds the way, / To form a great A.
B — By a bright thought, / To a B he is brought.
C — He's forc'd to strain his 4, / Left the C should be marr'd.
D — Now a D he is found, / With his Nose to the ground.
E — With the rest he'll agree, / And affist them with E.
F — From the Head to the Feet, / He's an F quite complete.
G — Look forward you'll fee, / He's in form of a G.
H — With his Hands in the Air, / An H does declare.
I — He looks mighty dry, / While in form of an I.
K — Do but look and you'll fay, / Here ftruts Comical K.
L — I, fits him down eafy, / And hopes for to pleafe ye.
M — Hah! Hah! here comes M, / To accompany them.
N — Now N follows after, / To excite you to laughter.
O — Any body may know, / He's in form of an O.
P — Pray look at me, / In the form of a P.
Q — Any Shape I can take, / So a Q here I make.
R — Here's an R to your view, / Which I hope fatiffies you.
S — Here he's twifted & twirld, / To make S to your mind.
T — T next does exhibit, / In form of a Gibbet.
V — V joins with the reft, / In their humorous jeft.
W — It is ftrange but moft true, / That I make W.
X — To pleafe every Sex, / I am forming an X.
Y — With his Arms full extended, / For Y is intended.
Z — It will ftick in my Gizzard / If I can't make an Z.

The Comical HOTCH-POTCH, or the ALPHABET turn'd POSTURE-MASTER.
Do but fee this Comic Set —
Of Fellows form the Alphabet.
Printed for & Sold by CARINGTON BOWLES.   at Nº 69 in Sᵗ Pauls Church Yard, LONDON.

Figure 42 *The Comical Hotch-Potch, or the Alphabet Turn'd Posture-Master.* Originally printed in London by Carington Bowles in 1782, this alphabet was a popular broadside in America. It was reprinted in chapbook form in Philadelphia in 1814 (a version I discuss in Chapter 3). Here the alphabet as a whole is a "posture-master," while the individual letters illustrate, using the bodies of schoolboys, the postures to be mastered. Typical of early alphabetic texts is this tension between orthodoxy—the student must conform to the physical configuration of the letter—and a raucous, festive undercurrent—he can moon you (see the letter M) while doing it. (Courtesy of the Williamsburg Foundation)

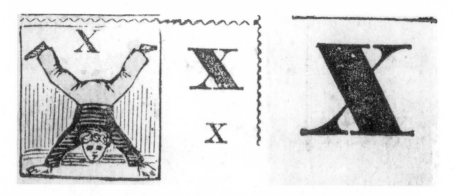

Figure 43 X from *Pictured A, B, C* (c. 1850). (Courtesy of the Rare Book Department, The Free Library of Philadelphia)

kin to the dancing-master, as well as at the fair, as an acrobat. The festive and somewhat bawdy combine with the disciplinary: "T next does exhibit, / In form of a Gibbet" as well as "He's forc'd to strain hard, / Lest the C should be mar'd" and "A D he is found, / With his Nose to the ground." Here, as elsewhere, the child has become the site or habitation of festivity, about which the culture is, precisely, ambivalent.

The alphabet's link to the human body has a long tradition.[53] The sixteenth-century French type designer Geoffrey Tory, for example, based his designs on the human form.[54] But the letters of typography are quite a different matter from the letters of literacy. Even when type designers place letters within a symbolic universe, they aren't likely to lose sight of the fact that type is a human technology. Literacy is another story; when the human form engages with the alphabet, as in the *Hotch-Potch*, it is always the human form that must conform to the size and shape of the letters, not the other way around.

In "The Alphabet Tattoo," a narrative alphabet (with no images) reprinted in a number of editions between 1787 and 1835, the personified letters are examined by "Great A" as likely recruits for a patriotic army. After lambasting most of the letters—"great D" is a "Drunkard" and his son, "little d," is a dunce, while "Mr. P [is] a prating Puppy," and so on—"Great A" finds three or four possible officers. "Great A," the narrative concludes, "being a person of Prudence and Penetration, never takes up with appearances only, but inspects . . . the very Hearts of Men" (26). *This* A, unlike its more famous, scarlet descendent, performs its office sufficiently well, for by power of "example" and "prudent management" he converts the rest of the letters to righteousness.[55]

The *alphabet array*, or the *worldly alphabet*, emphasizing the alphabet's function of ordering and arbitrary arrangement, is the one that has endured, the one most familiar to the modern reader, and the one most often encountered in primers after 1800, on the model of "A is for apple" (Figs. 44–46). Increasingly associated with a wide variety of external objects, both representative of and represented by the world, the new alphabet becomes a kind of world in itself. To take in the alphabet becomes a way of taking in the world. The worldly alphabet is the one that has won out in the era of secular reading instruction. With its apparent encyclopedism or scientism, its impulse toward organization and categorization, this is the alphabet most obviously a product of the Enlightenment. Whether objects, animals, or body parts, this alphabet represents, in words or images, the world at large, arrayed through the arbitrary but powerful order of the ABCs, forcefully producing a world that is knowable, graspable, and, most strikingly, obtainable. While through the medium of the swallow alphabets you might, fictively at least, have the power to consume the letters, to make them a part of you, the alphabet array alerts you to the vast quantity of things in the world up for consumption. At the same time, these images efface the elaborate operations of power required actually to bring these objects to one's doorstep.

The worldly alphabet marks an important moment in the history of

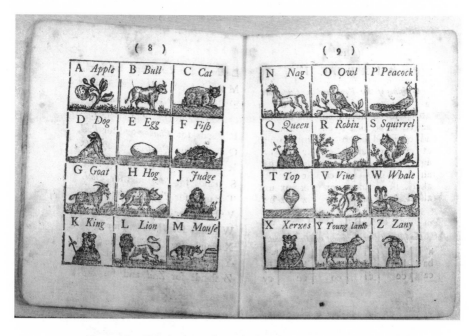

Figure 44 Alphabet array from *The Royal Primer* (1796). (Courtesy of the American Antiquarian Society)

the alphabet. If the orality of the alphabet reasserts itself through the swallow alphabets, in the alphabet array that orality is transferred to all things that can be linked to the alphabet, which is to say: everything in the world. Although this is the alphabet that may seem the most normal and ordinary and familiar to us, it is the one that most resembles Borges's "Chinese Encyclopedia," in which "animals are divided into: (a) belonging to the Emperor, (b) embalmed, (c) tame, (d) sucking pigs, (e) sirens, (f) fabulous, (g) stray dogs, (h) included in the present classi-fication . . . (l) *et cetera*" (quoted in Foucault, *Order*, xv). In a taxon-omy as fantastic as Borges's, the alphabet array groups animals, and everything else, by the dazzling randomness of their shared initial letter.

Figures 45–46 Alphabet array from "Youths' Battledoor" (c. 1828). *Figure 45 (left)*, A and B; *Figure 46 (right)*, I and J. (Courtesy of the Rare Book Department, The Free Library of Philadelphia)

Isolated from their usefulness, isolated as well from any binding imaginative narrative, and quite often from any kind of verbal play, the objects represented by these alphabets are atomized, adrift on the page, unmodulated by any assessment or evaluation beyond their association to a letter of the alphabet. Objects, animals, people, body parts, virtues and vices, tools, clothing—the alphabet array displays them all side by side, at its pleasure, in an aesthetics of accumulation and accretion.

Paintings of the period display a similar technique of representation.

Figure 47 Copley's *John Hancock* (in Rebora and Staiti, pl. 22, p. 212; courtesy Museum of Fine Arts, Boston. Reproduced with permission. © 1999 Museum of Fine Arts, Boston. All Rights Reserved.)

John Singleton Copley, for example, records the burghers of colonial America at the same time that the alphabet text is undergoing its shift. Benjamin West critiqued Copley's portrait of John Hancock (Fig. 47) for exactly its lack of modulation: "Each part being . . . Equell in Strength of Coulering and finishing, Each Making to much a Picture of its silf, without that Due Subordanation to the Principle Parts" (West to Copley, August 4, 1766, quoted in Rebora and Staiti, 40). Paul Staiti offers as a rationale for Copley's practice that he "structured his pictorial economy like a merchant's ledger" and "articulated and arranged pictured objects with equal emphasis, from buttons to eyes." Staiti sees these modes as

> analogous to the accounting methods of Boston's merchants. Copley's things, like the notations in the merchants' ledgers, were not set into a hierarchy determined by the importance of the individual objects but merely assigned positions of equivalent value on a surface. . . . It is in this relentless enumerating and stacking of visual elements that the characteristic concerns of Copley's colonial realism emerge. (42)

While something like "colonial realism" captures this mode, Staiti more formally calls this "numerical aesthetics" (42). Among Copley's precursors (and visual mentors)[56] are the Dutch painters of the Golden Age, who articulate what Roland Barthes has called "the empire of things," establishing the world, the secular, as painting's subject matter, cherishing representations of things for their utility. "Few substances" in these paintings, Barthes writes, "are not annexed to the empire of merchandise" ("World," 6). Objects in these works "articulate space"; at the same time, "this enumerative power constitutes certain men as objects." Barthes likens the "itemizing power" of these paintings to the French Civil Code, for its list "of real estate and chattels: 'domestic pigeons, wild rabbits, beehives, pond fish, wine presses, stills, ovens, manure and stable litter, wall hangings, mirrors, books and medals, linens,'" etc. (7). Alphabetized, this jumble of things forms the content of the alphabet book. Children of this epoch, then, are instructed to randomly enumerate in a way that seems normative and inevitable, because it is a procedure linked to other current modes and locations of representation in public records, account books, and paintings.

A number of encyclopedic alphabets based on this model emerge as well, among them alphabets of people, catalogs of types, stereotypes, and roles. *The Uncle's Present* (see Fig. 35), a catalog of peddlers' cries, falls under this category, as do some of the "A was an Archer" and "A was an Angler" rhymes. As we have seen, in these works carnival characters share the page with more conventional social, nontheatrical roles. While in many of these alphabets there is often a democratic leveling— with kings and rat catchers a few pages apart—there is also a less enticing sense of objectification: in these miniature "societies of the spectacle" everyone is valued, but valued only as an image.[57] In addition, there are many variations of alphabets performing a more explicit colonizing task, depicting "inhabitants of the world," representing national stereotypes (the Italian, presumably Catholic, is often shown as a peddler of "images"; the Frenchman as an idler; the African with an elephant tusk).

As these texts collaborate in the Enlightenment project of documenting the world, they participate in what Mary Louise Pratt has called a "planetary consciousness . . . marked by an orientation toward interior exploration and the construction of global-scale meaning" (15). Pratt is concerned with travel narratives and natural history, texts that recount movement through the world. The alphabet text gathers the bounty of these travels and produces them not only as knowledge, pure and simple, but also as language itself. That is, the alphabet book posits the world of imperial and capitalist enterprise as one that is already inside the language-learning child.

A Poetics of Alphabetization

"A is for apple"—this most recent and long-lived construction of the alphabetic statement, the foundational construction for the worldly alphabet, is based on synecdoche, the part-for-whole figure. Figural language is conventionally opposed to literal language, each presumably carrying a special kind of meaning. But the alphabetical trope takes a turn away from the letter's literal nonmeaning, its lack, to meaningfulness; without the trope, the alphabet lacks a language. Nontropic alphabet books, based on centuries of oral tradition, teach articulation independent of meaningful language: ab, eb, ib, ob, ub; ba, be, bi, bo, bu.

Printers and primer writers use verbal and visual figuration as alphabet mnemonics in a more or less chronological progression from the seventeenth through the mid–nineteenth century. First, letters are juxtaposed to images and rhymes (e.g., icon of Adam or Adam and Eve with "In Adam's fall / We sinned all"); based on the Renaissance emblem, these three parts are analogous to the emblem's visual image (the icon of Adam or Adam and Eve), its *explicatio* (the rhyme) and motto (which here takes the form of a letter). Historically, the next construction encountered in ABC books is prosopopoeia, or personification (A was an Archer; A Apple Pye). Finally, at around the start of the nine-teenth century the alphabet synecdoche makes its appearance.

Although a figure conveys all three functions of the alphabet—namely, representation, internalization, and consistent order—each tends to emphasize only one. Thus, emblem's strength is representation, prosopopoeia's is internalization, and synecdoche's is arbitrary arrangement. Generally speaking, the trope-function pair prevails in a given historical moment that most fully answers two criteria: it must respond to the symbolic requirements of its culture—that is, it must match the way in which the culture understands meaningfulness; and it must fit in with the current status of literacy—both its desired and real range—in that culture. While synecdoche and arbitrary arrangement seem to have won out over the long run, answering nicely the needs of, for example, bureaucracies, markets, and sound bites, in the first half of the nine-teenth century they vied with the internalization/prosopopoeia and representation/emblem pairs.

Prosopopoeia has an implicit visual element. Like the visual icons associated with the alphabet, verbal figures served to naturalize the al-phabet. *Prosopopoeia* is from the Greek for face, *prosopon*, a synec-dochic word meaning "at the side of or towards the eyes" (Partridge, *Origins*). Prosopopoeia is the trope of the close-up. This figure ani-mates both by bringing something abstract or absent before one's eyes and by giving eyes to the abstract/absent. "Although we cannot speak a word," goes an alphabet riddle, "We tell what others do."[58] The character of A in "The Alphabet Tattoo" "inspects . . . the very Hearts of Men" (31). These alphabets-come-to-life stare back, with eyes that are more than eyes, speaking knowingly of hidden things. While meta-phors of eating and consumption serve the alphabet's function of inter-nalization by representing that function, prosopopoeia does the work more subtly by allowing the alphabet a kind of X-ray vision. This trope circumscribes the child's world with witnesses, as if to say, if God or Mother or Teacher nods, the eyes of the alphabet are always open.

Alphabetic prosopopoeia, with its watchfulness, shares the field of antic personification with images of coins in eighteenth-century money satires like Joseph Addison's "The Adventures of a Shilling" and Charles Johnstone's *Chrysal* (in which a guinea gets into all sorts of intimate places and can see into people's hearts). The charm of these mock-heroics is akin to that of Donne's "The Flea" or Burns's "To a Louse," in which an appetite for special knowledge, especially erotic knowledge, gets displaced onto a parasite with unlimited access to the object of desire. Money is in the flea or louse position, as it endlessly circulates in a capital economy, with its traditional linkage to corruption, filth, and a kind of promiscuous or unregulated increase. As ABCs and primers become a Grub Street staple, the alphabet similarly establishes a vast range of circulation and accessibility; it borrows the tone of these satires along with the panoptical alertness and curiosity of their heroes.

If prosopopoeia extends the alphabet's graphic and peripatetic aspects into narrative, the synecdoche "A is for apple" gives the alphabet a mouth and a voice, binding the names of the letters to the names of things in the world. While synecdoche's list-generating capacity makes it a perfect transmitter of the alphabet's function of arbitrary arrangement, the trope has other powers as well. In Kenneth Burke's scheme of master tropes, synecdoche is the trope of representation. I would adjust this slightly to say that synecdoche is the figure of nonmimetic representation: A stands for apple because A is *in* apple, in the same way the senators from New York stand for New York. Synecdoche's sleight of hand makes the alphabet seem to have a syntax; the phrase "stands for" becomes an extension of the letter, its prop, or legs. "A stands for apple" would seem to be a more "rational" form of expression than the metaphoric prosopopoeia. Roman Jakobson links synecdoche, along with metonymy, to realism in fiction (111). For him, metaphor is based on similarity, and metonymy and synecdoche on contiguity, whether semantic or positional. The desire to naturalize the alphabet by adducing a putative similarity to something familiar (as in Comenius's "The Crow cryeth á á") leads to the metaphoric constructions of emblem and prosopopoeia. While these metaphorized alphabets create a fantastic world of animals crying out the letters and letters marching about like figures in a puppet theater, the world of the synecdochic alphabet is an infinite list of objects. If metaphor makes for striking *imagines agentes*, synecdoche makes of the world itself a vast storehouse, a *copia* of boundless plenty. When, in *Capital*, Marx describes the chain of substitutions that the value of a commodity generates, he articulates precisely the way in which the alphabet synecdoche operates: "The number of such possible expressions [of the value of a commodity in the terms of another commodity] is limited only by the number of the different kinds of commodities distinct from it." Serendipitously using the alphabetic character to substitute for any commodity, he seems to be defining the alphabet synecdoche: "The isolated expression of A's value is thus transformed into the indefinitely expandable series of different simple expressions of that value" (154). That is, "A stands for ——."

In addition to, and in part because of, the alphabet's new structure as a commodity, synecdoche becomes a kind of import-export device. At the same time, the alphabet becomes a conveyance, like other nineteenth-century technologies, for bringing far-flung objects up close, objects that in turn are the letters' visa out into the wide world. But in the process of alphabetization, that wide world becomes an anatomized map of isolated objects, for in what way are "apple, ant, arm" (for example) really representative of anything we might want to call the world? These isolated images make the alphabet seem "real," as real as this arm and this apple. "A stands for Apple" and its variations, "A is for Apple," "A as in Apple," while each has a slightly different nuance, all extend the associative world of the A to the very outer boundaries of language. While it surely makes a difference whether A stands for Adam or Apple, America or Argentina, Army or Abolition, Ann or Andrew, the very structure of the statement suggests that A inevitably will stand for all of these things and more.

The paradigmatic synecdoche, according to Kenneth Burke, is microcosm for macrocosm. A work of art follows this paradigm, especially in its opening, which "implicitly contains the future that is to become explicit" (509). The letter as it is represented in alphabet books is a model of this synecdochic relation to the world. The A, for example, "stands for" apple, arm, ant because it is contained *by* them and also seems to contain them; unfold the A, these books seem to say, and worlds will open to you.

Iconographically, I have charted in this chapter a movement from an affiliation with folk orality in the early alphabet books to a commercialized and, eventually, a sentimentalized, gentrified notion of literacy, beginning at the turn of the century and continuing to the midcentury and beyond.[59] Increasingly commodified in the culture, literacy is at the same time increasingly internalized by individuals. The alphabet, seemingly separate from human control, seemingly able to organize the world around itself, has become fetishized. The dominant feature of the fetish "is that, by being a material embodiment of a human aspiration or motive, it tends by the very fact of its objective form to cause its creator or employer to forget that he is himself responsible for its creation or continued existence" (Simpson, *Fetishism*, 11). We have seen some of the powers that, in the alphabet texts and images, have accrued to these fetish-letters. Personified and anthropomorphized, they perform actions; they provide food; they have material substance and appear to have weight in the world; they "tell what others do"; they see into people's hearts; they hold up for display various roles, both in and out of the ordinary course of social life; they promise rewards and punishments. In their relation to the festive, and in their functions of internalization and representation, letters promise sensual and emotional pleasures, they promise freedom, and they promise renewal. In their relation to discipline and in their function of arbitrary arrangement, letters exact bureaucratic and institutional conformity.

The all-seeing, all-representing tropic alphabet contributes to the creation of the literate world, while alphabetization initiates the individual into that world. Although there were many initiates of all ages (and many others systematically or circumstantially shut out from literacy), it is the child toward whom cultural programs are directed. Preschool instruction practices, classroom practices, and the performance of the language encountered in texts all contribute to rites of alphabetization. The poetics of alphabetization structures the language of these rites; the tropes and images that circulate the alphabet enact and embody the rituals of alphabetization within texts. The synecdochic letter—A, for example—unfolds to reveal the likeness of a world. Who grasps the A has in hand the key to that mimetic world, which in turn is meant to reveal the wide world beyond. But that wide world is, by turn, produced by the very forms in which it is represented.

She may sit as a queen in the empire of letters, for she must ever materially control the cause of learning. . . .

    —*Charles Burroughs (1827)*

When our land is filled with virtuous and patriotic mothers, then will it be filled with virtuous and patriotic men. She who was first in the transgression, must be yet the principal earthly instrument in the restoration.

    —*John S. C. Abbott (1834)*

A weak and ignorant woman will always be governed with the greatest difficulty.

    —*Benjamin Rush (1787)*

Chapter Three

"That Mother's Kiss":

The Alphabet, Gender,

and Narrative

By the early nineteenth century, reading has become what the popular nineteenth-century poet Lydia Huntley Sigourney calls "a necessity of existence" (*Letters of Life*, 39). In a recurring image in primers, a child tries and fails to teach an animal the alphabet; the characteristic moral is "Right glad am I, and thankful too, / I was not made a dog, like you," highlighting literacy as the key distinction between animal and child (Fig. 48). As literacy becomes embedded in an increasingly wide range of cultural practices, alphabetization becomes more than a rite of initiation. It is now the primary means of socialization, the lack of which renders one not just déclassé ("forever a blockhead be") but subhuman.

This chapter focuses on a central aspect of this assimilation: the function of the woman, especially the mother, in instituting and maintaining the new "reading world."[1] At the same time that women are becoming a historical presence in the transmission of the alphabet, they

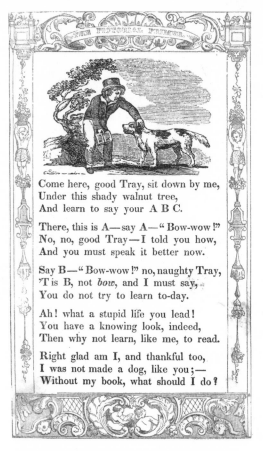

THE PICTORIAL PRIMER.

Come here, good Tray, sit down by me,
Under this shady walnut tree,
And learn to say your A B C.

There, this is A—say A—" Bow-wow!"
No, no, good Tray—I told you how,
And you must speak it better now.

Say B—" Bow-wow!" no, naughty Tray,
'T is B, not *bow*, and I must say,
You do not try to learn to-day.

Ah! what a stupid life you lead!
You have a knowing look, indeed,
Then why not learn, like me, to read.

Right glad am I, and thankful too,
I was not made a dog, like you;—
Without my book, what should I do?

Figure 48 "Without my book, what should I do?" from *The Illustrated Primer* (1847). The child-book-animal figure becomes part of popular iconography. On a bookcase in Susan Warner's house on Constitution Island, New York, for example, is a mid-nineteenth-century plaster statue of a boy showing his book to his dog. This circle of affection imitates the mother-child education model, and it helps preserve the dog, newly incorporated into the household on affective, not just utilitarian, terms, from abuse. (Courtesy of the Rare Book Department, The Free Library of Philadelphia)

are newly represented in relation to the alphabet—in visual images and in written discourse—across a range of genres. I will examine ABC books, primers, conduct manuals, and education treatises in this chapter, and a classic "women's" novel in the next. There are three, interleaved parts to the history of the alphabet's link to gender. The first concerns what happens to the alphabet when it is positioned in relation to women; the second, what happens to women when they are positioned in relation to the alphabet; and the third, what happens to men in this new scheme. As we shall see, the alphabetic functions of representation, ordering, and internalization are now accommodated and naturalized through representations of a maternal voice and body; this new configuration has consequences as well for the development of narrative between 1800 and 1850, which I discuss in the final section of this chapter and in the following chapters.

Gender and the Alphabet

In 1814, the Philadelphia printer James Webster issued an edition of *The Comical Hotch Potch, or the Alphabet Turn'd Posture Master* (Figs. 49–52), first published in Britain in 1782 (see Fig. 42).[2] This printer's choices of format, layout, and imagery register shifts in representations of the alphabet and in alphabetic learning after 1800, especially with regard to gender. American printers often simply copied British products, and much of the content of this chapbook indeed is identical, in text and image, to the broadside. The chapbook departs from the broadside, however, in ways that signal a new relation of the alphabet to gender. First, Webster has broken up the original "comic set" of twenty-four "fellows," arrayed in three rows on the sheet, into twelve pages with two letter-fellows each, and bound them into a sixteen-page signature, leaving them untinted. Second, the alphabet text is now framed by images of women.

To consider the more explicit shift first: the words of the title—originally a kind of caption to the broadside—share billing not, as in the original, with the letter-men, but with three "old wives," right hands directed upward, as though making "points" in their speech. These women are talking. This image appears on the new title page, positioned between the title and verse-subtitle. The central woman sits in a high-backed chair and looks directly out at the reader, right hand pointing up, left hand pointing down, as though, like one of the Fates, nominating sinners and saints. But if they've been weaving, measuring, and cutting, like the Fates, these figures seem to be announcing the results in the verse-subtitle: "Do but see this Comic Set / Of Fellows form the Alphabet." Are they narrating, as well, the alphabet rhymes that follow? Are they engendering the letter-men themselves?

It is well documented that women played an increasingly central role in the nation's literacy, as readers, writers, students, and teachers,

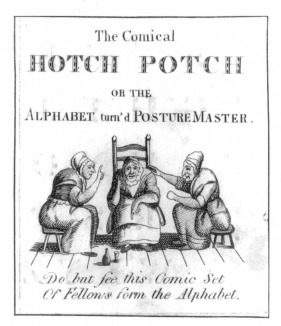

Figure 49 Old Mothers from *The Comical Hotch Potch* (1814). (Courtesy of the Connecticut Historical Society, Hartford, Connecticut)

between the Revolution and the Civil War. Women's literacy had "approximately doubled" between 1780 and 1840, according to Nancy Cott (15). The history of elementary education describes the rise of women as instructors and of mothers as home-instructors; girls were going to school; women were writing conduct books and educational treatises.[3] But if representations of women in alphabet texts may seem inevitable once women are historically present in alphabetization, two questions arise: How do these images function in relation to the alphabet and alphabetization? And how do these images function in relation to perceptions of women?

The *Hotch Potch* figures are clearly folk images,[4] owing more to Mother Goose than to previous images of women in association with the alphabet, such as Grammatica or Goody Two-Shoes. These "old mothers" inhabit their folk origins and carry traces of folk bawdiness and orality, such as the jug and cup sitting on the floor in front of them. If this alphabet somewhat precedes the reign of domesticity (by a decade or two, according to most scholarship of the period), it constitutes part of the cultural prologue to it. For it represents the new discursive space of the alphabet as explicitly feminized. I noted above in Chapter 2 the link between the trope of prosopopoeia and the alphabetic function of

He first finds the way,
To form a great A.

By a bright thought,
To a B he is brought.

Figure 50 A and B from *The Comical Hotch Potch* (1814). (Courtesy of the Connecticut Historical Society, Hartford, Connecticut)

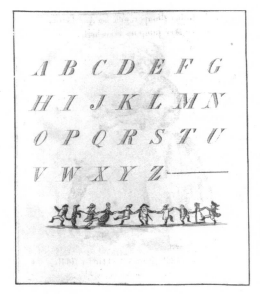

A B C D E F G
H I J K L M N
O P Q R S T U
V W X Y Z

Figure 51 ABC dancers from *The Comical Hotch Potch* (1814). (Courtesy of the Connecticut Historical Society, Hartford, Connecticut)

internalization in the original broadside. In the chapbook, while this trope is sustained, another mode of internalization is also represented: the figures have not only physically transformed themselves into letters; they have also come indoors.

The broadside emphasizes the collectivity of the "set" of "fellows," for they are presented all at once; the verses are subordinated to the bodies of the letter-men (or boys). Modulated differently, the chapbook elevates the alphabet rhymes to the same level as the alphabet's visual high jinks. After the title page comes a full-page alphabet in display type, updated with the letters J and U, missing from the broadside and hence missing from the nearly identical text of the chapbook's body-alphabet. Following the body of the book is another full-page alphabet, accompanied by a small festive image of dancers. The chapbook's frame closes with a full-page image of another "old mother" (Fig. 52):

> Here's old Mother Jumper, with her dog Thumper,
> You see they jump up very high,
> High diddle diddle, if they had but a Fiddle,
> I think they'd jump up to the Sky.

Webster offers a hodgepodge of alphabetic genres: variant texts of the alphabet, two with twenty-six, one with twenty-four characters, in an array of typefaces; an alphabet constituting the entirety of a little book; folk imagery mingled with the letters; the high-diddle-diddle cat (if it's a dog, as the rhyme claims, it's cross-dressing as a cat), associated with the alphabet at least since the first *New England Primer*. Details of this alphabet medley's composition are irreclaimable. Whatever the local constraints that made its new format a plausible one to James Webster's print shop, the overall frame and the mise-en-page of the alphabet in this chapbook signal a general cultural change over the life of this body-alphabet.

Like a narrative frame, the alphabet's frame positions the reader in regard to the text; in Chaucer's and Boccaccio's "frame stories," Walter Ong notes, "the reader can pretend to be one of the listening company" (*Orality*, 103). Webster's frame positions the reader in two ways: as an auditor and as the object of a woman's look. These two positions—listener and focus of a gaze—give a quarter turn to the commonplace "seen but not heard" of childhood. The child is meant to be seen listening.

As for that look, I would like to return to Roland Barthes's notion of the "empire of things" in Dutch painting. Barthes also

Here's old Mother Jumper, with her dog Thumper. You see they jump up very high,

High diddle diddle, if they had but a Fiddle, I think they'd jump up to the Sky.

Figure 52 Mother Jumper from *The Comical Hotch Potch* (1814). (Courtesy of the Connecticut Historical Society, Hartford, Connecticut)

considers what happens when Dutch painters turn to human subjects, and he finds that portraits are excepted from the rule of enumeration. The faces of the Dutch burghers evince a "*numen*," the gesture of the "divine nod," which is captured by the portrait's disarming gaze. These portraits consider you with the same coolness as they consider a length of fabric. As a consequence, when you look at a Dutch genre painting, yours is the organizing eye, but when the Dutch matron eyes you from her portrait, she puts *you* in order: "You become a matter of capital" ("World," 11). The "old mothers" of the *Hotch Potch* would seem to be taking a page from the Old Masters' book, with the notable difference that their "capital" consists of the alphabet. They are sizing you up as an object, not of commerce, but of alphabetization.

The letters seem to arise from the speech of these three women. And yet, though the women may be unlettered, the binding of these alphabet images within the pages of a book emphasizes textuality. A broadside, designed to be posted and read from a distance, is a public document, intended to be viewed by more than one person at a time. Broadsides provided occasions for the illiterate to participate in the public sphere by being auditors of the reading off of a text. In this second departure from the broadside, this alphabet shifts from a public or communal to a more private or domestic setting.

The title page of the chapbook directs attention to "hotch potch," which appears in large fancy capitals, twice the size of the rest of the letters, with a full line devoted to these two words. (In the broadside [see Fig. 42], the title appears underneath the array of images, as a kind of caption; the words "hotch-potch," "alphabet," and "posture-master" receive equal billing, in capital and small-capital letters, as distinct from the ordinary upper- and lowercase letters of the rest of the title.) The verb sense of "hotch"—to fidget, jump, or limp (*OED*)—associates its meaning with the original body-alphabet and "posture master" portion of the title. But the newly emphasized "hotch potch" has two senses. In the kitchen, it's a stew, and in the court, it's what the law calls a "collation" or "a throwing into a common lot of property for equality of division which requires that advancements to a child be made up to the estate by contribution or by an accounting" (*Webster's* 3d). The posture-master of the broadside has metamorphosed. No longer merely the disciplinarian-of-the-parlor, now this chapbook alphabet equalizes terms of inheritance. This chapbook captures in nascent form the reconfiguration that occurs when women enter the alphabetic picture: a formerly narrowly restricted patrilineal inheritance now becomes openhanded and matrilineal.

Women introduce gender difference—and gender roles—into the alphabetic environment. The male figures pose, perform, or embody the alphabet, while the women mark out the space for this activity. The potentially festive orality of the hotch-potch-as-stew is subordinated to a woman-organized space; the women of the title page, at any rate, are in a room, while the letter-men are suspended in space. The women have substance and volume: they cast shadows. The lengthened shadow of these women is the alphabet.

The women bind themselves to the letters with family ties. That is, the figures in the chapbook can never be seen all at once but appear two by two as you turn the pages. Their connection to one another, a given of the broadside, here depends on the reader and the women of the frame. In collaboration with the reader, the women provide a syntax for the alphabet.

While the figure of the woman had long been an alphabetic prop (Grammatica, for instance), she now manages the entire stage. The organizing principle for the alphabet is simply its conventional order. The feminized syntax of the alphabet is an elaboration of the alphabet's ordering function and suggests a fresh source for this order in the woman. The other alphabetic functions are also newly configured with the introduction of the woman. She counters the alphabet synecdoche's centrifugal potentiality with a centripetal draw, renewing the force of internalization. And she establishes for the alphabet's function of representation a materiality, so that the alphabet now exists like other objects, oriented in space.

The Space of the Alphabet

The alphabet rhyme "A was an Archer" is also reincarnated in a new format in the nineteenth century, exemplified by *The Men among the Letters* (see Fig. 26). The "men among" or tableau format becomes increasingly common and takes on architectural and monumental fea-

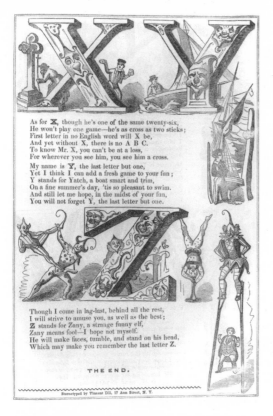

As for **X**, though he's one of the same twenty-six,
He won't play one game—he's as cross as two sticks;
First letter in no English word will X be,
And yet without X, there is no A B C.
To know Mr. X, you can't be at a loss,
For wherever you see him, you see him a cross.

My name is **Y**, the last letter but one,
Yet I think I can add a fresh game to your fun;
Y stands for Yatch, a boat smart and trim,
On a fine summer's day, 'tis so pleasant to swim.
And still let me hope, in the midst of your fun,
You will not forget Y, the last letter but one.

Though I come in lag-last, behind all the rest,
I will strive to amuse you, as well as the best;
Z stands for Zany, a strange funny elf,
Zany means fool—I hope not myself.
He will make faces, tumble, and stand on his head,
Which may make you remember the last letter Z.

THE END.

Stereotyped by Vincent Dill, 17 Ann Street, N. Y.

Figure 53 From *The Illuminated A, B, C* (New York, 1850s?). As the "tableau" or "men among" alphabet format develops in the mid and late century, it acquires a monumental and imperial affect. Here the letters organize the space architecturally. (Courtesy of the Connecticut Historical Society, Hartford, Connecticut)

tures later in the century (Fig. 53). In the "men among" model, people are represented on the same scale as the alphabet. As we have seen, the alphabet array throws objects out of relation with one another; their relationship to one another as well as to the reader is mediated by the alphabet, which also establishes the scale of the images. In *The Men among the Letters*, too, the characters determine scale. But the alphabet array subordinates real-world scale and proportion to alphabetic realism: a dog is as big as a house because it is not the relation of dog to house that counts but of dog and house, separately, to the letters. In *The Men among the Letters* and similar alphabets, the letters are arranged as though they are integral parts of the human habitat; the human figures are scaled in a consistent manner to the big-as-life (and bigger-than-life) letters. The butcher is to the B as the queen is to the Q. The alphabetic leveling of the "archer" rhyme finds its visual correlate.

In *The Good Boy's and Girl's Alphabet*, following the "men among" format, the letters function variously in the human habitat—or, rather, the human habitat adapts itself variously to the letters (Figs. 54–56). The letter may form a part of the landscape (weirdly, like Kubrick's 2001 monolith; see A, B, H, F, Y). The letter may form the boundaries of a space in which the person stands (C, D, O, Q). In the case of "R was a Robber," R swings from the top serif of the letter R: R hangs from R (Fig. 57). These letters don't go out of their way to accommodate the people, but, when necessary, they do accommodate the law. Like R, many of these are condensed monitory tales of discipline.[5] Darkly advising of its potential for punishment (and of alternative punishments, failing this one), this alphabetic image refers to a showier and graver form of bodily discipline. These images manifestly change the original, playfully absurd sense of the text. In combination with the images, the letter now not only identifies a person (R is a robber) but also restricts that person to a space, with occasionally fatal zeal.

As the tableau genre develops, the tone becomes sweetened and domesticated. As in the theatrical tableaux that were becoming popular at about the same time, in *The Illuminated American Primer* (1844; Figs. 58–61) small narratives are packed within the confines of the letters.[6] Most are drawn from secular emblems (Charity, Envy, Folly, Loving, Nonsense, Obedience, Patience, Temperance, Virtue, Wisdom, Youth) or religious emblems (Grace, Heaven); some are biblical (Aaron, Balaam, David, Isaac, Joseph, Korah, Mary, Samuel); others derive from natural history (Quail, Robin, Zebra). Xerxes is drawn from Bible history (and a long alphabetic tradition beginning with *The New England Primer*).

Only one letter is national: "Union" portrays George Washington and the flag (Fig. 61). But this image carries a lot of weight, for the alphabet's frame is a national story, opened by the title and the cover's medallion of Washington's profile, and closing with a picture and narrative of "Washington at Prayer."[7] The gender positions of the *Hotch*

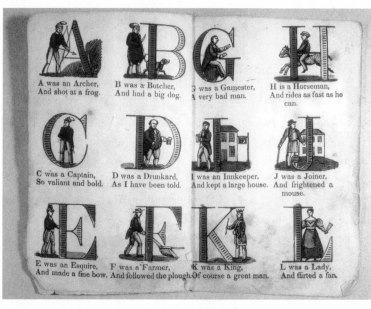

A was an Archer,
And shot at a frog.

B was a Butcher,
And had a big dog.

G was a Gamester,
A very bad man.

H is a Horseman,
And rides as fast as he
can.

C was a Captain,
So valiant and bold.

D was a Drunkard,
As I have been told.

I was an Innkeeper,
And kept a large house.

J was a Joiner,
And frightened a
mouse.

E was an Esquire,
And made a fine bow.

F was a Farmer,
And followed the plough.

K was a King,
Of course a great man.

L was a Lady,
And flirted a fan.

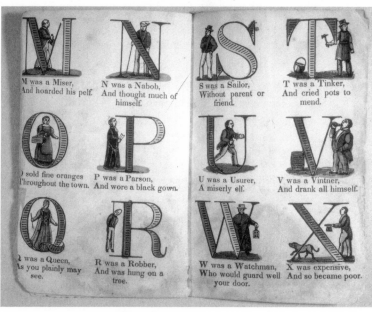

M was a Miser,
And hoarded his pelf.

N was a Nabob,
And thought much of
himself.

S was a Sailor,
Without parent or
friend.

T was a Tinker,
And cried pots to
mend.

O sold fine oranges
Throughout the town.

P was a Parson,
And wore a black gown.

U was a Usurer,
A miserly elf.

V was a Vintner,
And drank all himself.

Q was a Queen,
As you plainly may
see.

R was a Robber,
And was hung on a
tree.

W was a Watchman,
Who would guard well
your door.

X was expensive,
And so became poor.

Y was a youngster
That loved not his
school.

Z was a Zany,
And looked like a
fool.

Figures 54–56 *The Good Boy's and Girl's Alphabet. Figure 54 (opposite, top), A through L; Figure 55 (opposite, bottom), M through X; Figure 56 (left),* Y and Z. The tableau format becomes a concomitant of the domestic ideology of the mid–nineteenth century, which in this case evinces a painful tension between the mode and matter of illustration. Of particular interest here are the extreme poles of discipline and festivity in the graphic hanging of the robber, reminiscent of the "Tormenting of Malefactors" plate in the *Orbis Pictus* (Fig. 10), and in the antic zany. (Courtesy of the American Antiquarian Society)

Potch are here inside out. Patriotism and patriarchy provide the frame story; and yet, just as Grammatica might be positioned at the door of masculine literacy, Washington seems to be posted as the guardian or guarantor—and, in some ways, warden—of a female-oriented space.

The enclosed spaces of *The Illuminated Primer*'s letters are sometimes marked as explicitly domestic—as houses and rooms with women in them (Obedience, Grace, Heaven, the Magdalen). But regardless of their inhabitants' gender, these tableaux all express the alphabetic function of internalization through their representation of the spatial relations between people and the letters. As in *The Men among the Letters*, these letters are larger than life; more than this, the letters contain and may be said to be producing life.

If the alphabet array allures through its sense of an infinity of things, of boundaries transcended, the tableau conveys a sense of transcendent boundedness, of the desirability of enclosure, compression, and connection. The trope is still synecdoche. But in the tableau it operates in

R was a Robber,
And was hung on a
tree.

Figure 57 *(above)* R from *The Good Boy's and Girl's Alphabet*. The image of the hanged man in association with the alphabet persists in children's folklore. In a "Hangman" spelling game, one person thinks of a word and under a drawing of a scaffold, writes blanks for each letter of the word. The opponent guesses letters; the first player enters the correct guesses into the appropriate blank, and for each guessed letter not in the word, he draws a part of the hanged man. The object is to guess all the letters before completing the image of the hanged man. (Courtesy of the American Antiquarian Society)

Figures 58–61 *(opposite)* Tableau letter pairs from *The Illuminated American Primer. Figure 58 (upper left)*, C and D; *Figure 59 (upper right)*, E and F; *Figure 60 (lower left)*, M and N; *Figure 61 (lower right)*, U and V. (Courtesy of the American Antiquarian Society)

C is for Charity—which we all need:

D is for David,—who Israel did feed.

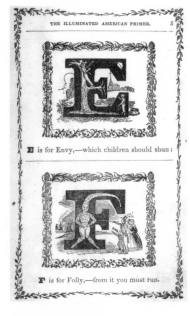

E is for Envy,—which children should shun:

F is for Folly,—from it you must run.

M is for Mary,—who chose a good part:

N is for Nonsense, which drive from your heart.

U is for Union,—this the good will approve:

V is for Virtue,—which I hope you will love.

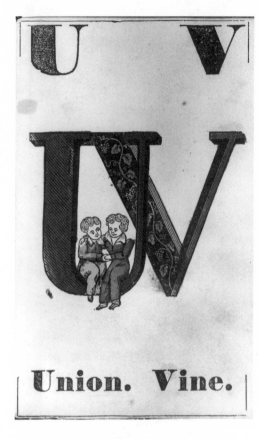

Figure 62 *Christmas ABC* (1835–1840). This panel of an accordion alphabet displays the "child within the letters." (Courtesy of the American Antiquarian Society)

the opposite direction, as from the far end of a telescope. In the alphabet array, the reader looks through the letter to a world, infinitely filled with, for example, A-words. In the alphabet tableau, however, "A is for . . . " opens onto a microcosm, contained within the letter. The entire image—the letter in which a drama is staged—is in turn meant to be taken in by the reader. But while children continue the task of internalizing the letters, the letters are increasingly represented as having internalized or consumed the children (Figs. 62 and 63).

In this dizzying exchange between inside and outside (the letters are in the children, the children are in the letters), between microcosm and macrocosm, we witness a culture struggling to picture to itself its evolving and complexly dependent relation to literacy.

Alphabetizing Things: The Narrating Woman

"Oh, Mamma, my things!"

—Susan Warner, *The Wide, Wide World* (1850)

Scale orients objects, visually, in space. Narrative orients them, through reading, speaking, or hearing, in time. But if scale can assist in the operation of internalizing the alphabet by representing kinds of internalization —a letter shaping a body, a man standing inside a letter—narrative creates for the ordering function of the alphabet a semantic field, a discourse. The "telling" of the alphabet begins to identify a monologic voice with the letters, linking the alphabet to an emotional tone and to particular actions or plots.

The pedagogical technique of the "object lesson," originating

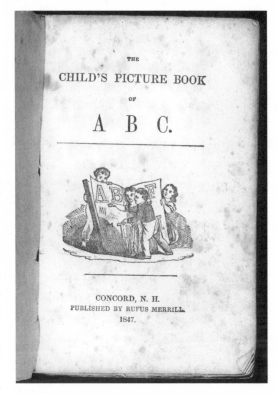

Figure 63 *The Child's Picture Book, of ABC* (1847). Characteristic of the nineteenth-century representation of literacy is this image of children miniaturized by the larger-than-life letters and book; the alphabet synecdoche invites entry into the world of the book. (Courtesy of the Rare Book Department, The Free Library of Philadelphia)

in *Emile* and refined by the widely influential Swiss educator Johann Heinrich Pestalozzi,[8] gives rise to a genre of pedagogical text in which images representing objects are accompanied by explanatory text. In the third book of Rousseau's *Emile*, a dinner party "in an opulent home" puts the susceptible student at risk of being intoxicated by luxury. By way of antidote, his tutor asks Emile: "Through how many hands would you estimate that all you see on this table has passed before getting here?" (190). The tutor extracts objects from the ambient scene, drawing Emile's attention to their origins as things in themselves and as objects of man's labor. The "vapors of the delirium" caused by luxury are dispersed as Emile considers all the places, hands, even lives that have contributed to what had seemed at first a seamless "apparatus of pleasure." Rousseau's technique is to counter worldliness with a directed reading of the world. Each object in the world becomes a window onto a vista worthy of the student's contemplation. While each object therefore shatters the apparent continuity of experience, the student's contemplation creates a renewed or reformed continuity, founded on his perceptions, which are in turn guided by his tutor.

In keeping with Rousseau's promotion of oral dialogue as remedy for the poisons both of images and of luxury, pedagogical texts of the early nineteenth century have titles like "rational dialogues" and represent situations in which a master, a father, or a mother questions and lectures children. One of Rousseau's English followers, Lady Eleanor Fenn, produced, under the names Mrs. Teachwell and Mrs. Lovechild, a number of these secular catechisms, which were imported and reprinted in America from around 1800 until the middle of the century.[9] Fenn's *Rational Sports*, which has a characteristically long—nearly forty-year—life in print, is, according to its subtitle, "Designed as a hint to mothers how they may inform the minds of their little people respecting the objects with which they are surrounded."[10] Here are Rousseauist dialogues in which children are guided to play at various trades and another in which a gift of a "Twelfth Cake" leads to a discussion of where the ingredients come from. (With these appear a much-reprinted sentimental tale of cross-species love, "The Lion and the Spaniel," and an encyclopedia-like entry, "Of the Wild Dog.") On the cover of this little pamphlet stands an image of the hero of the only novel permitted Emile, Robinson Crusoe, prince of things (Fig. 64).[11]

Fenn's *The Mother's Remarks on a Set of Cuts* presents itself not primarily as a book but as a wooden box inside of which are a pamphlet, a book, and fifty-four engraved sheets, with 324 images in all (Figs. 65 and 66).[12] Though formally hybrid and heterodox, partaking of broadside, game, book, pamphlet, even furniture (in its handsome wooden box), *Mother's Remarks* promotes a voice that is monologic. This multimedia combination has the effect of emphasizing the materiality of the objects while increasing the authority of the voice; we become absorbed in the oneness of the voice, for it will guide us to organize the many things in the wooden box. Eleanor Fenn is one of the inventors of the maternal voice, with

Figure 64 Lady Eleanor Fenn as Mrs. Lovechild: *Rational Sports, in dialogues passing among the children of a family* (1814). The cover shows Robinson Crusoe with Friday. (Courtesy of the American Antiquarian Society)

its genteel, penetrating authority, that echoes across the nineteenth century, encouraging mothers to encourage their children in the education of their senses, their sensibilities, and their sentiments.

Figure 65 *The Mother's Remarks on a Set of Cuts for Children* (Philadelphia, 1803). The wooden box containing *The Mother's Remarks* is decorated with a natural history image of a robin, associating the contents with nature, and the word "Douceurs," as though it's a box of chocolates, associating the contents with oral consumption. (Courtesy of the American Antiquarian Society)

According to Fenn, to "direct and regulate" children's curiosity is "the great business of education" (iv). Visual images—standing in for things—are the key to this direction and regulation: "Cuts are of great use to introduce proper subjects of inquiry . . . and, whilst we instill simple clear ideas of the nature of the objects with which he is surrounded, to infuse benevolence towards all animated beings" (iv). The lesson of this new infant curriculum is simply this: the world is full of things. This familiar message of the alphabet array is here given a new context and rationale by the narrating maternal voice. While the mother directs the child to a lucid vision of "the objects with which he is surrounded," she must carefully urge at the same time "benevolence," although distinguishing between "objects" and "animated beings" is not always easy, even for the author: "From every representation of a living object a lesson of tenderness may be inculcated" (v–vi).

"Living objects" are lessons too, like everything in the world. They are important in the project of educating "at once the head and heart" (viii). Among its other virtues, educating the "heart" reduces the need for physical discipline. The text to the illustration of the "rod," a recurrent image in alphabet books (sometimes as "birch"), notes its use "for

chastising refractory children"
(21). However, for the well-
trained child, "accustom[ed] . . .
to obedience," a frown "is punishment sufficient; an approving
smile a delightful reward" (22).
As it often does, the text now
turns directly toward the child-
auditor:

> I hope I have such an influence
> with you my dear boy, that in
> absence [you] reflect, how
> would my mother wish me to
> act; wicked boys will tell you
> that I shall not always know
> how you behave: but you will
> ever remember that there is an
> eye which sees every act: so
> live as to obtain His approba-
> tion: there is a hand that will
> most severely punish: fear His
> displeasure. (22)

Mother won't lay a hand on
the "dear boy," but "He" will,
in a big way. Mother binds the
child to her not only through a

Figure 66 From Lady Eleanor Fenn, *The Mother's Remarks*. (Courtesy of the American Antiquarian Society)

somewhat guilt-stained affection, but by associating herself directly
with omnipotent authority. Literalizing Barthes's *numen*, Mother aligns
herself with the eye of God; when Mother is absent, God will stand in
for her, as, otherwise, she substitutes for Him. Among other things, this
triangle establishes a chain of command that bypasses fathers.

In their handiness and materiality the cards are meant to mimic the world of objects. This world of objects must be entered through the alphabet, established in the first twenty-four cards. The unmodulated combination of objects on the page is a familiar one from the type of the worldly alphabet or alphabet array: pie, ink, fig. The text, which accompanies these loose card-images in a book, sometimes tunnels into the natural history of the object, as at Emile's dinner party. Still, the category "Things" or "Objects" is a perhaps not yet firmly established course in the infant curriculum, for old iconographic and sacred images keep breaking through. These images have not entirely shed their generic resemblance to emblems—nor has the mentality of the narrator. Ark, ship, tent are placed in an Old Testament context, while for the print of the Lamb, the text explains vaguely that lambs "are emblems of innocence" (58).

But the text for the "book" print (Fig. 66)—a wonderfully self-promoting mise-en-abîme image of *Mother's Remarks*—captures the up-to-date world this narrating mother wishes for her children:

> This is a book of cuts such as we are looking at; this book will suit little Isabella, who shall see all the pictures in time, as she keeps learning to read their names, and Elizabeth when she can spell the words. You, Ann, can find epithets or adjectives to suit some of those nouns. (66–67)

The book, no longer the sacred text, is newly associated with talk and interaction and visual imagery—and mothers.

This mother has acquired the traits of the all-seeing ambient mother who will rule the midcentury American "empire of the mother." For the paired images of "The Parting" and "The Return" (pls. 313 and 314) the text assures the mother's little boy as he goes off "that God sees you every where. He is about our path, about our bed, and spieth out all our ways; there is not a word in our tongue but God knowith [*sic*] it altogether" (77–78). When the child returns he is welcomed with the intelligence that "your countenance would have told me that you remembered and obeyed all my injunctions" (78–79). In his transparency, this child bears traces of his Calvinist origins. But the fluidity of his circumstances—his social mobility, his range of interests, his capacity for travel—makes the fixity of the gazes surrounding him all the more emphatic. These eyes have to stare harder and, like a surveillance tag team, keep the web of looks unbroken.

Like images in an alphabet book arranged within a woman-oriented space, the images of objects arrayed on loose cards in a wooden box are anchored and organized by the mother's "remarks"—the mother's speaking voice, represented by the text. The radical for *remark* is the Old English *mearc*, meaning "a limit or boundary, hence a boundary-sign" (Partridge, *Origins*). Mother's remarks place auditory boundary markers on everything and everybody in sight, pulling anything that can be subjected to representation under the sign of mother.

The mother's task is to surround objects with the sound of her voice, so that everything in the world adverts to her authority. If Adam names the animals, this Eve names everything else. Hers is the voice of a new Eve, an Eve of prolixity, for whom names alone have been insufficient. She doesn't name, but narrates. Every object is an opportunity for dilation; every object is pried open with the mother's voice and made part of the mother's story of what the world is. This mingling of the senses of sight and hearing through the medium of an affection-based authority establishes a mode of textuality that fosters an intense auditory and an intense visual experience.

The alphabetic-maternal procedure is striking. Things (of every kind: manmade, found in nature, imaginary, allegorical, living, dead) must first be wrenched out of the world, captured as images and set in a relation to one another that is both alphabetical and textual. They are afloat on the picture plane; their scale is organized to fit the format; they are stripped of any extraneous significance or association. What they have in common is the starkness of their presentation. Once they have been dis-integrated and alienated, they are re-integrated, through the medium of the mother's voice, into a world entirely constituted of and by, if not quite for, the mother.

The Technology of the Maternal: Alphabetical Order and Mother's Lips

> The measure of your power over your tongue is the test of your self-control.
>
> —Catharine Maria Sedgwick,
> *Means and Ends; or, Self-Training* (1842)

> The more freely we permit the tongue's movements, the more distinctly we can think the alphabet. If you stand before a mirror and protrude your tongue, you will see it either dilate or thicken, as each letter is pronounced in thought. The experiment must be made with letters whose articulation is lingual.
>
> —A. B. Johnson,
> *A Treatise on Language* (1836)

> Whatever the content of what is read, reading instruction from the Mother's Mouth is erotic from the beginning.
>
> —Friedrich Kittler,
> *Discourse Networks*

An important American promoter of romantic pedagogy, Lydia Maria Child, in her widely influential *The Mother's Book* (1831), recounts one of the most frequently repeated anecdotes in conduct manuals and education treatises for women. Following a long paragraph about teaching the alphabet, in which she proposes turning the letters into toys,[13] she urges that every step of infantile progress should be encouraged by expressions of surprise and pleasure. When a child is able to spell a new word . . . kiss him. . . . Sir Benjamin West relates that his mother kissed him eagerly when he showed her a likeness he had sketched of his baby-sister; and he adds, *"That kiss made me a painter!"* (54; emphasis in the original)[14]

Child associates the mother's kiss with alphabetic learning. As do many texts devoted to teaching and to parenting in this period, Child encourages maternal affection as the means to a specific end: "Nothing strengthens a child in goodness, or enables him to overcome a fault, so much as seeing his efforts excite a sudden and earnest expression of love and joy" (54). Underwriting this spontaneous burst of affection is a species of discipline directed toward the mother, rather than the child, that Lydia Child refers to in her opening chapter, "Bodily Senses": "You may say . . . that a mother's instinct teaches fondness, and there is no need of urging that point; but . . . mothers are sometimes fond by fits and starts" (5). The solution to inadequate and intermittent maternal love is "to govern one's feelings" (5). Pedagogical literature, in tandem with the burgeoning genres of women's self-help literature, prescribes conduct not only for the child, but also for the mother who is the primary instructor. Indeed, adjusting maternal behavior is literally a ground rule, for, as Lydia Child puts it, "the first rule, and the most important of all, in education, is, that a *mother* govern her own feelings, and keep her heart and conscience pure" (4; my emphasis).

The West anecdote is in a genre of testimony that recurs throughout the literature of female education and female conduct; these anecdotes underscore, by illustrating consequences of maternal influence, the necessity for maternal control. The success or failure not only of artists (Byron is the best-hated counterexample)[15] but also of military and political heroes, notably George Washington and Lafayette (with Benedict Arnold as counterexample), is attributed to the influence of mothers.[16] These biographical anecdotes generate a kind of cultural memory, reinforcing the creation, not to say the cult, of a personal memory of maternal influence.

Finally, the West testimony is notable for contracting the mother's actions metonymically to a kiss. The cause-and-effect narrative in which a mother's kiss or lips generate masculine heroism occurs frequently in this literature. Chief Justice John Marshall, for example, promoting an 1825 treatise on female education, writes:

> Precepts from the lips of a beloved mother, inculcated in the amiable, graceful and affectionate manner which belongs to the parent and the sex, sink deep in the heart, and make an impression which is seldom entirely effaced. These impressions have an influence on character which may contribute greatly to the happiness or misery, the eminence or insignificancy of the individual. (Garnett, 8)

Mother doesn't have to speak for her lips to have an effect. Another promoter of female education finds that Mother's "smile and her frown are the two strongest powers on earth, influencing human minds in the hour when influence stamps itself upon the heart in eternal characters" (Fisher, 30).

In the discourse of maternal influence, mothers seem, famously, imperious. Yet the physical presence of women is represented as being terrifically compressed and focused. Although maternal hands and bosoms float through these texts from time to time,[17] lips (along with the related terms, mouth, tongue, and voice) are more frequent—and more telling. If the mother's kiss generates masculine heroism, these lips would seem to have a kind of reproductive capability. Both the eroticism and the reproductive nature of the image call up the other, genital, set of Mother's lips. The mother's physical presence—which she must carefully discipline—is condensed to a feature triply associated with voice, birth, and sexuality.[18]

But if biological reproduction is suggested by "mother's lips," the kiss can assure a replica of the mother only by means of an increasingly necessary supplement to biology: the mechanics of imprinting. Catherine Beecher, echoing a common sentiment, wrote that "it is to mothers and to teachers that the world is to look for the character which is to be enstamped on each succeeding generation" (*Suggestions*, 7). While the classical pedagogical trope of cultivation persists (e.g., in the kindergarten movement), sentimental pedagogy prefers the trope of printing: "enstamp," "imprint," "impress." The prefix *in-* cloaks the dynamism of the root verbs: Print. Stamp. Press. But the prefix also emphasizes the insistent pressure that dissolves the boundary between inside and outside. "Stamping," juxtaposed as it almost always is to "influence," marks the fluidity of influence for the machine age; if influence "flows," "floods," "pours" (the verbs most often attached to it), stamping fixes, stops, interrupts, sets boundaries.

If Mother stamps, imprints, impresses, one might think of her as the printer or the printing press. But the tenor of these metaphors is rather this: the mother, like the printed-upon child, is caught up in the machine, her power restricted, as we shall see, to a certain kind of composing work, her venue confined, by an odd coincidence of terminology, to the galley and the bed.

Mother imprints whether she wants to or not: "You cannot prevent them from carrying into another generation, the stamp of those habits which they inherit from you" (Sigourney, *Letters to Mothers*, 10–11). But if Mother can't help herself from being an agent, she needs to put her agency—her "self"—in order. One teacher even uses "justify" in its printing sense to identify this process as it operates in a little girl: "Through my influence," the teacher writes, a child from an "ungenial home" was "in the end able to justify herself, and take a happier place in the family circle" (M. Mann, *Moral Culture*, 118).

To command, control, deny, govern, master, possess, regulate, sacrifice, subject, train—these are the verbs attached to that key word of modern subjectivity, the hyphenated "self-."[19] Inherently lacking on its own, the "self-" becomes a magnet (then as now) for the latest fashion in the lexicon of discipline.[20] To insert a hyphen is, the Greek root indicates, to bring "under one" the components in question. The woman is meant to construct, out of these components, a sex that *is one*, which is to say, not many, not individuated.[21]

To operate in the new "reading world," the woman has to perform a kind of maintenance on herself that brings her into a homology with the alphabetic functions. If these are representation, internalization, and consistent order, the mother, as the source of alphabetic learning, must align herself accordingly. That is, she "prints" (imprints, enstamps, impresses) representations on the child's memory; her voice and her actions, fully internalized, echo within the child's mind; and her presence is in order—static, consistent, and exactly repeatable—owing to the management of her "self-." The metonymic condensing of these operations to a mother's kiss, lips, tongue, and voice blurs their origins. The alphabet becomes permanently and paradoxically fixed to the maternal body and hence to memories that can't be memories—that is, to a prelinguistic stage of development that now has a memory written over it.[22]

Mother guarantees for the alphabet both a spatial and temporal ubiquity: in the present, mothers are everywhere, and they reproduce themselves exactly through "enstamping" into the future. The axis of the synecdochic alphabet is infinite in space, but temporally bound: "A is for" allows one to apprehend in an instant all objects on the A-list. But the axis of maternal influence is for all time; just as mothers are imagined to have the prescience of gods, their effect, too, is eternal. If through synecdoche the alphabet's self-generating power is limited only by language, mother's influence, the stream into which objects are placed, is infinite through time, as it permeates children, children's children, children's children's children.

This new genealogy so strikes nineteenth-century writers that they try to quantify it. William Alcott begins by positing modestly that if "one hundred only of each two hundred" women taught by a good teacher

> should live to have influence, seventy-five of them as mothers of families of the usual size, and twenty-five only, as teachers. There will then be five generations in one hundred and sixty years; and the number of children which will come under the influence of this line or succession of mothers and teachers, will be no less than ninety millions; or a number equal to six times the present population of the United States. (36)

By Alcott's reckoning, the imprint of the American woman of 1845 should still be everywhere visible today. Here is democracy's answer to aristocratic genealogies. Some use a theological rather than economic model for quantification: Mother "stamps on the plastic mind of youth an image that will remain forever. *The mother's influence will last through eternity*" (Wise, 176).

While the alphabet has acquired a body, the mother, with some conveniences in terms of range of influence (eternal life, for example), sees her own body sometimes reduced to lips—or less.

The Manns Among the Letters: Alphabet Plots

> There is no neighboring universe to fly to. If we forswear
> allegiance, it is but an empty form, for the laws by which we
> are bound, do not only surround us, but are in us, and parts of us.
>
> —Horace Mann, "The Necessity of Education in a
> Republican Government" (1839)

So far I have described a trajectory for the alphabet after 1800 that positions it within a female-inflected space and in narratives that set it afloat with other objects in a sea of maternal influence. But this is an influence that can be maintained only through a mechanizing of maternal personality and corporeality. Now I want to turn to texts that treat the alphabetic characters as entities capable of both motivation and plotting, and that evince an awareness of, verging on a resistance to, the special organization of the self required by alphabetization.

In a lecture of 1841 "on the best mode of preparing and using spelling-books," Horace Mann, the first secretary of the Massachusetts Board of Education and the most influential education bureaucrat of his day, presents himself as being overwhelmed by the alphabet and mounts an ad hominem attack against it. Spelling books were the mainstay of reading instruction from the mid–eighteenth century on, represented by such bestsellers as Noah Webster's *American Spelling Book*, the famous "blue-back" speller. The speller, as Jennifer Monaghan has pointed out, followed the ABC book and primer in the reading curriculum and was likely to be the first school text, strictly speaking, encountered by a child (*Common Heritage*, 13–14). The content of the speller was usually restricted to word lists, aphorisms, and short reading lessons, such as the fables in Webster's *Spelling Book*. While this system of reading instruction was firmly established in practice, there exists a tradition of screed against alphabetic learning in English to which Mann's essay belongs.[23]

Mann's own diatribe is a brilliant and vivid rant, which anthropomorphizes the letters and finds them guilty of being willful, calculating, deceptive, changeable, corrupt. First, he treats the phonic unreliability of the alphabet as a deception, attributing motive to the letters. The five vowels especially "ought to be called five harlequins," for they "have twenty-nine different sounds" and chronically "masquerad[e]"; compared to the alphabet, even Proteus "was no turncoat, but a staid, uniform personage" (2). Elsewhere, Mann uses "Proteus" as an epithet for his political enemy Orestes Brownson; from Mann's Whig perspective, the ongoing ideological debate between Whigs and Democrats aligned the former with stability and community interests, the latter with an atomizing individuality, which Mann sees as one of the threats of alphabetization.[24] It is partly this individuality that makes the letters unpredictable and unconventional:

> To conceive of a child's difficulty, in giving their right sounds to the alphabetic characters, as found in words, let us suppose any five articles of furniture or dress which we have most frequent occasion to use or to wear, were liable to change into twenty-nine articles of furniture or dress, the moment we should touch them; and, further, that this metamorphosis were not only arbitrary but apparently wanton. (2)

Among Mann's most serious charges is wantonness. "Wanton" means lacking in discipline but carries the additional sense of lewdness, promiscuity, lasciviousness. A suggestion of immoral sexuality infuses the motive Mann attributes to the alphabet. Mann's objection to the "wanton" unreliability of the letters is that it leads to an array of suffering for the child, including corporal punishment. He pictures a child who, logically taking the "a" sound in "falling" to parse the word "decay," "gets slapped, if not flayed for his stupidity" (12).

But while Mann is disturbed by the painful consequences of the alphabet's phonetic instability, he is also alarmed by its anatomizing effect: "When we wish to give to a child the idea of a new animal, we do not present successively the different parts of it,—an eye, an ear, the nose, the mouth, the body, or a leg: but we represent the whole animal, as one object" (14).[25] Mann introduces an analogy between two objects of the pupil's interest, a live animal and the alphabet. He proceeds to disassemble the animal "alphabetically," or anatomically. His suggestion is not that the alphabet might be treated as a living thing (although his tropes are animated enough), but rather that the alphabet inevitably dismembers living things.

Mann sees the arbitrarily disciplining and anatomizing effects of the alphabet coalescing into a generalized opposition to any pleasurable sensation. Following Locke and Rousseau, Mann hopes to draw children to learn through pleasure. Children, he writes, take pleasure in "brilliant and variegated colors, impressive forms, diversified motions, substances that can be lifted and weighed, and all whose dimensions, therefore, can be examined . . . objects which gratify the sense of taste and smell, together with melody or harmony of sounds." By contrast to these desirable objects, "letters and words present superficial form only,—form having dimension in a plane,—and incapable of being handled, weighed or examined." Not merely lacking in pleasure, the alphabet is a positive maw of displeasures: "There stands in silence and death, the stiff, perpendicular row of characters, lank, stark, immovable, without form or comeliness, and, as to signification, wholly void. They are skeleton-shaped, bloodless, ghostly apparitions" (16). Furthermore, the letters are too small to be seen, too similar to be parsed; the result is "emptiness, silence and death, [upon which] we compel children to fasten their eyes" (17). While Mann's rhetoric has invested the alphabet with life and substance, his core critique is of the alphabet's *in*substantiality and near invisibility.

Mann has a plan to vanquish the death-dealing alphabet, which he has positioned, in a rhetorical tour de force, as the villain of a kind of mock-epic or mock-gothic. First, he suggests creating material objects representing the letters, which the "child can handle, lift, carry hither and thither," and with which the "mother can amuse the child by sending it to pick out one of the letters, and thus gratify its love of bodily motion and exercise its power of search and discrimination" (18). In this solution, he brings the mother into the picture, sets the child in motion, and makes the letters into material objects. But he also proposes bypassing the alphabet altogether and teaching whole words.

Mann is so disgusted with the alphabet that he is obliged to justify learning it at all.[26] We must do so, he says, because "without signs, each mind would be local, insular, an individuality; signs bridge a chasm otherwise impassable . . . we use signs, instead of the things themselves, and in this way only is it that we achieve a sort of ubiquity and omniscience" (19). Without signs we are "insular," and yet the alphabet sinks us into "solitude" (17). If the alphabet seems fatal, we still need it, in order to master fate itself, and imperially so, with "ubiquity and omniscience." In addition, Mann figures the alphabet as a bridge to the world at large and to the common fund of sociability, and rails against its inadequacies. He likens learning the ABCs to learning the names in a city directory, "a mere bald catalogue of names from A to Z" with "no designation of residence or employment" (28). As the child must turn to texts with no knowledge of what the letters really are, he is like an apprentice with a list of undifferentiated names, sent "forth into the marts and exchanges of the city, as one acquainted with its people and ready to transact business with them" (28–29). For Mann, the alphabet in its current state unmaps the world, unhinging its elements from sociability.

And yet he also conceives of the alphabet as "but the supply of a natural want" (20), a desire precisely for an integrated and sociable grasp of the world. But this "natural want" seems somewhat scripted. Mann suggests that books for early readers should contain words "which are familiar, which excite vivid and delightful images or emotions, which are tasteful, as contra-distinguished from gross or vulgar terms, and which will be apt to bring kindly, social, and generous feelings in their train." Similarly, certain words and ideas must be excluded: "The words *kill*, *blood*, *gun*, *angling-rod*, *sword*, & c., may be very pleasant to the destructive propensity of a child, but for that very reason I would not have them in his book" (37). The prohibition suggests that the specificity of a child's "natural wants" lies rather with such violent and bloody images than with the ones Mann proposes.[27]

Having bypassed the alphabet and substituted words, Mann finds himself on a heading that logically leads him to transcend words as well:

> The teacher . . . may invite a group of little children to come around her *to think of pleasant things*; instead of forcing them to gaze at idiot marks. Such lessons will be like an excursion to the fields of elysium, compared with the old method of plunging children, day after day, for months together, in the cold waters of oblivion, and compelling them to say falsely, that they love the chill and torpor of the immersion. After children have learned to read words, the twenty-six letters, as they stand marshalled in the alphabet, will be learned in a few hours. (37; emphasis in original)

The goal of literacy training in this scheme is to soar over the alphabet, or to bridge it, like putting logs across a swamp. For the alphabet is associated on the one hand with immersion, plunging, drowning, being overwhelmed, on the other with coldness and military rigidity. The aporia brought on by the alphabet has a sexual element; the shift in the structure of internalization suggests that Mann is responding to the feminized space of the alphabet. The student, in this scheme, does not take in the alphabet but is, instead, plunged *into* the alphabet. The images of fluidity suggest that Mann is drowning in the waters of maternal influence.

But Mann is not just reacting to something abstractly feminine in this passage. These starkly masculine and phallic letters suggest a homoerotic sexual threat as well in the internalization of the alphabet. Mann's response is, in part, a result of his own transitional status. He is conflating his own memories (miserable ones)[28] of schooling with the present-day model of alphabetization, of which he is one of the main promoters. The older form of alphabetization—the agonistic Latin form[29]—no longer seems "normal." Horace Mann recalls his own early alphabetization with a kind of horror that seems to involve a recoil from the phallic and masculine emphasis of earlier educational programs. These earlier initiations, homosocial and to some extent homoerotic, are now perceived with homophobic horror and gothicized, as the new feminized mode of learning is becoming the norm. Later, Mann will decide that the problem of brutality and violence in schooling is attributable to schoolmasters devoted to corporal punishment; to their archaic, Latin-school brutality, he poses the romantic, maternal alternative.[30] But in this spelling lecture, his first idea is to lay this brutality at the feet of the alphabet.

If the traditional discourse of femininity (and its companion discourse of misogyny) glides into homology with the alphabetic functions, the discourse of masculinity—if Mann's voice might be considered representative—painfully resists. For Mann, the notion of internalization of these phallicized letters leads to disintegration, as though in a homosexual panic.[31] Mann attacks the alphabet from every quarter, seeing it as a menace to the individual through an array of sexual, psychic, and corporal violence. But Mann's solution constitutes a denial rather than a way out of the problem: he'll suspend the alphabet's existence until he decides (how will he decide?) the student is ready for it. In effect, Mann imposes a "latency period" on the alphabet. Mann exposes and then denies violence as constitutive of alphabetization.[32]

When Mann wrote this lecture, he had been for some years intimate with the Peabody family and was engaged to Mary Tyler Peabody. In 1841, while Horace Mann found himself trapped among the letters, Mary Peabody was also immersed in the mechanics, the philosophy, and the practices of alphabetization. In letters to fellow teacher Anna Lowell, she writes that alphabetic learning is simply too painful to inflict on children: "It is quite an effort for them to learn to observe closely enough to distinguish such small particulars even as words, with which they have such vivid associations, and altogether an unnatural one to learn arbitrary signs, to which nothing already known *can* be attached" (*Moral Culture*, 128).[33] She shares with Horace Mann what she calls "a great repugnance to *letters*, with their many different sounds, so puzzling to the brain" (129). Like Mann's "wanton," the hyperbolic "repugnance" is revealing, with its core meaning of resistance and its connotations of moral and sexual disgust.

Like Mann, Mary Peabody desires an escape from the alphabet and decides to take "the royal road to the attainment of this art, and teach *words* first, not letters":

> A word is a whole host of thoughts to a young child, and three words in a row a whole gallery of pictures. Bird, nest, tree! . . . The book that contains such words, and perhaps a story, of which they form a part, is itself an illuminated volume, and is immediately invested with a charm it cannot lose. . . . The warbled song, the downy breast, the sheltering wing, the snug retreat, have such an analogy with the mother's carol or lullaby, the brooding bosom, and the beloved arms, a child's dearest home, that every sentiment is enlisted. (127)

Peabody surrounds objects—"bird, nest, tree"—with a maternal narrative, flooded with affection. Through this suggested narrative, the chosen words are stamped on the mind of the child. The narrative, however, is always going to be the same, and therefore becomes a kind of antinarrative ("*perhaps* a story"). "Bird, nest, tree" translate instantly to "the downy breast, the sheltering wing, the snug retreat," and "the mother's carol or lullaby, the brooding bosom, and the beloved arms, a child's dearest home." Every word finds its affective link to home and mother in order to lodge in the memory.[34]

Peabody's effacing of the alphabet is a strategy of the alphabetized maternal. She doesn't experience the alphabet as a gothic "other." Rather, the alphabet is already incorporated, predigested, so to speak, through the medium of the mother. As Friedrich Kittler describes this procedure,

> An alphabetization in which all real work was taken on by the mother ceased to be an incision or pain; the latter, the forceable [*sic*] violation required to mark human beings with a storage or memory capacity, had always been forgotten because it was the precondition of memory itself. The discourse network of 1800 reversed this and made possible memories that reached back to a fully affectionate, maternal alphabetization. (51)

Mary Peabody's letter to Anna Lowell strikingly displays this process in its entirety; Peabody has, in effect, emblematized herself, metamorphosing into Mother. As Mother incorporates the alphabet, she also absorbs, or deflects, the pain of alphabetization; in return, she is memorialized.

Like the cross prefixing the "criss-cross row," in Peabody's scheme the associative chain that always leads to Mother anchors the alphabet. But while the institution of the Church already contains a set of symbols or signs to which the alphabet could easily become an extension, the maternal body undergoes a striking transfiguration in order to accommodate the alphabet. As the passage from Mary Peabody's letter suggests, the mother's body is transformed into a kind of institution (complete with architecture). This houselike body has no orifices (though presumably the "carol" is emitted through the maternal lips), the uterus is displaced outward into the womblike home, and all that remains of the body are "beloved arms" and the "bosom." The alphabet and the maternal body exchange some characteristics, eliding in the process their real natures. The alphabet, incorporated into the maternal body, hides its arbitrariness and meaninglessness along with any symptom of technology within imagelike words. Meanwhile, the mother's body loses its own syntax and articulation, its own meaningfulness, and acquires alphabetic qualities. For Mary Peabody every text is transformed into an allegory of motherhood. The alphabetized mother's sexuality—one of the other narratives her body could tell—becomes effaced along with the elements of alphabetization. Mother translates into text.

In their differently resistant narratives, Horace Mann and Mary Tyler Peabody struggle to reconcile the conflicts embedded within alphabetization. At the heart of their resistance, and signaled by their eroticizing of the alphabet, is their participation in a new systematizing of the self of which alphabetization forms a critical—perhaps even the essential—part.[35] The differences in their narratives are partly attributable to the differences in their own alphabetization. Horace Mann, like most educated men of his epoch, received a rhetorical education (in his case, in the law) that was not available to women, even very cultured and well-educated women like Mary Peabody.[36]

Horace Mann and Mary Peabody narrate two plots of alphabetization, aligned by gender. The masculine plot is gothicized, resistant, obsessively focused on a sexually charged alphabet. The feminine plot bypasses the alphabet, finding it "repugnant," relying instead on a fluid, maternal narrating voice to incorporate the alphabet into a heated, erotically charged emotional realm, focused on maternal love. Both of these are resistant plots: the first struggles hopelessly and self-consciously to remain outside of the alphabet; the other effaces the alphabet by reconfiguring women as alphabet-surrogates, or texts. The literary narratives that these theories and practices of alphabetization produce are the subject of the following two chapters.

Quel texte pour son instruction!

       ·   —*Jean-Jacques Rousseau,* Emile *(1762)*

The Wide World

      —*Ralph Waldo Emerson, journal title (1820–1823)*

"There is not the strength or courage left me to venture into the wide, strange, difficult world, alone!"

      —*Nathaniel Hawthorne,* The Scarlet Letter *(1850)*

Chapter Four

WWW: *The Wide,*

Wide World's Web

he *Wide, Wide World*: The alliteration of the title stresses the author's initial, the initial of her pseudonym, Wetherell (her grandmother's maiden name), and the initial of a patronymic (her father's middle name is Whiting). WWW. To ask the alphabetical question, what might W stand for—Warner, Woman, Writing, World?[1] W is the only letter in the alphabet that repeats another letter; within the endlessly repeating alphabet, W is a microcosm of alphabetic replication. As such, W itself operates as a trope across a range of texts. It reverberates, for example, throughout Edgar Allan Poe's tale "William Wilson" (1845), in which the protagonist's double is a replica exact in every detail but one: the doppelganger's voice is a *w*hisper.[2] While W carries the only polysyllabic name in the alphabet, its phonic value is a bare whisper (according to Partridge, *Origins*, the word *whisper* is itself an echoic formation). W is the interrogative letter; it is to English what Q (qui, quae, quo, quid, quale) is to Latin: who, what, when, where, which, why? As a letter "which is not one," W embraces itself within itself; W is a companion to U, V, Y, the "female" letters, shaped like vessels and diagrams of vulvas and uteruses. An erotics of the alphabet would position W as the autoerotic and female homoerotic letter.[3]

Within the narrative of *The Wide, Wide World* (1850), Warner, like Mary Peabody Mann, bypasses the letter of alphabetic learning. But the midcentury network of relations created and sustained by alphabetization is Warner's theme, and the synecdochic, doubling, female, repetitive W breaks through in the title. Today the sign *www*, the acronym for the World Wide Web, prefixes addresses, which we follow to find a "home" page; we "travel" by clicking on words and icons. This coincidence of letters is not entirely coincidental.[4] The Web and *The Wide, Wide World* communicate with each other from distant points along a medial arc. The identities created for readers and texts by such novels as *The Wide, Wide World* still resonate in our relation to new networks; my crude sketch of how the user navigates cyberspace might be an emotionally stripped version of how the reader and the heroine function within *The Wide, Wide World*, as they yearn for a home, relying on iconic representations and on a vision of human connectedness, structured by a media technology, that imagines a fluid melding of personalities.[5]

Nineteenth-century writers frequently accounted for their own sensations of disconnection and inundation by what was perceived as a flood of print media.[6] We have seen Horace Mann responding to the alphabet with a sense of resistant, enthralled bewilderment. Like other nineteenth-century technologies (the railroad, for example), widespread literacy in combination with a burgeoning print industry would appear to contract the world, and yet they contribute to the sense of the world as an often lonely expanse; the phrase "wide world" recurs in a range of literature in the nineteenth century, often conjoined with friendlessness and loneliness.[7] The crushing emotional tone of much of *The*

Wide, Wide World emanates in a complex fashion from the network of print and literacy that is also its subject matter.

While literacy is any novel-reader's prerequisite, *The Wide, Wide World* calls upon and calls up a structure of literacy that promises coherence, completion, and fulfillment. Warner's novel delivers a maternal plot of alphabetization, in which texts and mothers freely exchange attributes, raising the former to a sensuous life that transcends the alphabet, and sending the latter over the brink of alphabetic dispersal. This novel extends the web of literacy, articulating with unique force the longings variously created, excited, shaped, thwarted, and fulfilled through literacy.

In this chapter, I begin by considering the background to the writing of *The Wide, Wide World*, its growth out of the materials of pedagogy, and its echoes of and divergences from earlier modes of the novel. I then read the novel's play of reading and writing as a web of influence and interconnection that models and partakes of the technology of the maternal and other forms of alphabetization. In the final section, I consider Warner's divided authority within the text and the distinct narratives that this produces; I conclude with an analysis of the erotics of alphabetization within the novel.

A Renovated Crusoe

Take any individual . . . separate him . . . and look at him, apart and alone,—like some Robinson Crusoe in a far-off island of the ocean . . . and, even in such a solitude, how authoritative over his actions, how decisive of his contemplations and of his condition, are the instructions he received and the habits he formed in early life!

—Horace Mann, "The Necessity of Education
in a Republican Government" (1839)

Before beginning *The Wide, Wide World*, Susan Warner helped her sister, Anna Bartlett Warner, produce an instructional children's game for Putnam's. The Warners' *Game of Natural History* was the first professional writing from a team that between them wrote about a hundred books during the next sixty years.[8] Like Eleanor Fenn's *Mother's Remarks*, the Warners' game was a homegrown multimedia production, consisting of twenty-four cards, hand-painted by the sisters, with images of animals and questions about them, and a book, *Robinson Crusoe's Farmyard*, describing the animals in detail.[9] The Warners were not the first to cash in on Crusoe, for he had attained brand-name status by this time; chapbook abridgments of the novel and translations of Johann Wyss's *Swiss Family Robinson* (first published in English in 1814) were staples of the children's book market. But in the Warners' domestication of Crusoe, Crusoe's world is un-novelized, anatomized, reimagined, and reincorporated into a new narrative, which has left all of Crusoe behind and yet, in a way, captures him completely in a renovated inventory of animated things. In a word, they alphabetized *Crusoe*, by fixing him within the model of the maternal narrative.

Motivated primarily by desperate financial need, but also by literary ambition and evangelism, Susan Warner began *The Wide, Wide World* in 1848. Raised in New York to expectations of ease and urbanity, Warner found herself, after her father's decade-long downward skid, socially outcast and financially shipwrecked on Constitution Island, in the Hudson River near West Point.[10] From the rich materials and reduced prospects of her own narrowed world, Warner produced *The Wide, Wide World*'s child-hero, Ellen Montgomery. Ellen's name scans like Robinson Crusoe's, and her success in the marketplace would lead to a series of books called, echoing *Robinson Crusoe's Farmyard*, "Ellen Montgomery's Bookshelf."[11] If, in the Warners' version, Crusoe's island curriculum was the discipline of natural history, with animals, necessary to human survival, as its objects of study, Ellen's course through the world required the skills and materials newly necessary to the white, middle-class girl's existence: reading and books. *The Wide, Wide World* would be one of the books that would deepen and extend the range of this new necessity, affixing it to a set of personal and cultural memories.

Crusoe captivated Anglo-American readers with its entrepreneurial prodigal son in a "drama of filial disobedience" (Fliegelman, *Prodigals*, 67). *The Wide, Wide World* charmed them differently: in the place of the man, the girl; in the place of filial disobedience and shipwreck, adoring obedience and home-wrecking abandonment. The similarities between the works are striking:[12] both develop narrative through acts of reading and writing; in both, the Bible is positioned just beyond the edge of the text, as the crucial supplement. An ideal of self-government motivates both heroes, due to (in *Crusoe*) exile from and (in *The Wide, Wide World*) inadequacy of patriarchal institutions. But if the man voyaging outward and organizing an island for his use metaphorically captures a utilitarian function of reading in the eighteenth century, the girl adrift in the "wide world," while struggling to organize her interior world, describes the new nineteenth-century reading protocol.

Gender, Genre, and Replication in The Wide, Wide World

The hero of *The Wide, Wide World* is, of course, a girl, even, perhaps, an emblematic *She*, as her name Ellen (sometimes Ellie) plays on the French *elle*.[13] Her gender attests to the obvious fact that she has many precursors other than Robinson Crusoe. From Richardson, to Rowson, to Austen, to Radcliffe, to Sedgwick, to Gaskell, to Thackeray, British and American authors writing across a range of genres had put women at the center of fictional narratives. There are fewer precedents for child-heroes—at least in novels, at least for adults.[14]

The European *Bildungsroman* focuses on a young adult's progress into the world of adult activities—finding work, finding love. Bakhtin defines, as the most significant type of the novel of emergence, one organized "by the future," in which the hero "emerges *along with the world* and he reflects the historical emergence of the world itself" ("*Bildungsroman*," 23). Franco Moretti regards the *Bildungsroman*, in its focus on the "material sign" of youth, as the symbolic form of modernity, because it "accentuates modernity's dynamism and instability." If Europe, in this formula, "plunges into modernity, but without possessing a *culture* of modernity" (5), America is modernity's immanence. But for Americans, forming themselves on the run, accelerating European "dynamism and instability" into a blur, "youth," with its suggestion of suspenseful liminality between childhood and adulthood, is a problematic category. The culture expresses its apprehensions by strewing its children's literature with the abandoned, lost, burned, crippled, and dead bodies of children in monitory tales, pious fables, pedagogical stories, and popular ballads. At the same time, pedagogical tracts are typically prefaced with nervous accounts of European anarchy and revolution,[15] as the inevitable consequence of inadequately educated children. When American writers represent the anxiously monitored "rising generation," they almost always choose children, not twenty-year-olds.[16] For the antebellum American writer, the transition from child to adult—that moment when the individual emerges into history—defies representation. Instead, childhood becomes constructed, not as a period of transition, but as a site of stability and knowability, as writable and legible text. While the novels of childhood can be full of event—and horrific ones[17]—these events are manageable because they are represented as being in the past—behind us, resolved.

The Wide, Wide World has been called "a kind of bildungsroman in reverse,"[18] and Warner expends an enormous amount of narrative energy in stopping the clock on "real-world" historical time.[19] Although *The Wide, Wide World* conforms to the realism of Bakhtin's model, it more nearly falls under his category of the novel of "cyclical emergence" (22), in which the world is a school through which everyone must pass, with the same result. But *The Wide, Wide World* might be called, instead, a novel of alphabetization, a special and somewhat compressed *Bildung*, in which Bakhtin's "cyclical emergence" depends on a particular replication of literacy. This genre takes as its hero a smaller, younger, less formed protagonist, who must struggle not to map and navigate the world, but rather to read and write herself into existence.[20]

In *The Wide, Wide World*, the desired stability and coherence of childhood is manifested through a reassuring replication. Not only does Ellen repeat her mother's emergence,[21] but Ellen herself is replicated in the text. Mrs. Montgomery is quite likely named Ellen as well (she signs a letter "E. Montgomery," 227). And there is still another Ellen in the novel: Ellen's best friend, her only friend among her age peers, is the younger Ellen Chauncey. Scenes of the two Ellens together in the novel are disorienting to read. But the girls are meant to be interchangeable. When they meet, Ellen Chauncey asks the ontological question, "'How shall we know which is which?'" Ellen Montgomery answers that when they each say "Ellen" they will mean the other one: "'I shouldn't be calling myself, you know.'" Ellen Chauncey gets to the heart of the matter: "'But when somebody else calls Ellen, we shall both have to run'" (284). The two girls can distinguish between themselves, but when a call goes up for a generic Ellen they will both swing into action.

There are two paradigms for the process of exact replication resulting in the proliferation of Ellens, or of *elles*: the alphabet and print.[22] As I suggested in Chapter 3, emblematic enstamping is an effect of maternal alphabetization. In a supplement to, and replacement for, biological reproduction, the mother is meant to be stamped into and onto the child. The technology of the maternal assimilates crucial operations of modernity in order to counter the distressing velocity of modernity; maternal replication assures that human nature remains recognizable and consistent down through the generations. In *The Wide, Wide World*, rather than assimilating historical time in the Bakhtinian model, Ellen's emergence constitutes an attempt to stop history. If modernity would seem to *belong* to America, Ellen represents American culture's conflicted resistance to modernity's velocity. As if, as Wlad Godzich puts it, "language could slow down the world,"[23] Ellen's development consists in increasing strictures on reading, writing, and speech. The heroine's formation in and through language assures the ongoing stability both of language and of personality.

The novel depends for its existence on operations that it resists; it copes with its resistance by replicating a sanctified version of what it fears. If the world speeds by chaotically, if persons are becoming alphabetized cogs, then the novel will hurl an unprotected girl out into the world, who will then standardize herself internally, but according to a righteous model. She will use the new mass market's capacity for the broadcasting of images to transmit an emblem of maternal orthodoxy. That this emblem is created out of the materials of literacy assures that it can homeopathically counter literacy's anatomizing, standardizing, and secularizing effects.

Textual/Maternal/Commodity Networks

It seemed to her as if she were caught in a net from which she had no power to get free.

—Susan Warner,
The Wide, Wide World

"'Mamma, what was that I heard papa saying to you this morning about his lawsuit?'" Mamma, papa, child, and lawsuit open the novel, mediated through the voice of the child. We might be in the world of the *Comédie humaine*, with this suggestive mingling of public/legal and private/family interests. "'I cannot tell you just now,'" Mamma replies, and will never tell, really. The details of the lawsuit never emerge (now we know we're not in a Balzacian world), though some consequences of it quickly do.

Ellen is a well-trained Emile-like child, an unworldly student of the text of the world. In the interlude of a few paragraphs between Ellen's catechizing of her mother and her mother's version of an answer, we encounter the world of Ellen Montgomery: "Face pressed against the windowframe," Ellen becomes absorbed in "the moving world without," for she has "seriously set herself to study everything that passed" (9). When at last Ellen turns her attention back inside, it seems as though the world has passed her by: "The room was dark and cheerless; and Ellen felt stiff and chilly." But she quickly pokes up the fire, puts books, curtains, work-box, shutters, table-cloth, and chairs in order: "'There, go back to your places'" (10).

Warner presents Ellen as a practiced observer of the world outside and a good manager of the things in the room, including her adored, sickly mother: "Ellen tried stroking her mother's cheek very gently; and this succeeded [in rousing her], for Mrs. Montgomery arrested the little hand as it passed her lips, and kissed it fondly two or three times." The maternal temperature rises. Following the expressive logic of motherly lips, Mrs. Montgomery's next utterance explains an aspect of the wide world's disciplines, which sets the maternal replications in motion. For the loss of the lawsuit requires that Mrs. Montgomery and her husband go to Europe ("'Not, and leave *me*, mother?'"), leaving Ellen behind (11).

The law provides the novel's frame, but transmitted through the voice of the child, it positions the reader in a space that rebukes the law. The lawsuit constitutes a set of texts—legal codes, contracts, briefs, the court records—that Warner would have known all too well: her father was a lawyer and, for a time, a court reporter.[24] If one set of texts can disconnect mother and daughter, another set will bind them in a way that can transcend the law. The failure of the law requires a new kind of writing, one that will continue to replicate and circulate across great distances the embrace of mother and daughter.[25]

Patrilineal and patriarchal heritage proves inadequate all around, and is replaced by a new textual and maternal network. To fund a shopping trip to outfit Ellen for her long separation, Mrs. Montgomery sells her mother's ring, for Captain Montgomery's allowance has been "barely sufficient for her mere clothing" (29). In the face of bare sufficiency, the Montgomery women will pose fluid excess. Funded matrilineally, their shopping trip is founded in a kind of outlawry: when Ellen worries that the doctor won't let her mother go out, Mrs. Montgomery replies (echoing her youthful rebellion?), "I shall not ask him" (26). After the jewelry store, they enter the bookstore where Ellen chooses a Bible "with unusual care, as though a nation's fate were deciding" (30). For Warner, the nation's fate is better placed in such details than in the network of patriarchal professionals who thwart and prevent such choices, while organizing things so cruelly or, at best, ineptly.[26]

Books are represented as offering sensual pleasure: "'Oh, what a delicious smell of new books!'" (29). Although the Montgomery women are called passionate, when mother and daughter are together their appetites are turned toward each other and they subsist largely on tea and toast. (Ellen's appetite increases when she's away from her mother.) As the bookstore stimulates physical sensations, it also kindles extreme emotion: Ellen is "in ecstasy" (29), "in love," with "flushed cheek and sparkling eye" (30), while her mother struggles with "rising emotions of pleasure and pain" and finally sheds "some of the bitterest [tears] she had ever shed" (30).

Although they know they are to be separated by an ocean, until now mother and daughter have been in complete sympathy. In the bookstore the potential for disconnection rises up between mother and daughter for the first time, for here they are distinctly out of sympathy, unconnected:

"Her little daughter at one end of the counter had forgotten there ever was such a thing as sorrow in the world; and she at the other was bound beneath a weight of it that was nigh to crush her." Mrs. Montgomery recovers by remembering "the words Ellen had been reading to her . . . that very morning" (30). In the resulting triangulation, the mother remembers the daughter reading the (mother's) Bible, and this memory helps her to compose herself enough to relate to her daughter face to face. The recollected reading experience mediates between mother and daughter. It is the bookstore and its exciting inventory that have infused mother and daughter with emotions that threaten to separate them; it is a reading experience that re-mediates between them, making it possible for them calmly to coexist within the "reading world." This scenario fully captures the double bind of midcentury literacy.

In the bookstore, Mrs. Montgomery's bitter tears fall "thick upon the dusty floor" (30). The space of the bookstore is now sanctified with the evangelical holy water of maternal tears. Mrs. Montgomery's tears counter the sensuality of the commodities in the bookstore with the sensuality of the mother's body. But her tears also express a painful assent to the network of relations represented by books and bookstores. Although mother and daughter are emotionally at odds in the bookstore, Mrs. Montgomery must have a Bible for Ellen, for it will be her surrogate. When, before sending her out on another shopping mission, Mrs. Montgomery tells Ellen that "a great deal of skill and experience is necessary for a shopper" (44), she means a proficiency not only in discriminating among the array of bindings or fabrics, but in mastering the economics of emotional expenditure as well.

The famous tears of *The Wide, Wide World* flow into the inevitable gaps in language; they are the syntax of the unsayable. They replace Ellen's words of gratitude for her mother's purchases: "Words failed her, and tears came instead" (32); "'I don't know what to say; I can't say anything. Mamma, it's too much.' So it seemed for Ellen sat down and began to cry" (37). Tears reorganize an anatomized world through sensation. For the susceptible reader, tears function as a deep mnemonic, suturing the representations in the novel to personal memory.

Mrs. Montgomery's purchases are in support of Ellen's reading, Ellen's writing, and Ellen's ongoing, across-the-miles embrace of her mother. Every article is identified with the feminine: Ellen calls up the authorities of a Miss Allen and a Miss Pichegru (unidentified, but perhaps her teachers) in the purchase of a writing desk. Moreover, these objects are explicitly identified with the maternal body. Mrs. Montgomery always chooses, and guides Ellen to choose, the color red: the work-box is "crimson-lined"; Ellen picks a red Bible because "it will put me in mind of yours" (31); after resisting red sealing wax ("'it is so common'"), Ellen accedes to her mother's preference: "'a stick of red on purpose to seal to you'" (35). Marked with mother's-lip red, these objects will be able to reproduce the full maternal affect;[27] they will speak in the mother's voice, perform as mnemonics, and fulfill mother's precepts: "'My gifts will serve as reminders for you if you are ever tempted to forget my lessons . . . the desk will cry shame upon you . . . the sight of your work-box will make you blush'" (37).

When the objects are brought into the house, removed from the "bewitched" (32) commodity setting of the store, they are positioned within the maternal narrative, which increases and yet directs their bewitching power by sanctifying it with "mother." A quick study, as though in training for her eventual supplanting of her mother, Ellen surrounds the objects with her voice: "She first went through the desk and every thing in it, making a running commentary on the excellence, fitness, and beauty of all it contained" (40). Ellen would use all of her new objects to ransom her mother, if she could: "'Oh, dear mother . . . I wish they were all back in the store, if I could only keep you'" (41). She recognizes the exchangeability of mother and her surrogates, but still values the original over the representations.

Warner establishes relations between objects and persons that are akin to her sense of the relations between texts and persons; objects and texts circulate similarly and carry similar meaning.[28] Describing Harriet Beecher Stowe's "sentimental possessions," Gillian Brown considers that

> a thing becomes a personal possession, supplemental and hence special to the owner. Possessions might be said also to be a personification, or, more precisely, a personalization of things which supplements and transmutes the things' objecthood. . . . The narrative of the beloved thing is a narrative of entitlement because it projects the possessive principle of the owner's freedom: it restages self-possession. (42)

While "sentimental possession may rationalize—by personalizing—market relations" (43), Brown modifies this critique in relation to Stowe. Sentimental possession "shares the liberal ideal of self-realization in property, but [Stowe] would secure this goal by replacing market relations with familial ones"; Stowe grounds "the principle of possessions in interiority" (44). Warner is certainly more open to the critique that she "rationalize[s]—by personalizing—market relations" (43). But for Warner, certain objects, often related to writing, become full surrogates for people, and it is this quality that transforms the alienating potential of the marketplace. At the same time, the need for surrogates—because people die, or the law sends them away—leads to the necessity of attaching to these store-bought objects emotions previously assigned only to persons. Warner's objects don't "restage self-possession"; rather, like images in alphabet books and objects in pedagogical maternal narratives, they help to organize the owner's subjectivity, as these objects become signposts in an internal landscape.[29]

Ellen herself operates as an object of "sentimental possession" within the novel, for she is herself "owned" and exchanged over the course of the narrative. Through Ellen, Warner transforms Benjamin Rush's decree that the child must not belong to himself but to the community: "'I am glad to think I belong to you, and you have the management of me entirely, and I needn't manage myself, because I know I can't; and if I could, I'd rather you would, mamma'" (18). But Rush's idea was a republican fantasy, never a legal reality.[30]

The attachment of children exclusively to their mothers, and the drawing of mothers into a sphere with its own public responsibilities, activates Rush's idea, but with an unforeseen side effect. That children belong to their mothers commodifies children. As in Brown's description of Stowe's "sentimental possession" the redemption of the commodity from capital depends on its being properly owned. After her parents' deaths, Ellen is taken up by the genteel and British-born brother and sister John and Alice Humphreys; Ellen and the Humphreys mutually choose to "belong" to one another. Aunt Fortune Emerson resists relinquishing Ellen, staking her claim in pragmatic farmer's terms: "*She* had the first and only right to her; and Ellen had no more business to go and give herself away than one of her oxen" (458). Ellen is, literally, chattel, a useful adjunct to the farmyard. Fortune, however, is out of her depth, or out of her time, and forfeits any possible rights to Ellen by interrupting the maternal-textual network: she withholds from Ellen Mrs. Montgomery's letters. Ellen is cast again into the wide world when one of these long-deferred letters from her mother consigns her to the maternal homestead in Edinburgh. In this upper-class household, for the first time Ellen really resists being owned. While she is the household's "newly acquired treasure" and her adoptive father insists "you belong to me entirely" (504), Ellen worries that she "'gave myself to somebody else first'" (520). At first dutiful, Ellen reasons that her parents "'had a right to give me away if they pleased'" (504).

Ellen's resistance comes not from having discovered ownership in herself, but from a combination of allegiance to previous owners and a sense of being improperly owned by the Lindsays: "She was petted and fondled as a darling possession—a dear plaything—a thing to be cared for, taught, governed, disposed of, with the greatest affection and delight." And though she is an object of perpetual "watching, superintending, and admonishing" by them, she longs for John's "higher style of kindness, that entered into all her innermost feelings and wants; and his was a higher style of authority too, that reached where theirs could never attain" (538). While Ellen's resistance derives partly from the Lindsays' belated arrival on the scene, they, like Fortune Emerson, represent out-of-date views of childhood. Fortune's is nearly feudal, whereas the Lindsays' is an early capitalist view of children as charming and amusing objects. John Humphreys's ownership is active; it is founded on the labor he has invested in Ellen. But more than this, the erotic reach of John's authority establishes his ownership over Ellen's interiority. Ellen seems almost to recognize, indeed to honor and cherish, the degree to which she has been fabricated by her mother and by John; it can never occur to her to own herself.

Seeing Through Women

Her disembodied spirit entered the hearts of her young disciples,
who, rising from their knees, perceived the heavenly messenger
had left in their hands the revelation of which she had spoken,
a volume of divine origin—the Bible.

—Catharine Maria Sedgwick,
  Means and Ends; or, Self-Training (1842)

She is the very medium by which she pleases.

—John Bennett,
  Strictures on Female Education (1793)

Mrs. Montgomery shapes Ellen into her own replica. Early in the novel, while Ellen is still in New York, she sees out the window "a poor deformed child, whom she had often noticed before. . . . Besides his bodily deformity, he had a further claim on her sympathy, in having lost his mother within a few months" (16). The sight of the motherless deformed child turns Ellen's mind to an exuberant catalog of ways to please her mother while they are apart, which ends in tears "of mingled sweet and bitter" (16). The equation of motherlessness with deformation underscores the penetrating forming activity of her mother on Ellen's body. If a mother's kiss made Benjamin West a painter, Ellen needs her mother for a more homely reason: to keep her body intact.

But if the loss of the mother threatens Ellen's physical organization, Ellen's internal organization can threaten the mother's body. The narrator warns that Ellen's "passions were by nature very strong, and by education very imperfectly controlled" (11). When Ellen collapses with "a wild cry . . . hiding her face in her [mother's] lap" at the news of impending separation, Mrs. Montgomery soon "saw the necessity . . . of putting a stop to this state of violent excitement; self-command was restored at once" (12). And if self-command were to fail? "'Try to compose yourself. I am afraid you will make me worse, Ellen, if you cannot,—I am, indeed'" (13). If Ellen cannot "compose" herself, that is, align herself internally, her mother will die.

High stakes, in a way; in another way, not high at all because her mother is sick unto death already. But what does it mean to represent a failure of *self*-discipline as entailing the death of the loved object? This proscription gives a final turn of the screw to superego formation via what Richard Brodhead calls "disciplinary intimacy."[31] As the mother attaches her own enfeebled body to Ellen's young healthy one, Ellen masters this insurmountable burden, as she is meant to, by fully internalizing her mother. She embodies her mother, as her mother's own body fades into nonbeing.

In effect, not only failure of the law, but failure of the maternal body frames the novel. The failure of paternity to protect, the failure of maternity to thrive. One failure is external, worldly, the other internal, corporeal. From the worldly failure, there is no redemption, for one can hardly imagine an inward turn by Captain Montgomery. The corporeal failure, however, continues the trajectory the self-governed woman has been on all along: toward an internal emblematic stasis and an external dispersal of the body. In the "reading world," death simply increases the metonymic force of the mother's already circulating body. If in life she was reduced to metonymic body parts, in death her metonymic powers can be conferred on any object in the world. And more: having emblematically imprinted these objects with her lips and voice, the mother lives on, as William Alcott predicted.

Ellen's mother-surrogate, Alice Humphreys, also fated for an early death, exemplifies an ideal operation of the feminine. She is "like the transparent glazing which painters use to spread over the dead colour of their pictures; unknown, it was she gave life and harmony to the whole" (205). Woman is spread thin across the visual field itself; she is the glazing, material and yet invisible, giving "life and harmony." For Alice and Mrs. Montgomery, the full maternal flight from the corporeal accomplishes two things: first, it frees woman from the visual field; and second, it increases her capacity as a medium.

The woman as a primarily visual entity—an adornment or embellishment, or figured as part of a morally pleasing and visually enticing scene—is a commonplace of conduct manuals and women's education treatises, as well as of the traditional misogynist tracts sometimes bound together with them.[32] To fall ill might be seen as a fortunate fall halfway out of the visual field, into transparency. But this is more than the "sentimental transparency" that posits a reassuringly honest see-through woman, whose thoughts and feelings are always visible.[33] Rather, this female transparency is what makes the visible possible. In the previous chapter, I described the way in which the advent of women in alphabet-ization positioned the woman as a kind of syntax for the alphabet—a ground for alphabetic discourse—through her visual, aural, and oral presence. Now we see the female serving as the medium through which the world might be perceived. The novel's closing sentence finds Ellen becoming for the Humphreys "the light of the eyes" (569). In Ellen's ascension to pure light, she is like Mary Peabody Mann's ideal of al-phabetization: "I well remember the shining pages of my childhood's books,—a lustre never emitted by white paper alone" (M. Mann, 127). While Mary Peabody Mann finds a sheer light emanating from the al-phabetic page, Susan Warner resolves Ellen's alphabetization by having her transcend both the alphabet and text to become the very medium of vision.

Ellen as Emblem of Literacy

"The Bible is in my head, my head is in the Bible."

—Resident of an insane asylum, 1778
(quoted by Friedrich Kittler)

The inherent visuality of women, according to the discourse of feminin-ity, combined with Ellen's extreme youth (she's ten as the novel opens), makes Ellen accessible to annotation, literally in the marking up of her books, figuratively as she is scrutinized and assessed by everyone she en-counters. That she is so accessible to annotation makes her legible. In-deed, by the 1850s childhood has emerged as a text that, then as now, the culture reads as runes through which it imagines its own destiny. If the child is father to the man, the child is also the living parent of the culture. Early in the novel, Ellen, exemplifying this inversion of roles, nurses her mother. A kindly doctor teasingly criticizes Ellen's nursing: "'She [Ellen's mother] looks to me as if she had been too much excited. I've a notion she has been secretly taking half a bottle of wine, or reading some furious kind of a novel'" (19). The wine Mrs. Montgomery has been drinking is made of her daughter's tears; and it is her daughter, a "furious kind of novel" in the making, that she's been reading.

Mrs. Montgomery is just the kind of mother that, as Chief Justice Marshall had put it, "does so much towards making . . . her daughter to resemble herself" (Garnett, 8). Mrs. Montgomery defines the emblematic mother: "'Do you know my mother, sir?'" Ellen asks a sympathetic stranger who describes, in affecting abstractions, the ideal mother to her (72). Mrs. Montgomery influences and shapes Ellen by binding herself physically to written texts—her own script, the Bible, and all the accoutrements of writing that Ellen will take away with her.

In Ellen's new red Bible, Mrs. Montgomery inscribes two passages from the New Testament. As Mrs. Montgomery sinks her head "upon the open page," she silently prays: "'Let these words be my memorial'" (42). Later, when she is separated from her mother, Ellen remembers the first quotation: "Then came some words in her memory that her mother's lips had fastened there long ago" (261). Mrs. Montgomery has so composed herself that the maternal lips successfully printed these words in Ellen's mind.

In the novel's conversion scene, after Mrs. Montgomery has died and Ellen has begun to transfer her passion for her mother to John Humphreys, he instructs her to "'carry your heart and life to the Bible and see how they agree'" (352). This is how, he assures Ellen, to discover whether "'the Holy Spirit has changed you and set his mark upon you.'" Alone, as Ellen ponders whether she is "changed," she "bent her head upon her little Bible to pray" (350). Replicating her mother's gesture, physically aligning herself with her mother by putting her head in a book, brings Ellen to her conversion. Her relation to the book, as to her mother, is metonymic and synecdochic: she is juxtaposed to the book, she is inside of the book, the book is inside of her.

Once Ellen has incorporated her mother, she has taken another step toward becoming the same kind of medium as her mother. To use the spiritualist sense of *medium*, Ellen has "channeled" her mother. When the farmer Mr. Van Brunt is laid up with a broken leg, Ellen reads *Pilgrim's Progress* and the Bible to him in a special, transcendent way, "not only with her lips but with her whole heart" (413). When it seems that Mr. Van Brunt has dozed from boredom, Ellen "sank her head upon her book and prayed that a time might come when he would know the worth of those words" (413). Ellen's ritual invocation of the emblem of literacy—head in book—succeeds in winning a new convert. Ellen discovers some time later that this moment for Van Brunt, with the additional fixative of Ellen's sensuous, sanctifying tear falling on his hand, was the start of his conversion, which he owes to Ellen's "instrumentality" (569). Ellen's inner life, aligned through her mother and the Bible, soon becomes—as in the mechanics of stamping—able to be impressed on others. At the same time, Ellen fosters a kind of literacy that transcends the alphabetic text.

Writing and stamping operate in one direction along a social and spiritual hierarchy; Ellen can be an "instrument" of Mr. Van Brunt's conversion, but continues to be written and read by her mentors. Constituted by her mother's imprinting, Ellen is an emblematic text. John makes explicit the relation between feminine visuality and textuality. John suggests to Ellen that "'from any works we may form some judgment of the mind and character of their author'" (480). The highly literate Ellen assumes he means "from their writings." But John has other works in mind as well. First, he says, from the Eddystone lighthouse one might form an opinion of its builder; and one can judge women through "women's works" (480). What might John offer to match the supreme phallic example? So much work gets done in the novel; one could dream, at least, of Warner forcing John to say that novels are "women's work." But novel-writing aside, there is a vast array of work performed by the tireless women of John's acquaintance, which Warner, in fastidious and riveting detail, represents.[34]

But John explains: "'I cannot help forming some notion of a lady's mind and character from the way she dresses herself.'" For it is here that she manifests "the style of her thoughts" (480). Such is woman's work, the outcome of all of Ellen's internal labor. Her text is in plain sight, right on her body. But not only "styles of thoughts" are visible on women's and girls' bodies. Ellen is wholly transparent to Alice; just as a kindly stranger was able to guess all of Mrs. Montgomery's attributes simply by asserting the stereotypes of ideal motherhood, Alice is able to judge Ellen's mother by looking at Ellen. She's sure to let Ellen know, as she praises the traces of Mrs. Montgomery's gentility in Ellen's behavior, that Ellen ought not to "'take home the praise that is justly her right and not yours'" (240). Ellen is having a self written for her, stamped upon and into her by others, and must not be permitted pride of authorship.

While Ellen has incorporated her mother through a process of replication, it is John Humphreys who writes Ellen. Warner connects John's writing to oracles and hieroglyphics, to, that is, an essential spoken and an essential written language, making him a plausible annotator of the emblematic Ellen. Ellen asks him to decorate a homemade New Year's present—a needlebook that Ellen's young replica Ellen Chauncey has sewn for her mother—with inscriptions in his elegant writing. When Ellen asks him to keep his work a secret, so the present will be a surprise, John promises to be "as obscure as an oracle" (302). A schoolroom dialogue follows as John defines *oracle*, with a commentary on paganism. But John's alignment with oracles is telling, for he proves to be nothing if not oracular, especially at the end of the novel. He next proposes to write Ellen Chauncey's name "in hieroglyphics" (303), and again pauses to explain the word ("'I mean written in some difficult character,'" 304) and to pursue a dialogue about Egypt. Similarly, when Ellen asks him for a copy of one of his sermons, he explains that "'they have never been written yet'" (409), thus aligning his oracular gifts with oratory; he shows her his half-page of shorthand notes, which look to Ellen like Hebrew. Warner would have associated shorthand with the law (her father used shorthand in his practice), and while here it forms one of the links between John and the "worldly" world, Warner also redeems shorthand for John by associating it, through its affinity to Hebrew, with biblical law. The suggestion is that John writes his sermons in God's own language; but it must be noted that the *fact* is that John makes notes for his sermons in the up-to-date alphabetic technology of shorthand.[35] Nonetheless, Warner positions John in terms of sacred languages, compressed, authentic, mysterious to the uninitiated, and widely perceived in nineteenth-century philology to be closer to natural language.[36] These forms of speech and writing are available to and come naturally to John, while Ellen has constantly to struggle, under the relentless regulation of John and Alice, for correctness in her language; the network of maternal alphabetization operates upon a language that is itself still figured as thoroughly patriarchal. Through his corrections, John writes Ellen, as he writes the hieroglyph for "Ellen Chauncey"—compressing her into an emblem.

As in the example of Ellen Chauncey's needlecase, the maternal writing network offers John another opportunity to shape Ellen through the regulation of her reading and writing. Ellen's reading is interrupted one day by a young Irishman needing help to write a letter to his mother; Ellen wants to brush him off, but John insists that she help the young man. Later, out riding, Ellen admits that she was "very wrong," and the oracular John ("his keen eye saw that the confession . . . came from the heart")[37] concurs: "'You are right now. . . . But how are your reins?'" (462) The juxtaposition of interior alignment with control of animals indicates the nature of the self that has to be "reined in," and also allies the concept with the emblematic tradition in which Temperance is figured with a bridle in her hand (see Fig. 11). John makes the connection explicit: "'No more lose command of your horse than you would of yourself'"—a particularly dark warning, given that John has a history of beating unmanageable horses.

As if acknowledging the artifice of his own authorship of Ellen, and to maintain his copyright, John prevents her from reading fiction, where she might disturbingly encounter other Ellens and Johns. John orders English periodicals for Ellen with "no fiction in them" (464).[38] John knows that novels will tell Ellen all about men like him. But more than this: he knows that novels can stand in for him. Mrs. Montgomery, through a triangular relationship with the Bible, has been incorporated by Ellen; John has picked up where she left off, and continued to write Ellen. If Ellen were to turn these powerful susceptibilities toward novel-reading, she might begin to refurnish her inner life. She might discover, for example, that she has a sexuality apart from the one John has constructed for her, which is designed to fit him to a tee. While Ellen is depicted as being "lost in her book," she is permitted to get lost only in certain parts of the "reading world": "perhaps hunting the elephant in India or fighting Nelson's battles over again." When John appears in the flesh, "Back she came, from India or the Nile; down went the book; Ellen had no more thought but for what was before her" (468). The excitement of John is equated to the excitement of reading colonial and military adventures. But John insists on being Ellen's only textbook to sexuality or to any other kind of emotional adventure—indeed, any kind of interior existence at all. When John finds Ellen engrossed in a "curious story" in an old copy of *Blackwood's Magazine*, he asks her to read no more *Blackwood*s. Ellen has to smother "a sigh of regret" (477).

When, after a long delay, John comes to see Ellen in the maternal family home in Scotland, he watches her without her knowledge and sees "the writing of the wisdom that looks soberly and the love that looks kindly, on all things." Indeed, "her mind was resting itself in one of the verses she had been reading that same evening" (559). The looked-at, listening child is fully transformed into a written, reading child, who reads even when she doesn't have a book in her hand. Here is the ideally alphabetized creature in the new model of alphabetization, which absorbs and then transcends text.

"The Dividing Line":
Alphabetic Realism, Narrative Authority, and the Erotics of Alphabetization

An artist's use of language is the most sensitive index to cultural history, since a man can articulate only what he is, and what he has been made by the society of which he is a willing or an unwilling part.

—F. O. Matthiessen,
American Renaissance

"I wonder what in the world they will make me do next?"

—Susan Warner,
The Wide, Wide World

The narrative of *The Wide, Wide World* is doubly divided against itself: first, the novel prohibits novel-reading; second, the narrative is partitioned between the plot of Ellen's alphabetization and a realistic chronicle of great interest and detail. As the focus of the novel's thematizing of a particular structure of literacy, Ellen holds the narrative together. But if Ellen, as an emblem of alphabetization (head in book), centripetally pulls at the narrative, the narrative is pulled centrifugally as well, by the dispersing force of what I will call alphabetic realism.

Statistically, the bulk of the novel is given over to nearly paratactic descriptions of animals, work, landscapes. No one—not even the Irish boy—is illiterate in this novel. But the second narrative of *The Wide, Wide World*, which has given it a deserved reputation as an early "local color" novel, takes place outside of the "reading world," with the taciturn Mr. Van Brunt, the wild Nancy Vawse, the unsentimental Fortune Emerson—characters not susceptible to the full maternal alphabetization that Ellen undergoes. The realistic narrative of *The Wide, Wide World* expresses another literacy, an aesthetics of enumeration, that derives from earlier novels (most notably *Robinson Crusoe* and *The Swiss Family Robinson*) as well as from the kind of pedagogical writing that the Warners produced for *Robinson Crusoe's Farmyard*. *Robinson Crusoe's Farmyard* has an inherent usefulness and meaning because of its genre. But in the parallel narrative of *The Wide, Wide World*, composed of unmoralized, merely pleasurable "reality effects," Warner is writing a realistic novel.

In "The Reality Effect," Barthes distinguishes this mode from early kinds of descriptiveness sanctioned by the rhetorical tradition (e.g., epideictic oratory and ekphrastic set pieces). Barthes asks what the significance can be of the structurally insignificant details that occur in novels. Using the example of Flaubert's painterly description of Rouen in *Madame Bovary*, Barthes concludes that such a feature is justified "if not by the work's logic, at least by the laws of literature: its 'meaning' exists, it depends on conformity not to the model but to the cultural rules of representation" (145). Alphabetization supports the special mode of representation manifested visually in the "worldly" alphabet array and verbally in the figure of synecdoche; alphabetic realism, the new, postrhetorical mode of description, becomes in *The Wide, Wide World* a discursive counterpart to the drama of alphabetization that is played out through the body of Ellen Montgomery. The "meaning" of the scenes of alphabetic realism bears no relation to the intensely emotional agon of the other narrative. And yet they are both consonant with "cultural rules of representation" derived from alphabetization.

Excerpts from two scenes will show what I mean. In the first scene, Ellen finds her way into the "lower" kitchen of Fortune Emerson's farmhouse and watches Mr. Van Brunt and a helper at work slaughtering hogs:

> "Have they been killed!" was her first astonished exclamation, to which Sam responded with another burst [of laughter].
> "Be quiet, Sam Larkens!" said Mr. Van Brunt. "Yes, Miss Ellen, they've been killed sure enough."
> "Are these the same pigs I used to see you feeding with corn, Mr. Van Brunt?"
> "The identical same ones," replied that gentleman, as laying hold of the head of the one on the table and applying his long sharp knife with the other hand, he while he was speaking severed it neatly and quickly from the trunk. "And very fine porkers they are; I ain't ashamed of 'em." (232)

Ellen proceeds to get comfortably settled in to watch, asking the occasional scientific question: "'What do you mean by "laying them down," Mr. Van Brunt?'" (232). Overall, the Ellen formed in the molten emotionality of her mother's training is here nowhere to be seen. Of note as well is the characteristic structure of such passages. In a later scene, Van Brunt and Ellen head out to feed salt to sheep:

> They crossed two or three meadows back of the barn to a low rocky hill covered with trees. On the other side of this they came to a fine field of spring wheat. Footsteps must not go over the young grain; Ellen and Mr. Van Brunt coasted carefully round by the fence to another piece of rocky woodland that lay on the far side of the wheat-field. It was a very fine afternoon. The grass was green in the meadow; the trees were beginning to show their leaves; the air was soft and spring-like. . . . It was slow getting through the wood. [Van Brunt] was fain to stop and wait for her. (420)

Because of the rather clear-eyed charm of such scenes, one could simply say that they constitute a narrative relief between the more fervid passages. But in their paratactic structure and in the lucidity of their descriptiveness, they utterly refuse every opportunity to interpret or moralize even upon so fine a topic as sheep. These scenes so radically contrast to the typology that rules other passages about nature in the novel that the two kinds of narrative seem not to belong together in the same book.[39]

The descriptive passages seem to belong to a realistic novel. That is, to the kind of novel that Warner is not permitted, by her other narrative, to write. But it is not the narrative voice that prohibits such novels. It is John Humphreys's voice. One must suspect that Warner sends Ellen Montgomery to Scotland for the final portion of the book in an effort to detach herself from the superegoistic voice that threatens to overwhelm her narrative.[40] John's function as a kind of shadow-narrator is represented in the text by the image of a "dividing line." After Alice Humphreys dies, Ellen is comforted for the loss of this second mother by John. As John holds Ellen, his "arm that held her was more than all words; it was the dividing line, between her and the world—on this side everything, on that side nothing" (443). "More than all words"—this is the spiritualized literacy, transcending words themselves, that Ellen has been schooled to. Meanwhile, the "nothing" that is the "wide world" is the substance of that two-thirds of the narrative discussed above: salt-licking sheep, rebellious children, dunkings in streams, adventures in snowstorms, slaughtered hogs, milking cows—all the elaborate details of rural life.

John would seem to exert his authority not only over Ellen but over Susan Warner as well. But though he sometimes seems to exceed his creator's will, John serves Susan Warner well. His association with sacred language balances the draw of the strictly secular alphabetic realism, which has no beginning or end and threatens merely to develop into an infinite catalog of object and event, with *no meaning*. John signifies for Warner the significance of language; without John's oracular and hieroglyphic grounding, Warner could not justify her own sojourn into the plotless accounting of the reality effect.

In addition, John is the requisite male of a conventional marriage plot. In the end, however, Warner thwarts the marriage plot, suggesting another resolution to her narrative of feminine alphabetization. At the end of the novel, when John visits Ellen in Edinburgh, he tells her, "'I shall try you in two or three things, Ellie'" (563).[41] His "two or three things" are, first, "'Keep up a regular and full correspondence with me'" (563) and, second, "'Read no novels'" (564). Ellen happily complies, adding that she doesn't read novels because she knows he wouldn't like it. (An English periodical agrees with John about novels and finds *The Wide, Wide World* "too emotional for children" [quoted in Jordan, 89].)

John refuses to state any third thing; in an access of submission, Ellen decides that "whatever it were, she was very sure she would do it!" (569) In what category would this third thing fall? Reading, writing, and. . . . The arithmetic of the plot might lead one to suppose that the third thing is marriage; it would add up, as a consummation of the sexually charged relationship between John and Ellen. But in fact, the third thing is that there *is* no third thing. Reading and writing: the circuit is complete.

Jane Tompkins, in her afterword to *The Wide, Wide World*, is correct to see this novel as kin to the *Story of O* (599).[42] But we misread the novel if we fail to see that the erotic energy that infuses it has been invested exclusively in its new model of literacy. It is this investment, as well as John's strictures against exactly this investment, that keeps Warner from pursuing her "realistic" narrative, for without the eros there may be description, but there would be no plot. The eroticized alphabetization also prevents Warner from resolving the conventional marriage plot. While marriage may be assumed, it is not articulated (the postnuptial chapter was not published). What *is* articulated is that personality is furnished through literacy with everything it needs. Indeed, this form of alphabetization is profoundly autoerotic.[43]

Even in the unpublished final chapter, this tendency is apparent when Ellen and John set up household as husband and wife. In Ellen's new study, the central item of furniture is an escritoire that "belonged to [John's] father's mother and grandmother and great-grandmother" (583). Through this symbol of matrilineal alphabetization, John enters the network of maternal texts; it is this, rather than Ellen's putative happiness with her husband in himself, that permits the chapter to close with Ellen's complete fulfillment: "'I am satisfied . . . that is enough. I want no more'" (583).

These are all the characters . . . unless we add the scarlet letter. . . .
It is the hero of the volume.

　　　—*Evert A. Duyckinck,* Literary World, *March 30, 1850*

It is, in its visual character, not merely a sign of what is to be known
but it is itself an object worthy of knowledge.

　　　—*Walter Benjamin,* The Origins of German Tragic Drama

Chapter Five

THE STORY OF A:

ALPHABETIZATION IN

THE SCARLET LETTER

The Importunate Letter

From its title, its prefatory conceit, and its major plot elements, from its initial word to its final sentence, *The Scarlet Letter* turns on the first letter of the alphabet. Yet the figure of the letter A slips in and out (mostly out) of critical close-up and remains unelaborated in the extensive literature that has grown up around the novel. The early reviewer quoted above wrote it large: "The scarlet letter . . . is the hero of the volume."[1] Roy Male's "Hawthorne's Literal Figures" asks, "What other literary work has been so successful in breathing life into a letter?" (87). Invoking the graphic sense of "character," Nina Baym proposes that "taking this primary definition, the chief character of *The Scarlet Letter* must be, of course, the scarlet letter itself" (*Scarlet Letter*, 83). Most recently, Sacvan Bercovitch asserts that "the letter has a purpose and a goal" (x) and that the "A is first and last a cultural artifact, a symbol that expresses the needs of the society within and for which it was produced" (xiv). A century ago Henry James lamented the risk Hawthorne ran, with his insistence on the many powers and venues of the A: "When the image becomes importunate it is in danger of seeming to stand for nothing more serious than itself" (408). The allegory-hating James regrets this aspect of Hawthorne's art, but his analysis is correct: the "importunate" letter does "stand for nothing more serious than"—and nothing other than—"itself."

The assertion that critics have drawn from the letter responds to the imagined question: "What does the A stand for?" In his essay about "The Minister's Black Veil," *Hawthorne and History: Defacing It*, J. Hillis Miller notes in a passing reference to *The Scarlet Letter* that "'A' stands for adultery, but black is more ambiguous" (67). Similarly, Richard Chase, in his 1957 *The American Novel and Its Tradition*: "The scarlet A is an ordinary symbol (or sign). . . . We can say with relative certainty what the scarlet A stands for. It stands for adultery or . . . it stands for the inevitable taint on all human life" (80). Chase's contortions to get the A to stand for what he wants it to—not quite A for Adultery, but maybe A for tAint?—characterize the problem. What the A "stands for"—a near-infinity of A-words, for starters, and then everything that the A-words represent—is a red (or scarlet?) herring. The critical commonplace that the A "stands for" adultery seems inevitably to lead on to what adultery "stands for" and so on. The assumption that the A is a stand-in, or cipher, that it must "stand for" something else, is a by-product of the figural structure of the alphabetical statement. "A is for . . . ," "A stands for. . . ."

An alternative to this interpretive cul-de-sac is to consider the question that Henry James raises: if the letter "stands for itself," what is the letter? Like the police scouring the minister's quarters in "The Purloined Letter," we have looked and looked without being able to see the scarlet letter where it hides in plain sight in the alphabet itself.

In this chapter, I take up Hawthorne's own apprehension of the letter prior to writing *The Scarlet Letter*. Both as a literary artist and as a fellow traveler within New England's pedagogy of literacy network, Hawthorne finds in the alphabet an artifact that reflects his sense of how people move through and are shaped by what he calls "the world's artificial system." In the following sections, I analyze Hawthorne's allegorical mode and the poetics and erotics of alphabetization within the novel, to demonstrate how the novel itself performs the work of alphabetizing. Representations of alphabetization in *The Scarlet Letter* and the novel's particular alphabetization of the reader have operated to keep it suspended at the core of institutional literacy in America for a century and a half.

A Priori:
Hawthorne's Letter before The Letter

Hawthorne was alphabetized by a master: Joseph Emerson Worcester, who went on to compile geography books and dictionaries.[2] While Hawthorne's cultural milieu put him in touch with the advanced thinking of his day on elementary literacy, he also pursued a more arcane interest in the alphabet itself. Perhaps it was Worcester's early influence that led Hawthorne, as a young adult, to read the classic treatises on the alphabet, John Wilkins's *An Essay towards a Real Character, and a Philosophical Language* (1668) and Charles Davy's *Conjectural Observations on the Origin and Progress of Alphabetic Writing* (1772) (Kesserling, 48, 64). Hawthorne also knew the work of Charles Kraitsir, a physician and linguist, whose 1846 *The Significance of the Alphabet* was published by Elizabeth Palmer Peabody and promoted in a long article by her in her one-issue literary periodical *Aesthetic Papers* of May 1849, in which Hawthorne's "Main Street" first appeared.

Kraitsir played a role in the Peabody circle, but more importantly he enters the Hawthorne family's imaginative life and Hawthorne's own imaginative life in the months preceding the composition of *The Scarlet Letter*. An entry in *The American Notebooks* for February 1, 1849, links Kraitsir to Hawthorne's domestic universe. Here Hawthorne, as he often does in this period, records observations of his children as they career about the house; his notebook captures them, almost snapshot-style, as they circle about and clamber over their writing father. On the morning of February 1, Hawthorne records, he had taught the days of the week to Una, then nearly five and, her father complains, "not quick in acquiring any set lesson" (421). Hawthorne notes that his wife reads a story to Una, who responds with "'Oh, how my leg does ache, hearing reading!'" (419). Una asks her father "to write sixty-four on her hand"; observing this, Julian asks, "'What somebody make that mark on you?'" (421). Hawthorne reads over Una's shoulder as she writes to "her Grandmother Peabody": "'Dear Grandmother, Is Dr. Kaitser [*sic*] free of his wife?'" (421). Kraitsir's close association with Elizabeth Peabody had led his wife, and possibly others as well, to draw a scandalous conclusion. (The wife was soon institutionalized, and Kraitsir went off to wage revolution in Hungary.)[3]

This entry bears on issues that emerge more fully in *The Scarlet Letter*. In the form of the undocile Una we can see the embryonic Pearl; in the shadowy Kraitsir, a hint toward Chillingworth. Six months before beginning *The Scarlet Letter*, Hawthorne observes Una responding with physical pain to being read to (as her mother will more famously when Hawthorne reads her *The Scarlet Letter*);[4] her father teaches her a primer lesson, writes on her body, and hears her inquire about doctor/scholar Kraitsir's marital discord. Capping these evocative associations is Una's sympathetic interest in a man who might be a model for Chillingworth, both in his profession and in his marital blisslessness, and whose area of scholarship (Chillingworth's is never specified) is the alphabet.

Hawthorne's visual imagination had been drawn to the alphabet some years before he wrote *The Scarlet Letter*. A number of Haw-thorne's 1839 notebook entries have long been recognized as sketches toward future works. This entry, which has largely been overlooked, strikes me as a meditation central to a new understanding of *The Scar-let Letter*. Here Hawthorne exposes the burden of alphabetization and finds in the alphabetic character a paradigm for the tension between ar-tificial systems and consciousness that is so crucial to his fiction-making:

> Letters in the shape of figures of men, &c. At a distance, the words com-posed by the letters are alone distinguishable. Close at hand, the figures alone are seen, and not distinguished as letters. Thus things may have a positive, a relative, and a composite meaning, according to the point of view. (*American Notebooks*, 183 [Jan. 4, 1839])[5]

Perhaps remembering an "Alphabet Turn'd Posture-Master" (Fig. 42) from his own boyhood, Hawthorne finds in this fanciful alphabet an image for what was a familiar theme in his tales: the dissonance or slip-page of meaning between individuals and groups, units and systems. Here Hawthorne imagines an explicit act of reading. At a distance, words; close up, men; only in the middle range are the letters visible. When Hawthorne reads the "A stands for" idiom literally, he in effect refigures it, finding a dark allegorical pun at the heart of the trope. Men have subjectivity, a sense of themselves; words give a sense of their rela-tion to one another; letters mediate between these two positions. Letters are the medium by which men are metamorphosed into words —that is, into meaningful units of a system. At the same time, only by overlook-ing the letters can one pursue meaning, even if the letters one must over-look are men. Hawthorne introduces an implied reader who can change point of view or perspective. Meaning doesn't inhere in the unit or in the system, but is rather a creation of the shifting field of vision of the reader-in-motion. I may be standing near the "letters in the shape of fig-ures of men" and see them as men, while you are standing at a distance and read the words they form. Both I and the letter-men are oblivious of the meaning that, for you, lies on the surface and is, for you, the whole point, indeed the only point. By the same token, you are incapable of perceiving the men or, for that matter, of understanding my point of view. As a communications theory, a politics, or an epistemology, this could hardly be more despairing, for it opens up an abyss between the subjective sensations of the men and the meaning they unwittingly convey as a group, as well as between the perceptions of different "readers."

The letter-men passage offers, nonetheless, a coherent semiotics. The entry concludes with the observation that "things may have a positive, a relative, and a composite meaning, according to the point of view." Hawthorne's "figures of men" convey "positive" meaning; letters, a "relative" meaning; words, "composite" meaning. Modern semiotics, following de Saussure, has similarly found a triadic structure in the sign. Roland Barthes, for example, identifies for the sign "three relations":

> To start with, an interior relation which unites its signifier to its signified; then two exterior relations: a virtual one that unites the sign to a specific reservoir of other signs it may be drawn from in order to be inserted in a discourse; and an actual one that unites the sign to other signs in the discourse preceding or succeeding it. ("Imagination," 211)

Barthes links a particular "consciousness" to each of these relations, which he identifies as the symbolic, the paradigmatic, and the syntagmatic, respectively. These terms are the professional semiotician's version of Hawthorne's "positive," "relative," and "composite."[6]

For Hawthorne, the important feature of the sign is its relation to persons, and his signs intimately share the landscape with persons. The basic unit, the alphabetic sign, is bonded to men's bodies. In addition, the perceptions of an observer, a reader, establish the meaning of the picture, regardless of the fact that the essential units of his perception are men with their own subjectivities. In association with signs, then, persons not only behave as meaning-makers themselves, as readers, but they also function as readable units, that is, as texts.

Hawthorne typically conflates signs and persons. As a consequence, his characters' meaning and identity shift depending on how they are "read," as in "Young Goodman Brown" or "My Kinsman, Major Molineux"; or a character's identity may become melded to an external sign, as in "The Minister's Black Veil." The singularity, subjectivity, or interiority—in the semiotics of Hawthorne's letter-men entry, the "positive" meaning—of a character thus collides with the place of that character within a larger scheme, the "composite" meaning. In the case of the letter-men, this larger scheme or system is alphabetic learning.

The letter-men are, strictly speaking, alphabetized, and their fate is the general fate of the literate, who, as they bend to the task of literacy, become participants in the system, or the institution, of literacy. In a sense, Hawthorne takes the alphabetic synecdoche—"A stands for Arthur," say—and asks: What happens to Arthur? When Arthur becomes representative, what can he any longer mean to himself? What can Arthur know about what his body really signifies? The breach between the individual and society is a commonplace of Hawthorne criticism. What the letter-men passage tells us is that alphabetization, as a point of contiguity and exchange between the individual and society, and as a process that continually transforms them both, is paradoxically fundamental to creating and to spanning this rift.[7]

Hawthorne's notion of literacy contrasts with that of the sentimental pedagogy of, for example, his sister-in-law, Mary Tyler Peabody Mann.[8] In her 1841 letters to Anna Lowell, Mary Mann speculates that "the ancient fancy of illuminating the works of great minds with gilded and *scarlet letters* grew out of some . . . early association with printed, or rather written thoughts" (*Moral Culture*, 127; my emphasis). Mary Mann's "scarlet letters" (eight years before Hawthorne's novel)[9] are associated with "printed, or rather written thoughts," intimating warm and sensuous memories of early reading. In this scheme, thoughts transferred by hand or print to a page are "illustrated" or "illuminated" by the reader's imagination. Mary Mann's pedagogy of literacy is based on this principle: "If the printed word is pointed out at the same time [as the child discovers how to say a word], it is still more interesting, because then it becomes an object of the senses, a real thing, just as much as the book it is printed in" (126). The word becomes "an object of the senses, a real thing" through its aspect as visual image. Mary Mann posits a response to the real-thingness of the word that somewhat exceeds the stimulus. Friedrich Kittler describes this kind of reading effect as "hallucinatory sensuousness" (117). The child's imagination is called into play, not freely, but in a highly disciplined way: the hallucination is scripted so that everything in the world might be positioned within the domestic house of memory. In Mary Mann's notion of "scarlet letters," manuscript illuminators literalized the relation among thoughts, words, visual images, and emotions and, in a sense, transcribed their hallucinations.

Mary Mann's is a semiotics in which the space between the sign, the signifier, and the signified collapses into the reader's imagination. In her "whole language" practice, Mary Mann repudiates the letter; she promotes, in effect, a theory of the syntagm—the unit of discourse—rather than of the sign. If Hawthorne is at home in a semiotic middle distance, with the paradigmatic, Mann promotes the syntagmatic, the discursive. Signs are subordinated to a maternal syntax, which keeps the relationship between the elements—letters, words, things—consistent and stable by referring them back to mother and home.

Domestic ideology and its accompanying theory of learning anchors the sign, while for Hawthorne the sign shifts about until shiftlessness is its signal trait. Yet Hawthorne's semiotics coincides with that of domestic ideology in three significant ways. First, both attribute a power of agency to the reader that has consequences for and upon the bodies of others. Domesticity's everychild, disciplined by the maternal allegory of reading, creates and sustains a powerful vision, dependent on a particular configuration of the mother's body. Hawthorne's everyman similarly draws meaning from the bodies of men bent to the shapes of letters. In both cases, reading entails violating another's bodily integrity by the superimposition onto that body of a sign whose general meaning is not "relate to me" or "look inside" or "MWF seeks SWCM for forest walks." The sign says simply, "Read me," and the bodies have been turned into public spaces. Second, Hawthorne and Mary Mann (for example) attribute to this situation a distinct pathos: for him, it amounts to suffering, while for Mary Mann, love overwhelms and overwrites pain. The third point of contact emerges fully in *The Scarlet Letter*, and that is the relation between alphabetization and feminine spaces and artifacts. As we have seen, domestic ideology aligns literacy with an ideal of maternal reproduction and replication; the text of elementary literacy is always an allegory of mother-love. For Hawthorne the individual's entry into the world of written signs is as inevitable as being born of woman; but he shares with Horace Mann a grim sense of the strenuous artificiality of alphabetization. Like Horace Mann, Hawthorne seems almost to stand outside of language, looking in with resistance and longing.

When Hawthorne was removed from his government job at the Salem Custom House—excised, so to speak, from that system of meanings—he responded with a mixture of regret and relief. Hawthorne was in correspondence with Horace Mann, who, it was thought, might use his bureaucratic pull to do something for his brother-in-law. On August 8, 1849, Hawthorne wrote to Mann that he hoped to write a "school book—or, at any rate, a book for the young."[10] What he began writing no more than a month later was not a schoolbook, not quite, but *The Scarlet Letter*.

Memories of Alphabetization in "The Custom-House"

When the narrator of "The Custom-House" comes upon the A he treats it not as the familiar nursery and schoolroom image, which it would seem to resemble, but rather as an inscrutable artifact of an unfamiliar culture. Just before finding the letter, the narrator, by now a bored functionary, a parochial flâneur-manqué, has been "poking and burrowing" into old papers, "glancing at such matters with the saddened, weary, half-reluctant interest which we bestow on the corpse of dead activity" (29). The pitch of his concentration shifts from desultory to avid when he lays his "hand on a small package, carefully done up in a piece of ancient yellow parchment." He finds that there "was something about it that quickened an instinctive curiosity, and made me undo the faded red tape, that tied up the package, with the sense that a treasure would here be brought to light" (29). The "corpse of dead activity" has been animated, it turns out, by the letter A.

Before the letter emerges from its ancient parchment, its influence is felt; it quickens curiosity and suggests hidden bounty. Severed from the alphabetic system, the letter draws upon the power of its isolation. In his discussion of the isolated allegorical image, Angus Fletcher suggests that the separation of a unit from its system, so far from canceling its meaning, distills or concentrates it. Such a metonymic or synecdochic image "tends toward a *kratophany*, the revelation of a hidden power" (88). Like Fletcher's allegorical image, the A conveys a sense of imminent kratophany, a sense that a hidden power will "be brought to light." Hawthorne amplifies the aura of the packet by exaggerating the age of the yellow parchment from the merely old to the "ancient."

What hidden power, what "treasure," might come wrapped in truly ancient parchment? A clue appears in Hawthorne's "The Village Uncle" (1835, 1842).[11] Subtitled "An Imaginary Retrospect," the tale contrasts the narrator's present existence, that of a solitary, reclusive writer, with an imagined biography, in which the narrator repudiates the isolated writer's life to become a beloved and loving family man, elevated finally to the status of revered village elder. In this "retrospect," the narrator imagines the children he would have had, if he were to choose this sociable alternative to the lonely literary life, and worries that "I feared to trust them even with the alphabet; it was the key to a fatal treasure" (223). In this tale, the narrator regards the alphabet as holding out to the children the threat of a writer's isolated and dreamy destiny, in which they would be shut out from the "warm affections" and "honest toil for some useful end" of the village uncle (227).[12]

The hidden power, in the ancient parchment, "fatal" enough to raise the dead, is the power of alphabetization, here distilled to a very potent form, steeped in the casks of Puritan, republican, and capitalist-democratic institutions.

The narrator's response to the discovery of the A comes in stages, as his own place or point of view shifts in "The Custom-House" from surveyor's to child's to literary artist's. As an artifact of the customhouse, the letter is naturally linked to borders and boundaries; the letter's relation to these boundaries changes with each of the three "Hawthornes."

First, automatically behaving in his official role as customs surveyor, the narrator measures the letter: "Each limb proved to be precisely three inches and a quarter in length." The A, for the moment, is another commodity (from *commodus*, "conforming to measure"; Partridge, *Origins*) that must come under the scrutiny of the customs office. A specialized kind of reader, a customs surveyor reads places and objects; to survey is to bring the world into a textual relation. To survey at a national border is to translate all objects passing over that border into the nationally legible text; any object or person that can't be made to conform to the text is refused entry. In Hawthorne's own semiotics we might say that the "positive" meaning of an item attempting to cross a border has to be left at the border; only the "relative" and "composite" meanings can cross over. After the surveyor reads, he writes, for his job is to take the products of what we now call the Third World and stamp them with the imprimatur of the First: "The Custom-House marker imprinted [his name], with a stencil and black paint, on paper-bags, and baskets of anatto, and cigar-boxes, and bales of all kinds of dutiable merchandise, in testimony that these commodities had . . . gone regularly through the office" (27). Hawthorne's name is synecdochic for the government; he "stands for" Uncle Sam. These objects become both legal and legible as they are translated, by the device of Hawthorne's name stamped on them, into commodities. The sign that these objects have been commodified is that, like recalcitrant children made docile, they have been alphabetized.

The letter A exists within the Custom House as a kind of contraband. It has traveled not from Latin America or China or India, but from that other foreign country, the past. On its journey, while crossing a temporal border, the letter has crossed the national border between a colony of Great Britain and the United States. Considered "official" by the heirs of Surveyor Pue, it has escaped biography and antiquarianism; read as "unofficial" by the Custom House when documents were transferred to Nova Scotia during the Revolution, it has escaped history. Previously illegible to readers representing private and public realms, the liminal letter finds its ideal reader in the shape-shifting Hawthorne. Indeed, as the author of *The Scarlet Letter*, Hawthorne stamps his name on the A, claiming with magisterial confidence the story of its origins as his own.

In the second stage of the narrator's relation to the A, as if the narrator were very small and the letter very big, it fills the field of vision: "My eyes fastened themselves upon the old scarlet letter, and would not be turned aside. Certainly there was some deep meaning in it . . . which . . . streamed forth from the mystic symbol" (31). Though merely the everyday letter A, it is figured as unique as well as inscrutable and illegible, quite severed from the alphabetical system. While this isolation increases its allegorical or magical force, it taps a more homely source as well. In the natural history of the A, there is one time when such absorption is appropriate and necessary, and attention to its attributes, its primary exteriority, is the order of the day. That is at the very first stage of elementary literacy, when one learns the ABCs.[13] Hawthorne recovers the primal strangeness and *un*familiarity of alphabetization, but with the intellectual and investigative equipment of an official and scientific adult. The child who pauses over the ABCs is merely delinquent; for the adult, a speculative attention to an unfamiliar object is not only permissible, but admirable, as being scholarly, scientific. If the child is constrained *not* to ask, the adult is permitted to dilate and dawdle. The child is expected to accept the A, like so much else, without inquiring into its nature.

Hawthorne, as an adult, fills his eyes with the A. The child, whose experience is being echoed and reenacted here, would perhaps try to put this interesting object in his mouth, but a different impulse overtakes the adult Hawthorne. He intensifies the sensuous materiality of the letter by picking it up and placing it on his breast. Fascinated and mystified by the A, he has associated it with female artistry: "It had been wrought, as was easy to perceive, with wonderful skill of needlework; and the stitch (as I am assured by ladies conversant with such mysteries) gives evidence of a now forgotten art" (31).

The repetition of "rag" ("this rag of scarlet cloth. . . . little other than a rag," 31), along with its redness, points to another of the "mysteries" the ladies are conversant with, that is, menstruation. The "rag of scarlet cloth" belongs to another set of signs besides the alphabet, signs of female reproductive sexuality. The narrator can't tear his eyes away from the A, in part because the red rag returns him to aspects of his mother's lap. The A might be construed as a graphic sign for and a screen image of the mother's genitals. While symbolically menstruation is the "curse of Eve," and as such a marker of Original Sin, it as pertinently links the A to female sexuality, understood both as desire and as reproductive potential. In nineteenth-century medicine, menstruation was evidence of a periodically recurring wound and was aligned with the "heat" of the lower mammals.[14] The hint that the A is fabricated of a rag dyed in menstrual blood suggests as well that the A is not only an intimately womanly creation, but a woman's castoff, her superfluity, her excess; menstrual blood is about egress, not internalization. Moreover, surrounded by silence and taboos, menstruation is the definitive marker of women's sphere. For Hawthorne, raised in a family of women, menstruation and the alphabet might well have been met with at about the same time, both cloaked in mystery, secrecy, and the enticing and excluding realm of adult knowledge. Hawthorne, then, like Minister Hooper with his black veil, takes the radical step of wearing something gendered female. But the stain of female reproductive sexuality and female sexual desire, both symbolic and corporeal, is, in the case of the letter, colorfully explicit. More than this, although the letter is here depicted as unique and solitary, by linking it to menstruation Hawthorne reasserts the cyclical, repetitive nature of alphabetization.

No sooner does the narrator bring the letter to his breast than it seems to change substance; "as if the letter were not of red cloth, but red-hot iron," it seems to have heated up. Hawthorne literalizes the maternal "stamping" effect. The narrator "shuddered, and involuntarily let it fall upon the floor" (32). When the narrator places the letter on his breast, "It seemed to me,—the reader may smile, but must not doubt my word, —it seemed to me, then, that I experienced a sensation not altogether physical, yet almost so, as of burning heat" (32). The narrator's stammer—"It seemed to me . . . it seemed to me, then"—depicts a representational predicament. With a wink of collaboration ("the reader may smile"), the narrator draws attention to his difficulty in finding words to describe his experience. This difficulty resolves into a riddle: When is a sensation not a sensation, when is heat not hot? Three solutions come to mind: when one dreams, when one speaks figuratively, when one reads. But the narrator also reports the definite physical experiences of a "shudder" and a lapse in motor control when he "involuntarily" lets the letter fall. The A apparently has the power to induce physical sensations—seemingly sexual—but it can merely suggest or represent others.

A reader may be physically engaged by reading through tears and arousal. While tears were seen in Hawthorne's culture as comparatively benign, sexual excitation was widely seen as a distinctly adverse consequence of reading.[15] Sophia Peabody Hawthorne educated her children at home, but, sharing the anxiety of the village uncle, she postponed teaching Una to read, in an era when middle-class children as young as three were expected to know the ABCs. She was perhaps following the notions of Amariah Brigham, whose 1832 *Remarks on the Influence of Mental Cultivation upon Health* Hawthorne had taken out of the Salem library before his marriage in 1835 (Kesserling, 45). Brigham worried about the overexcitation that the nascent mass media induced and recommended postponing literacy training:[16] "Let [parents] rejoice if their children reach the age of six or seven with well formed bodies, good health, and no vicious tendencies, though they be at the same time ignorant of every letter of the alphabet" (50). For Brigham, the hidden power of the alphabet is excitation. While avoiding direct reference to genital arousal, he finds the brain a relentless erogenous zone, stimulated by too much study. Citing one M. Broussais, he writes that "'every thing which only exercises thought by requiring a lively and constant attention, keeps up in the brain a state of vital erection, by which it is sensibly transformed into a permanent focus of irritation'" (100). Another self-help writer that Hawthorne turned to in 1828 (the year of his alphabetic studies) equates mental and sexual arousal; in his *Remarks on the Disorders of Literary Men*, Chandler Robbins considers that, like the eye and ear, the "brain, too, has its causes of excitement. The exercise of the mental powers determines the blood to this organ, and produces a temporary orgasm" (17). It would appear that Hawthorne's uncovering of the A in "The Custom-House," leads to "a state of vital erection" ("My eyes fastened themselves . . . and would not be turned aside"), and his attempt to merge with it by putting it on his breast leads to a "temporary orgasm" ("I shuddered").[17]

The A, a product of female artistry and sexuality, induces a physical response—first a desire to touch, to bring the letter to the breast, and then an autonomic response. The letter, too, seems to have a response; if the surveyor stamps his name on commodities, the A seems to be trying to stamp itself onto the surveyor. In the poetics of alphabetization, the A of "The Custom-House" performs within the trope of prosopopoeia; it is "motivated" by the alphabetic function of internalization: it wants to get under Hawthorne's skin. But the A is also operating according to the technology of the maternal. In this fantastical scene of discovery Hawthorne's "letter-men" have met up with sentimental pedagogy's "mother." The ambient scene of desire created by the letter leads Hawthorne to bring it to his breast; this is the affective universe of "mother." But lacking the mediation of an actual mother to superintend the proceedings, the A answers back hotly and the narrator responds sexually; the letter makes itself desirable and then abandons its reader. This is the atomized, divided world of the letter-men.

The discovery of the letter in "The Custom-House," shrouded in mystery, inducing sexual desire and yet repelling touch, has the structure of a primal maternal scene, with its taboolike combination of desire and danger. Hawthorne tries on the maternal signifier, as though in a gesture of what feminist anthropology calls "saignade,"[18] a male imitation of menstruation, which foreshadows Dimmesdale's "bloody scourge" (144) and apparent self-mutilation in the novel. As if subject to the regulations of taboo, Hawthorne soon "assumes the nature of the forbidden object as if he had absorbed the whole dangerous charge" (Freud, 31) and gets cut off from the Custom House. But Hawthorne's fictive ritual of re-alphabetization may have had the effect he desired: the symbolic "mother's kiss" of the A generates his masterpiece.

In the third phase of Hawthorne's identity-shifting, as an artist in "The Custom-House," the A "recalled my mind, in some degree, to its old track" (33). The discovery of the A has led to a hallucinatory state, in which dreaming, figuration, and reading coincide. Hawthorne describes the breakdown of everyday boundaries, in this famous passage in "The Custom-House," as his ideal state for producing romance:

> Moonlight, in a familiar room, falling so white upon the carpet . . . is a medium the most suitable for a romance-writer to get acquainted with his illusive guests. There is the little domestic scenery of the well-known apartment. . . . A child's shoe; the doll, seated in her little wicker carriage; the hobby-horse;—whatever, in a word, has been used or played with, during the day, is now invested with a quality of strangeness and remoteness. . . . Thus, therefore, the floor of our familiar room has become a neutral territory . . . where the Actual and the Imaginary may meet, and each imbue itself with the nature of the other. (35–36)

The maternal-domestic world of "small" and "trifling" things, especially those belonging to children, as they are translated by moonlight, acquires "strangeness and remoteness," losing "their substance" in this "neutral territory." "Neutral" is a middle term, from "neuter," *ne uter*, not either; the "not either" of the neutral territory is defined by whatever exists beyond its borders. A zone of exchange, akin to a marketplace, this liminal site suggests transfers of every kind between opposites. In the feminized darkness, the moonlight of the neutral territory, a ghostly figure appears that might be identified with Hawthorne's mother who died in the house a short time before:[19] "Ghosts might enter here, without affrighting us. It would be too much in keeping with the scene to excite surprise, were we to look about us and discover a form, beloved, but gone hence, now sitting quietly in a streak of this magic moonshine" (36). The "neutral territory," Hawthorne's ideal ground for composition, is rich with the suppressed, ambient maternal-feminine. Indeed, in terms of gender, the "neutral" territory is not neuter but rather a distinctly feminine "medium" required for the "romance-writer." Only when the letter is reincorporated into the feminine-maternal medium can artistic composition take place. Hawthorne is incapable of invoking this desirable state while working for the government, whose very existence depends on the boundaries that the feminine "neutral territory" dissolves in a flood of moonlight.

Three phases of the narrator's personality come together in "The Custom-House" like the three points of the letter A: the official, the infantile-erotic, the literary. Each persona puts a distinct value on the A. In the customhouse, the government functionary reads and writes commodities as they cross a national border; this persona establishes the A as a quasi-illegal border crosser and as a commodity. The child reads the isolated letter, erotically linked to the mother's body, while the letter writes on the body, creating a wounded boundary between outside and inside; the A becomes a fetish charged with volatile powers of female sexuality. The literary artist reads and then transcribes an aesthetic text in a maternal "neutral" zone between the Actual and Imaginary; the letter operates as a catalyst, which then, through the medium of a feminized space, merges into the artist's text.

The autobiography of "The Custom-House" is not restricted to Hawthorne's sketch of the bureaucracy, but tells a more private story as well, about Hawthorne's own formation as an alphabetized person. When he "remembers" a moment overlooked by official histories, the event belongs to a metaphorical rather than a real house of customs. The customs of a literate culture are grounded in its rites of elementary literacy. Though a creation of the public sphere, these rites tend to take place, particularly in the American mid–nineteenth century, at home and, coinciding as they do with the child's early erotic fantasies and discoveries, seem intensely private. And yet it is into participation in the public sphere that they are meant to propel the newly socialized, alphabetized child. This is Hawthorne's kind of paradox: what we think of as our most private moments are actually writ large for others to read, though not necessarily in a script legible to us. Critical to the establishment of Hawthorne as an author and for the fate of *The Scarlet Letter* as a cultural artifact is the fact that it is the actual customhouse, an icon of the public sphere, that empowers Hawthorne to imagine a secret origin for the A, in an unwritten gap in national history and in a written-over primal scene of the maternal body.

Allegory, Adultery, and Alphabetization

In "The Custom-House" the A is "twisted" around the "small roll of dingy paper" that contains "a reasonably complete explanation of the whole affair" (32). Like the microcosmic A in an alphabet book, suggesting the macrocosm of A-words, the scarlet letter both is contained by and contains the narrative of *The Scarlet Letter*. This synecdochic relation of the narrative to its origin in the alphabetic character lays the groundwork for Hawthorne's allegorical mode in the novel. As the ur-letter, the A unfolds to produce writing, and it subjects all within its purview to the strictures of written or printed discourse. It is in this active sense rather than in any set of one-to-one correspondences that *The Scarlet Letter* may be read as an allegory of alphabetization. The binding of the alphabetical character to the bodies of Hester, Pearl, and Arthur requires varying degrees of bodily conformation or distortion and the infliction of various kinds and degrees of pain; this binding and conformation constitutes their alphabetization.

"Allegory," as Angus Fletcher describes its etymology, derives from "*allos + agoreuein* (*other + speak openly, speak in the assembly or market*). *Agoreuein* connotes public, open declarative speech. This sense is inverted by the prefix *allos*" (2). *Allos*, "other," modifies the radical for speaking publicly (in the *agora*, the forum or marketplace) in "allegory." If allegory describes the translating efforts of the author as well as the interpretive efforts of the reader, what translates the characters in *The Scarlet Letter* from one state or status to another is adultery. The words share an etymological bond. "Adultery" is rooted in an unadulterated "other"; according to Partridge (*Origins*), the sense of the Latin *adulterāre* is *adalterāre*, literally, "to alter." If allegory means to *speak* "other," adultery means to *be* other. When the letter translates Hester's body into a public space, she has become "the other" in the marketplace, there to be read and interpreted. Allegory, adultery, and alphabetization all require a transformation from one state or status to another; in each case, the realms of official conduct and private experience exist in tension with each other, or come into open conflict.

The liminality inherent in these three terms is captured in the opening chapter of the novel, "The Prison-Door." The narrative emerges from the customhouse, both figuratively, since there the narrator finds the A and the bare bones of his story, and literally, as "The Custom-House" introduces the novel. The customhouse opens onto a world of commerce with faraway places, but it is also, as the house of custom, the site of cultural rituals. As the novel opens, however, the venue has shifted from "The Custom-House" to "The Prison-Door." In a metonymic reduction, the house distills down to a door, and all its customs to the disciplines of the prison.

Hawthorne arrays a catalog of ill-lettered figures, in nearly primerlike alphabetical order, who might issue from the prison into the marketplace in chapter 2: "bond-servant," "child," "heterodox religionist," "Indian," "witch" (49). In the place of these malefactors, Hester emerges. The bloodthirsty matrons in the crowd want to strip Hester (54), brand her on the forehead, kill her (51). The A deflects, suppresses, and compresses within itself these radical solutions. The A's first task is to contain, and eventually dissipate, the violent desires of the crowd. The only discipline Hester will receive is the discipline of the alphabet. The A thus substitutes for fatal punishment; it "stands for," stands in the place of, death. At the same time, by deferring Hester's death the A gives birth to the narrative. The first power of the A, then, to give life, is aligned with Hester's maternity. Hester's adultery would never have been discovered if not for her pregnancy. If her fertility has engendered the A, the A returns the favor, extending Hester's life.

Hester begins as a Bellerophon figure, bearing a written sign, like his, and like his meant to discipline her for illicit love.[20] Through epic endurance Hester, like Bellerophon, outstrips her punishers and her punishment. Like Bellerophon, Hester undergoes heroic struggles and wanders alone like him, whom Homer describes as "devouring his own soul, and shunning the paths of men" (6:200–203). Like him, Hester is "banished and as much alone as if she inhabited another sphere, or communicated with the common nature by other organs and senses than the rest of human kind" (84). Bellerophon carries his "baneful tokens" from the writer to the reader, remaining, himself, outside the realm of text, though influenced by it. But Hester wears her A with a difference because she is able to read her own sign.

"Tall," a woman "on a large scale," with "abundant hair . . . a marked brow and deep black eyes," Hester has "impressiveness" and "a certain state and dignity" (53). The outsized female figure, especially in the "figure or body of a female enchantress," according to the Renaissance scholar Patricia Parker, is associated with "the dilation of romance narrative" (10); a reining in of female largeness and largesse is a way of "mastering or controlling the implicitly female, and perhaps hence wayward body of the text itself" (11). But Hester's size is overdetermined. Hester is large as a reminder of her recent pregnancy, and she is large to distinguish her from woman in the nineteenth century. She is large to provide a canvas for the A; she is a sculpture, a painting by Raphael, a picture in an emblem book: Grammatica, for example. She is large, like a monument, to hold the gaze of the audience; she is large because she has to remain visible from afar. She is large so that Hawthorne, and the reader, can be small.

Moreover, Hester is large because the A has transformed her into a public space. The modern form of capital letters originates in letters incised in stone; the capital letter is inherently monumental.[21] In his work on the German *Trauerspiel*, Walter Benjamin finds that the written language of allegory appears in fragments, or ruins.[22] Like Fletcher's allegorical image, Benjamin's fragments are "fateful": "In this way language is broken up so as to acquire a changed and intensified meaning in its fragments." Benjamin connects this fragmentation to the fact that with "the baroque the place of the capital letter was established in German orthography" (*Origins*, 208).

Hester is "transfigured" (53) by the fateful letter on her bosom: "It had the effect of a spell, taking her out of the ordinary relations with humanity, and inclosing her in a sphere by herself" (54). The A submits Hester to a rite of transition, but her liminality dilates for the length of her life.[23] The isolated letter, as if by contagion, isolates Hester. But isolation is an effect, too, of silent, solitary reading. As though undergoing a ritual process, Hester "felt or fancied, then, that the scarlet letter had endowed her with a new sense." The A "gave her a sympathetic knowledge of the hidden sin in other hearts" (86). Like McLuhan's "extensions of man," the A allows Hester to exceed the limits of her body by giving her the power to read people as texts, to enter into them without their knowledge. Not only does Hester read others, but she must patiently endure being read by them. "Both men and women, who had been familiarly acquainted with Hester Prynne, were now impressed as if they beheld her for the first time" (53). The A's melding to Hester defamiliarizes her and at the same time gives her the power to "impress" or imprint, as if the A were a piece of type and the crowd Hester's blank page. But more often, Hester herself is the page: Chillingworth sees her becoming "a living sermon against sin, until the ignominious letter be engraved upon her tombstone" (63). At church, "it was often her mishap to find herself the text of the discourse" (85) as she is presented as an allegory for the congregation.

For Walter Benjamin allegory is bound to the graphic aspect of script: "In the context of allegory the image is only a signature, only the monogram of essence, not the essence itself in a mask. But there is nothing subordinate about written script; it is not cast away in reading, like dross. It is absorbed along with what is read, as its 'pattern'" (215). If allegory "speaks other" in the marketplace, one way to encode is simply to bypass speech, for all to hear, and produce instead silent script, for some to see and read. Those who read absorb and are shaped by the written script. *The Scarlet Letter*'s characters "absorb" the "pattern" of the A, with various consequences. For Benjamin the tension between "signifying written language and intoxicating spoken language opens up a gulf in the solid massif of verbal meaning and forces the gaze into the depths of language" (201). In Hawthorne's allegorical mode, Hester stands by, if not quite for, signifying, written language; given a chance to substitute speech for the letter by revealing her lover and being released from the A, Hester declines. She almost instantly internalizes and possesses the letter, announcing her ownership in the opening scenes: "It is too deeply branded. Ye cannot take it off" (68). Hester and the letter are both transformed. The A now has a habitat, a context, a place from which to be viewed and exert influence; Hester acquires some of the power, permanence, and inviolability of text.

In the binding of the alphabetic sign to the adulterous woman the two exchange some qualities: the alphabet becomes sexualized while the woman is alphabetized. The letter emblematizes her sexuality, leeching it, as it were, of its experiential value for Hester. In a sense this effect preceded Hester's adultery and is a by-product of her femininity; Chillingworth chillingly tells her "'I sought to warm thee by the warmth which thy presence made [in my heart]'" (74). Just as preachers turned Hester into "the text of the discourse," so had Chillingworth used Hester as a medium through which both he and she could experience life. Like the letter-men, Hester, by becoming a sign, has become a medium for the experience of others.

In sentimental pedagogy, the mother is radically desexualized. Hawthorne counters the chaste mother with the adulterous mother. When the mother's sexuality is transgressive it becomes visible, as if it can only become visible while crossing a border. And as it crosses the border, like a parcel coming through the customhouse, it gets the A stamped on it. In *The Scarlet Letter* the state posts on Hester the ultimate synecdochic or metonymic sign, and as usual in Hawthorne's fictive world, the sign melds with the person. In a kind of homeopathic therapy, the state's alphabetizing of Hester resexualizes the maternal body even as it attempts to desexualize it.

Hawthorne treats Hester and Pearl as letter-men, for they are precisely in the predicament of having a relative and composite meaning that is outside them. More than Hester, who is painfully initiated into the alphabetical world, Pearl is the product of alphabetization as much as the progeny of Hester and Arthur, as though she were the offspring rather of

Grammatica and Rhetorica. The ultimate alphabetized child, Pearl is like an isolated image in an alphabet book. In her isolation, she creates a "visionary throng" of playmates: "She never created a friend, but seemed always to be sowing broadcast the dragon's teeth, whence sprung a harvest of armed enemies, against whom she rushed to battle" (95). Hawthorne turns Pearl into Cadmus, famous for this mythic moment as well as for introducing the alphabet into Greece from Phoenicia.[24]

Hawthorne describes what he calls "a peculiarity of the child's deportment" (96), which proves to be not what one would think of as "deportment"—how Pearl might carry her body, Pearl's posture, Pearl's behavior. Rather, by "deportment" Hawthorne means something like Benjamin's "absorbed . . . 'pattern,'" or what I have been calling "alphabetization," for he uses the term to introduce Pearl's discovery of the A:

> The very first thing which she had noticed, in her life was—what?—not the mother's smile, responding to it, as other babies do, by that faint, embryo smile of the little mouth, remembered so doubtfully afterwards, and with such fond discussion whether it were indeed a smile. By no means! But the first object of which Pearl seemed to become aware was—shall we say it?—the scarlet letter on Hester's bosom! (96)

Like the child-man Hawthorne finding the letter in the customhouse, baby Pearl is full of desire for the mother's A: "Putting up her little hand, she grasped at it, smiling, not doubtfully, but with a decided gleam that gave her face the look of a much older child" (96). And as in "The Custom-House," the narrator stumbles over his language, opening gaps in the flow of the text, gaps that open onto a preliterate orality, in an attempt to describe the scene of Pearl's discovery of language. Rather than finding her mirror in the mother's face, Pearl finds it in the A. Rather than an "embryo smile" in mirror-response, Pearl gives "a decided gleam that gave her face the look of a much older child." "Gleam" is associated in *The Scarlet Letter* with the letter: "It was whispered, by those who peered after her, that the scarlet letter threw a lurid gleam along the dark passage-way of the interior" (69). Pearl "imprints," as naturalists say of animal relations, not, as is the usual case, on her mother, but on the A.

In essence, Pearl reads before she speaks; she literally rather than figuratively takes in the alphabet with mother's milk. By the age of three, without books, Pearl knows the contents of the Westminster Catechism and *The New England Primer* (112). Having so early imbibed the letter, Pearl forms an indissoluble unit with the A. More even than Hester, Pearl has become a sign, "the scarlet letter endowed with life, only capable of being loved" (113). Hester and Pearl have so conformed to the written sign that they have no existence outside or beyond it.

"Behold a Spectacle of Blood": The Erotics of Alphabetization in The Scarlet Letter

In [Böhme's] view A was the first letter which forces its way from the heart.

—Josef Nadler, quoted by Walter Benjamin,
   Origins of German Tragic Drama

And all he saies, a Lover drest
In his own Blood does relish best.

—Andrew Marvell,
   "The Unfortunate Lover" (1681)

Thus this cross-stroke covers the man's organ of generation, to signify that Modesty and Chastity are required, before all else, in those who seek acquaintance with well-shaped letters, of which A is the gateway and the first of all in alphabetical order.

—Geoffrey Tory,
   Champfleury (1529)

In its twenty-fourth chapter, as though having exhausted the twenty-four-character seventeenth-century alphabet, Hawthorne's allegory of alphabetization closes with a reading lesson, of a very advanced sort. His last words on the first letter of the alphabet in *The Scarlet Letter* describe the stone that marks the graves of Hester Prynne and Arthur Dimmesdale. This seemingly dry summary conclusion to the novel serves to extend the life of the A beyond that of the human characters. But Hawthorne compresses within the letter that remains on the tombstone all the drama, especially the erotic drama, of its history within the romance.

The tombstone "bore a device, a herald's wording of which might serve for a motto and a brief description of our now concluded legend" (264). The image on the gravestone will be described in language that will provide both a supplement and a condensation or a mnemonic for the entire novel. What are the words that promise so much?

"On a field, sable, the letter A, gules."

Hawthorne (as Harold Bloom has said of Dickinson) makes the visible very hard to see. If on the one hand reading provides hallucinatory experiences, on the other hand, reading can shut us out entirely from the hallucinatory, leaving us stranded in the literal, as this does. It may help to consider these parts of the puzzle Hawthorne leaves us with: the heraldic emblem; the epitaph; the exotic "gules," Hawthorne's last word on the A.

The narrator has promised to condense the novel into an emblem described in words, whose pictorial element will thereby be formed in the minds of readers. But are readers really likely to get the picture? Before an image can be created, the novel's final sentence needs to be translated from the technical language of heraldry into plain English. Hawthorne's nineteenth-century readers would have been better equipped to do this than we are, but even they might have paused. The editors of a modern school text, foreseeing student bewilderment, offer this note: "'On a black background, the letter A, in red'" (Norton ed., 1302). True enough. But Hawthorne's "simple slab of slate" with its "semblance of an engraved escutcheon" surely lacks paint or inlay, unlikely ornaments anyhow in a Puritan graveyard. The editors have left off too soon, for in heraldic engraving color is coded in lines: sable, black, is indicated by crosshatched horizontal and vertical lines; gules, red, by vertical lines. Hawthorne is attuned to such iconographic distinctions, and here wraps the A in the national flag as he described it in "The Custom-House": "thirteen stripes turned vertically, instead of horizontally, and thus indicating that a civil, and not a military, post of Uncle Sam's government, is here established" (5). The A and the national flag are put on the same picture plane, so to speak; the A, having transcended and outlived Hester, has shifted into the public, monumental realm.

Etched on a tombstone, the letter forms part of a memorial, and speaks to the remaining community: "its story and admonitions are brief, that the thoughtless, the busy, and indolent, may not be deterred, nor the impatient tired: the stooping old man cons the engraven record like a second horn-book;—the child is proud that he can read it" (59). Thus William Wordsworth, in "Essay upon Epitaphs," associates epitaphs with elementary reading instruction. He explains that monuments among "savage tribes unacquainted with letters" (49) simply used stones or raised earth to protect and memorialize the graves. The epitaph presumes literacy but at the same time, in its simplicity, constitutes a reading lesson: "The stooping old man cons the engraven record like a second horn-book." Wordsworth associates first things, the ABCs, with last things; alpha with omega; in the second childhood, the second hornbook is a memento mori.

Gules, pronounced like "jewels" but with a guttural g as in gullet. A specialized word for the color red in heraldry, gules derives from Middle English *golet*, gullet, throat. The redness of gules, then, is a fleshy red, the red of the interior passages of the human body. It is in this throaty tincture that we are meant to conceive Hawthorne and Hester's A. The physicality embedded in this technical term is a Hawthornian touch: flesh, blood, body, buried in language. Gules has two aspects: redness and throatiness. Gules frequently means simply "bloody." In *Timon of Athens*, for example, which one might say is Shakespeare's most "Hawthornian" play: "Follow thy Drum, / With man's blood paint the ground, gules, gules" (4.3.59). I have noted above the link between the scarlet letter and menstrual blood in "The Custom-House." The association of the letter with blood-redness and specifically menstrual-blood-redness recurs throughout the novel. When Hester is leaving the prison, one of the matrons tells her to take off her overly fanciful A and replace it with one of her own "rheumatic rags," while referring to the A as a "red letter," which is slang for menstruation (54). "Rheumatic rag" is a version of "snot-rag," but while "rheum" is associated with the common cold, it refers to anything that "flows." Red rag is also slang for tongue, a double meaning that links mouth and womb. On Hester's "red-letter day," at the prison door are red flowers, another slang term for menstruation. The leech, Chillingworth's sobriquet, is a blood-sucking worm used in many cultures as part of menstrual rituals and rituals of "saignade," and in the nineteenth-century United States it was used to treat menstrual difficulties (Delaney, Lupton, and Toth, 168–169). Hester's namesake, the biblical Esther, refers to her crown contemptuously as a "menstruous cloth."[25] The blood-redness of the A thus binds the letter indelibly to the woman's body and to female sexuality.

Furthermore, Hawthorne's closing line is a literary borrowing from a bloody baroque poem, Marvell's "The Unfortunate Lover," which is itself based on an emblem.[26] In this love-allegory, the hero is born in the midst of a stormy shipwreck, of a mother "split against a stone / In a *Caesarian Section.*" The lover is "brought forth" only to be "cast away." With the ocean his tears, the wind his sighs, he is nurtured by cormorants, traditionally emblematic of lust, who "receiv'd into their cruel care / Th'unfortunate and abject Heir," feeding him on "hopes and despair." While one feeds him, another pecks at his heart, so that "He both consumed and Increas't." Hawthorne substitutes the A for the lover in the last lines of the Marvell poem:

> This is the only *Banneret*
> That ever Love created yet:
> Who though, by the Malignant Starrs,
> Forced to live in Storms and Warrs;
> Yet dying leaves a Perfume here,
> And Musick within every Ear;
> And he in Story only rules,
> In a Field *Sable* a Lover *Gules.*

Marvell's "Story," meaning both history and narrative, is figured as the signal triumph, indeed the empire, of shattered love. Hawthorne adopts this conceit for the A, which stands in for, stands for, and writes over the passion-riven, blood-drenched lover.

As for the throatiness of "gules," the Chillingworth-like Dr. Kraitsir wrote this dithyramb about the gutturals:

> The *gutturals*, in the first place, name the *guttur, gurgel, gorge, gosier, kehle, gula, collum*, and express what resembles the throat physically, . . . the *capacious, covering, hidden* or *hiding* . . . symbolical of the *internal, essential, central, causal*; the *key*, the *unknown*, the *creative; growing, connecting, action*, the *cutting into anything*, the first personal pronoun, and the *interrogative*. (15; emphasis in original)

Associated with the throat, for Kraitsir, is all that is hidden and internal, along with "the *key*" and the action of "*cutting into anything*," the pronoun "I" and the "interrogative." If Hawthorne turned Kraitsir into Chillingworth, such might be Chillingworth's ruminations when he shudderingly discovers what is, we are led to believe, bloodily etched on Arthur's breast.

In the alphabetic treatises with which Hawthorne was familiar, A is treated as throatily "apert" or open. Kraitsir describes the vowels as "sounds not peculiar to man, and not expressive of his reason" (13). Both Charles Davy and John Wilkins associate with the letters images that link letters naturally to bodies (Figs. 67 and 68). For Davy, citing Dionysius of Halicarnassus, each vowel graphically illustrates the mouth, the lips and teeth held "with a considerable aperture of the mouth," the position required to make the letter's sound: "Nothing could more exactly represent the opening of the lips in profile for the purpose, than the character of this letter [Alpha] reclined, in which the cross bar delineated or pointed out the situation of the teeth" (84–85).

In *The Scarlet Letter*, the A appears in a variety of media—cloth, sky, flesh, stone—and yet at no point is the A itself voiced. If Hester's lips are sealed by the A, however, Arthur Dimmesdale's are notably "apert," and, as Hawthorne reiterates, "tremulously" so. It is Arthur who expresses what Walter Benjamin called "the ecstacy of the creature" in the spoken word (*Origins*, 201); and yet he is nearly mute in the actual narrative. Hawthorne tells us about his eloquence, but we are barred, by the medium of print, from being able to experience "the gift that descended upon the chosen disciple, at Pentecost, in tongues of flame; symbolizing, it would seem, not the power of speech in . . . foreign and unknown languages, but that of addressing the whole human brotherhood in the heart's native language" (142). Dimmesdale's gift of the "tongue of flame" allows him sympathetic knowledge, akin to the kind Hester gets from the A. His "heart vibrated in unison with [the sinful brotherhood of mankind], and received their pain into itself, and sent its own throb of pain through a thousand other hearts, in gushes of sad, persuasive eloquence" (142). The preacher's vibrating, throbbing, gushing (and elsewhere, breathing, swelling, crying) voice may well articulate the very A in "The Minister's Vigil." Here, on the scaffold in the

Figure 67 From John Wilkins, *Essay towards a Real Character and a Philosophical Language* (1668). (Courtesy of the Newberry Library, Chicago)

Figure 68 From Charles Davy, *Conjectural Observations on the Origin and Progress of Alphabetic Writing* (London, 1772). (Courtesy of the Newberry Library, Chicago)

middle of the night, Dimmesdale "shrieked aloud; an outcry that went pealing through the night" (148). A long A-A-A-A-A-A-A-A-A?

Hawthorne depicts Dimmesdale's speech in exclusively sensual and sexual terms. His "vocal organ was in itself a rich endowment. . . . Like all other music it breathed passion and pathos . . . in a tongue native to the human heart" (243). His voice "gushed irrepressibly upward"; listeners "could detect the same cry of pain," while his audience "had been bourne aloft [on his voice], as on the swelling waves of the sea" (248). Dimmesdale's sensuous orality sharply contrasts with Hester's alphabetic rigidity; her "life had turned . . . from passion and feeling, to thought" (164). But for Hawthorne's Dimmesdale, the *cri de coeur* is not enough, *speech* is not enough. Dimmesdale must have the A etched onto his body, becoming, in imitation of Hester and Pearl, script himself. Only after Arthur reveals what is on his breast does the narrator allow that the scarlet letter had done its office.

Hawthorne ruefully iterates the A's imprinting capacity as well as the permanence of its imprint: "We . . . would gladly, now that it has done its office, erase its deep print out of our own brain; where long meditation has fixed it in very undesirable distinctness" (259). Identifying with the reader, as witness to the novel's scenes of instruction, Hawthorne describes his own and his reader's uneasy but irremediable alphabetization. The A reaches beyond the confines of the novel, just as, within the novel, the A exceeds the boundaries of Hester's lifespan.

Hawthorne's "fatal token" both substitutes for Hester's death and memorializes her death. If the novel counts on a screened primal scene, the lovemaking of Hester Prynne and Arthur Dimmesdale, to produce narrative, it counts on the grave to close the narrative. In this way, the novel is an imitation of life, or at least of the life cycle. But the big events are encased in writing: A is for sex, A is for death. Hawthorne's allegorical mode exaggerates the usual case: when we read words that describe experiences, we may feel as though we are absorbed in these experiences, but what we're absorbed in is reading about them. Hawthorne breaks this experience into its elements by forcing us to contemplate the letter A. The letter A substitutes for, becomes shorthand for, absorbing scenic descriptions of the lovers' bed or the deathbed. The A is a kind of lightning rod, absorbing our readerly attention, deflecting it from the moments of life-being-lived that Hawthorne withholds from us.

Hawthorne shuts down this aspect of the A, writes over it. Although both the materiality and the sensuality of the A are implicit within the text, its sound, its throatiness, is effaced. In Benjamin's terms, Hawthorne focuses on the tension "between signifying written language and intoxicating spoken language" and "forces the gaze into the depths of language" (*Origins*, 201). Indeed, the layer of allusiveness that Hawthorne inserts at the end of his romance makes one feel that he wants the reader to tunnel through the text, to become absorbed in the puzzle that its literariness presents.

The Scarlet Letter *as a Rite of Institution*

In "The New Adam and Eve" (1843) Hawthorne gives his most blatant warning about worldly systems:

We, who are born into the world's artificial system, can never adequately know how little in our present state and circumstances is natural, and how much is merely the interpolation of the perverted mind and heart of man. Art has become a second and stronger Nature; she is a step-mother, whose crafty tenderness has taught us to despise the bountiful and wholesome ministrations of our true parent. It is only through the medium of the imagination that we can loosen those iron fetters, which we call truth and reality, and make ourselves even partially sensible what prisoners we are. (746)

Given "what prisoners we are," it is no coincidence that the letter emerges from the "Prison-Door" of the first chapter of *The Scarlet Letter*. In "The New Adam and Eve," Hawthorne replants the original couple amid the remains of a depopulated Boston and environs. When Adam and Eve come, in their wanderings, to the books in the Harvard library, Hawthorne's language will be familiar to readers of "The Custom-House": "The unintelligible thought upon the page has a mysterious relation to [Adam's] mind, and makes itself felt, as if it were a burthen flung upon him" (760). These books are like the A, whose "deep meaning . . . streamed forth . . . subtly communicating itself to my sensibilities, but evading the analysis of my mind" (31). Eve persuades Adam to leave Harvard before "he lingered there long enough to obtain a clue to its treasures" (761), riches that Hawthorne elsewhere—as in "The Village Uncle"—explicitly, and throughout this tale implicitly, characterizes as "fatal." Hawthorne poses the "medium of the imagination" as the saving balm, the antidote to the "world's artificial system" as it is represented by the productions of literacy. Hawthorne expresses a kind of double consciousness about his position as an author and as a literary artist. His awareness of the strictures and distortions that literacy can demand of its initiates combines with his sense of an erotic draw at its heart: the new Adam and Eve can stay in Eden as long as they can resist being alphabetized.

Hawthorne's use of Cambridge and Boston as sites of these conflicts links them to his own position as an author. The "Cornhill" in the "vicinity" of which Hawthorne accurately plants the prison and the marketplace in *The Scarlet Letter* had more than historical verity to its account. The corner of Cornhill and School Street, where in the seventeenth century had stood the house of the "sainted" Ann Hutchinson, was a spot Hawthorne knew well; in the nineteenth century it was the house of Ticknor & Fields, his publishers.[27] Cornhill is the quarter of printers and publishers in the nineteenth century, and Hawthorne underwrites them, so to speak, with the disciplining technologies of the earlier culture: the prison and the scaffold.

Both in its prehistory, in the form of entries in Hawthorne's American notebooks, and in its one-hundred-and-fifty-year life as romance, novel, and, importantly, school text, *The Scarlet Letter* holds a central position in the literacy life of its culture. The alphabet, perhaps even more forcibly than printing, had became the technology of the United States in the antebellum period. Thus it is not remarkable that one of the founding texts of American literature has as its fundamental element—some say its protagonist—the first letter of the alphabet.

Richard Brodhead has pointed out that Hawthorne is the only canonical writer of the American nineteenth century whose star has never dimmed, starting bright and twinkling along steadily now for a century and a half (*School*, 63). Occasional shifts have occurred in the Hawthorne canon, but *The Scarlet Letter* has always been its sun. It is an institution. For Sacvan Bercovitch "it is not too much to say that *The Scarlet Letter* began the institutionalization of an American literary tradition" (xix). As Brodhead and Jane Tompkins, among others, have noted, Hawthorne, as an "institution," has always had an easy relation to literature as an institution and to related systems of schools and universities.[28] This is because Hawthorne's replication of the process and consequences of alphabetization has continued to match the symbolic requirements of American culture.

In this chapter, as I have focused on a central text of advanced literacy in America, *The Scarlet Letter*, and its adaptation of what I am calling "the story of A," the scene has changed from nursery and schoolroom to adult institutions. Hawthorne makes the origins and ends of the alphabet explicit; his A emerges from and lives out its life in the customhouse, the prison, the marketplace, the cemetery. The A has grown up—with a vengeance. While the genre of *The Scarlet Letter* may be allegorical romance, it functions as a foundation epic of American literacy. This is its cultural work.

*We may thus expect a thorough exteriorization of knowledge with respect to the "knower," at whatever point he or she may occupy in the knowledge process. The old principle that the acquisition of knowledge is indissoluble from the training (*Bildung*) of minds, or even of individuals, is becoming obsolete and will become ever more so.*

—*Jean-François Lyotard*, The Postmodern Condition

EPILOGUE:

F, ETC.

red capital letter F hovers in front of a suburban house; the house is lit from within, windows aglow against a dark scene of barely distinguishable shrubs, trees, yard, and sky. Set back, away from the thoroughfare, the house extends a path from its doorway outward and downward to the edge of the canvas, toward the beholder. But much in the image runs counter to this hospitality. In its volume and amplitude, the house is the emblem of suburban safety; in its illuminated emptiness, an emblem of suburban menace. The stop-sign-red letter is a billboard rendering of a traditional capital. In their different ways, letter and house are both icons of modernity, and here they exist in the same register, applied with the same commercial or industrial technique of airbrushing. Edward Ruscha's *F House* (1987; Fig. 69), painted while the artist was also working on a public art commission for the Miami–Dade County Library,[1] belongs to the genre of what has been called the "imagetext,"

Figure 69 *F House*, by Edward Ruscha (1987). Acrylic on canvas. (Courtesy of the artist and The Art Institute of Chicago. Photograph © 1999, The Art Institute of Chicago. All rights reserved.)

central to the linguistic and representational revolutions of twentieth-century art and literature.[2] This particular imagetext resonates with the history of alphabetization and the condition of the postmodern alphabet. In "Language, Images, and the Postmodern Predicament," Wlad Godzich observes that in current literacy debates there has been "a failure to appreciate the fact that literacy, as a specific relation to language, has had a defining role within modernity. Any changes in our relation to language would thus spell the end of modernity" (355). Part emblem, part alphabet tableau, part dissociated worldly alphabet, *F House* emerges far down the road from the alphabets that have been the subject of this book and registers the disruption and obsolescence of the modes of alphabetization that they encouraged.

F House. The juxtaposition in the title echoes pedagogical alphabets, which read: A Apple. Here, though, the letter has fallen out of the alphabet's order. It's as though, in a kind of printer's error virtually unknown in alphabet books,[3] two statements had been conflated: "F F***" and "H House." But the fact is that this F is not playing the traditional alphabetic language game. If F "stands for" anything, it is this fall out of the representational order. Ruscha removes the letter from the paradigm of the alphabetic statement. One cannot expect the loss of connectedness to the world of human meaning to have poignancy for the F. This purposive failure of the alphabet's synecdoche insists on another existence, an autonomous existence, for the F, which no longer grovels for sense among objects. Freeing the F from a specific referent, the painting at once invokes the letter's whole chain of semantic associations, while at the same time calling attention to the formal qualities of the letter as a visual image. As for the house, it perhaps needs the letter less than the letter needs the house—or rather, than the letter once needed the house. The self-sufficient house, bristling with cultural prestige, doesn't require a caption or a voiceover, or the emblem book's *mot* or *explicatio*. The addition of such a red mark as F does, however, irrevocably, if indeterminately, qualify the house, both visually and syntactically. If this house is a home, the path to it is foiled by the F, as the scarlet letter interposes between beholder and house, or traveler and destination. Depleted as the sentimental scene of instruction, the house now becomes a setting for other dramas and other lessons.

F House is steeped in popular culture, its technique and imagery echoing ads, movies, TV, children's alphabets. One is used to such gargantuan letters, and even used to not making much sense of them. The ubiquity of letters in the landscape and in every medium reduces but does not entirely efface the allegorical intensity of the solitary letter. In its combination of familiarity and strangeness, the F renders the house uncanny and knocks the B-movie aura of the black-and-white house into a more complex, if less sensational, psychological zone. The letter seems at first to impose on the house, creating a barrier between it and the beholder. This is an effect both of its eye-stopping legibility as an alphabetic character and of its color rather than the technique of painting, for on inspection, the impression of impermeability of the red letter is seen to be an illusion; the F is nearly transparent, a veil or scrim. This overlay of familiar image on familiar image creates a third image, characterized by a kind of implacable dissonance.

The painting positions the letter in a separate pictorial realm from the house, which is more or less objective or realistic (it looks like a blurred photograph). Letter and house seem beholden to different physical laws, but they are melded together by a shared gravitational force, a third reality, or field of meanings. The letter, by contrast with the house, isn't weighed down by the laws of nature. Nor do we wonder, as we might about the house, about the letter's medium (what would it mean to photograph a letter?) or the letter's "original." If we consider this primarily a painting of a house, the letter "floats" or "hovers," defying gravity, suggesting the supernatural or, in the idiom of art history, the surreal. Still, the letter operates in utter consistency with its own weightless two-dimensional alphabetic nature. The letter draws attention to the surface and to the materiality of the canvas. F functions toward the medium of painting in the same way that Hawthorne's A functions toward the medium of print. Just as the A siphons attention onto the techniques of reading and interpretation, so the F reminds one that depth in painting is a fiction. The F flattens. And yet, paradoxically, the vibrating red figure of the F enforces, through a phenomenon called color stereoscopy, the illusion of three-dimensionality.[4] The F, like the mutable A, creates a special effect. To the degree that F operates as text, it slows down, even arrests, the velocity of the image. The vibration thus set in motion between these two incommensurable modes engages the spectator in the work of resolving them. The focal point of *F House*, again somewhat like that of *The Scarlet Letter*, veers between the displaced and vivid letter, on one hand, and the banalities of the scene it finds itself in, on the other; or, to put it another way, from the beholder's point of view, between the irresolvable conflicts presented by this painting and a desire for the fluent narrative experience associated with text. Someone looking at this painting might find herself, as I have and others have, flooded with some of the many hundreds of words that F stands for, and more than this, with stories about the scene, treating the painting as an illustration for a half-remembered text. The image-text conflict throws one back upon oneself, to seek a foundation from which to perceive the world with less dissonance.[5]

F House advertises the exteriority of the letter; it imagines the letter outside. If the house might be said to represent the human habitat—the house of language, the "custom" house—F is external to it, a truant. Promoting visualization without internalization, this alphabetic sensorium differs radically from the nineteenth-century model, so invested in internalization. This is a letter not participating in or seeking to affiliate with a discourse or a semantic field. But although this is a letter without benefit of a trope, it has little in common with the nontropic alphabet of the premodern era, in which the visuality of the letters is a prop for repetitive oral rituals.

The painting articulates a new paradigm for the alphabet's relation to language and to the world, a relation full of paradoxes, in which literacy practices are no longer the pulse of cultural practices or even of language practices. As Godzich has observed, "the decisive proposition for modernity" is that "language is the originally instituting institution; it provides the framework within which the practice of the subject will be that of a self-positing of the Self in language" (366–367). Postmodernism, in

Godzich's description, has witnessed an unlinking of the world from language and from the subject. In this view, the availability of modes of representation based on images, more immediate than language, creates a situation in which the "imaginary becomes free of the *logos* since the world speaks itself in its own terms. . . . Such a world is defined without us" (368).

The letter has always been the nexus between the image and the text. *F House*, like other postmodern alphabetic representations, claims a position for the letter as an image unhinged from its textual function. Nonetheless, textuality clings to the F, as a haunting rather than a presence. A human creation, the letter is ejected from the human habitat and at the same time overwhelms the human with an array of dissociated meanings that can't be shed. The letter exists exterior to—no longer generating—culture. While I am extrapolating from the F to the alphabet, whose increasing separation from human practices has a genealogy, one branch of which I will now briefly sketch, the F's "outside" status resonates with another usage. For F is, of course, notorious as a mark of the outsider.

F. The worst grade. F for failure, flop, and fuck-up. F for fallen, forlorn, forgotten. F for folly. F is the grade equivalent of the old alphabet Zany, the personified and secularized Omega, the ultimate (and requisite) outsider to the culture of literacy. Only six steps down the alphabet ladder, but Judgment Day has struck and you might as well be in hell. In most contemporary grading systems, a crevasse ominously opens up between D and F. (E has dropped out, resonating perhaps too strongly with the E-word *excellent*.) Nineteenth-century school bureaucrats weren't the first to spot F as a mark of punishment. F is noted since the Renaissance as a brand burned into criminals judged to be "fighters" and "fraymakers." But F was also paradoxically constituted as a sign of literacy. The felon who could give evidence of his literacy, which was a signifier of a clerical vocation, could claim "benefit of clergy," and deflect the gallows by carrying instead a brand of F for felon.[6]

Letter grades are an innovation of the mid–nineteenth century, appearing just at the end of the long period of alphabetization that has been my subject, contemporary with the common school movement, "graded" schools that grouped students by age and ability, and the trend toward compulsory education.[7] Historically, letter grades inscribe pedagogy's transition from oral/rhetorical to print/alphabetic media, expressed as well by the replacement of printed and written examinations for the oral examinations that had been the ancient inheritance of school ritual. Letter grades and report cards to parents create an official record and a written correspondence that dispenses with face-to-face communication. In an increasingly professionalized bureaucracy, grades position students themselves as objects of knowledge, as data, and as commodities whose worth is determined by others in a system of comparative pricing. Letter grades produce the experience of the student as a specialized text, one that is abbreviated and encoded.[8] What the student learns is newly constituted—"marked"—as an objective acquisition separated from him: something within him that is nonetheless available to visualization, to scrutiny, and to inscription. As capital letters, marks echo with the memorializing and monumental sense of the inscription, turning the child into a public space.[9]

As I have argued, verbal and visual figuration of the alphabet in the seventeenth, eighteenth, and nineteenth centuries, in ABC books and primers, as in novels, had extended the letters and installed them as participants in the doings of everyday life, as players within and even generators of social and intimate life. Agents of action, affiliated with consumption, aligned with money and capital, the alphabetic letters had become ubiquitous. Bound with the passions and incorporated into personality, such letters produced a form of literacy in which the self is both mirrored and created through silent, solitary reading. The ABC book of the nineteenth century positioned the child within a system of knowledge production and organization that presented to him the world as a spectacle. Grades hypostatize the discipline of letters with the clear reminder that the regime of knowledge produced by alphabetization embraces the child among its objects. Grading draws on all the alphabetic functions and the values that have accrued to the alphabet during modernity's literacy campaigns and compresses them into a regulatory shorthand, in which the letters themselves are asserted as new signs, in a new hierarchy: ABCDF. The anomalous letter in the grading system is at the same time the one that illustrates the superiority of letters over numbers for such a system.[10] The first four letters transform the equipollent alphabet into an axiology. But the really ingenious move is to enliven this new hierarchy with figuration, focusing all of the alphabet's discursive potential on narratives of failure.

F stands for fail. *Fail* has a long life in English. Its etymological constellation includes error, deception, and death. From an early meaning in the thirteenth century ("Of crops, seeds, etc.: To be abortive or unproductive") to its prestige in the annals of capitalism since the seventeenth century ("To become insolvent or bankrupt"), it narrates a miniature history of economic systems (*OED*). *Fail* thus incorporates the pedagogical trope of cultivation, as well as the more recent economic model, which makes *fail* a busy keyword of the American nineteenth and twentieth centuries in and out of school.

Grading is the part of my job as a teacher that makes me feel the most desperate about my affiliation with the institution.[11] Marking— what a word! what an activity!—makes me experience myself most vividly as an object of institutional discipline, while at the same time my relationships with students create a conduit for the institution's power over them. Many of the most conscientious teachers (or at any rate those who can't produce within themselves the authoritarian personality, even for an afternoon) are frantic about grading and yet strangely passive too, as though mesmerized. One's struggles with grades seem merely personal and neurotic; grades seem to depoliticize everyone's relation to the institution at precisely the institution's most politically charged site. Encoded in these letters is the entire social contract of Enlightenment and nineteenth-century pedagogy, with all of its assumptions about forming children and reforming society; grades and marks are a compressed archive as well of structural social inequality in the United States.

The letters on *Sesame Street* "present" and, in effect, sponsor every show as well as segments within shows. "M," for example, "proudly presents Melvin the Moving Man," in a cartoon that closes with the announcement that it "has come to you courtesy of the letter M."[12] Imagined as a corporate entity, the letter claims production rights to the very medium whose images threaten to supplant the letters. "Proudly presenting," the letters are no longer represented as substitutes for or cues for the real thing; they *are* the thing.[13] To the extent that the letters thus become mock–corporate logos, they are positioned outside of the scene of instruction, as a ground or condition for all such scenes. To the extent that the letters are figured as brands, they echo earlier meanings of "brand" and enter into the mnemotechnique of consumer culture; the letter is positioned in the same register as the Nike Swoosh, whose vast associative power relies in part on its very inarticulateness. Its attribute as a brand enlists the letter as an object of consumer desire and as an exemplar of cultural capital. The premier episode of *Sesame*

Street beautifully captures this relation when Bob (one of the adult humans in the cast) shows his magic tricks to a visitor; after making some coins appear, he produces a dollar bill as if from thin air. With a series of deft origami-like foldings he creates out of the dollar the letter W. W, as I suggested in an earlier chapter, is a letter that resonates with the alphabet's repetitiveness and self-reproduction; in its self-compounding, it is the letter that most resembles money, exemplifying the letter's aspect as the folding green of cultural capital.

In its early days, *Sesame Street* relied on the governmental and nonprofit support of the U.S. Department of Education, the Carnegie Corporation, and the Corporation for Public Broadcasting. Theirs was explicitly a social action mission, and their goal was a kind of redistribution of cultural capital. Designed to benefit the "disadvantaged" preschool child, *Sesame Street* was meant to close the "achievement gap" between poor and middle-class children.[14] The values conveyed by the show are familiar to students of the nineteenth century, for its set imagines an inner-city neighborhood imbued with all the affective attributes of the nineteenth-century home.[15] The Muppet Ernie acts out the affective program of the nineteenth-century literacy universe, with his passionate emotional attachment to letters: "E is my favorite letter in the entire alphabet," he cries in the first show, establishing his character.[16] Part of the charm of Ernie's attachments is that they are inexplicable, conveying at once Ernie's affectionate nature and the impassioned randomness of consumer desire. Nineteenth-century literacy training helped to forge these very desires, as it aligned the heated experience of reading and the furnishing of a rich interiority with the consumption of books. Marking a sea change in the place of both children and education in United States culture, the show is now funded by commercial enterprise, through, for example, a product and promotion deal with the chain store K-Mart.

There's no library, newsstand, or bookstore along Sesame Street. Virtually no one reads there. *Sesame Street* seems to support a literacy grounded in sociability rather than interiority.[17] The sociability represented on the show, however, is drawn not from life in the nineteenth or twentieth century but from other TV shows. Parodically reflecting on its own medial world, *Sesame Street* offers an anthology of TV genres: variety shows, commercial breaks, game shows, melodramas, highbrow programming, talk shows, documentaries, cartoons, cable channels. Not surprisingly, *Sesame Street* thematizes the communications modes with which it communicates to the viewer: performance, music, and images, rather than letters and text.

At the end of each *Sesame Street* show the "brought-to-you-by" letters are superimposed over the set in the same visual gesture as Ruscha's *F House*. This commonplace advertising technique—text superimposed on an image—updates *The New England Primer*'s positioning of the letter in the marketplace, which served to commodify the alphabet as it alphabetized the market. The problem faced by earlier literacy campaigns was to put the letters into circulation, to enforce their readability by establishing their connection to everyday practices and to current visual culture. In the real streets from which *Sesame Street* emerges letters are ubiquitous on every surface, in every medium. *Sesame Street*'s response is to pull the letter out of circulation, to single it out from the crowd of letters and arrest its motion. This singling out concentrates the sheer presence of the letter and its ontology as an image at the same time that it submerges the letter's textuality.

The reigning alphabetic function on *Sesame Street* is visual representation. Sequencing is no longer a culturally significant function of the letters, since, among other reasons, digital information can be accessed at random; alphabetical order is as unimportant to the current organization of knowledge as it was to the rhetorical commonplaces.

My ABC's

Big Bird found the letter A.
Find some other letters of
the alphabet hidden in
the picture below.

Figure 70 From *On My Way with Sesame Street*. Vol 1: *My ABC's*.
(© Children's Television Workshop, Sesame Street Muppets, and the
Jim Henson Company)

The alphabet's internalizing function has been similarly, if more complexly, transformed. Internalization appears to be represented by its opposites: externalization, exteriorization, ejection.[18] But this is to conceive of internalization only from the human point of view. The fact is, the alphabetic function of internalization is no longer exclusively addressed to the human.

In one episode, Big Bird and Elmo ask the letter of the day, V,[19] who is, like them, an animated Muppet, to come live on Sesame Street. V hesitates until they explain that the whole alphabet resides there. The other letters appear on cue, superimposed across the screen, soaring quickly past. "The alphabet, my family, wait for me," cries V, who flies off after them. In its capacity and will to flee the scene, at a velocity that outstrips language, this is the alphabet aspiring to be an image, a flow of data, perhaps even motion pure and simple. This strikingly aloof alphabetic behavior contrasts sharply with nineteenth-century alphabetic practices, which were integrated into and often dominated human spaces. The alphabet in motion gives the impression of having, even more than its corporate manifestation, an existence in some other place, "outside of everything."[20] This alphabet is exterior to its human inventors and belongs to a zone that is inhospitable to language.

On *Sesame Street*, speed-hungry letters, like this V, share the field of alphabetic representation with their opposite, images that can only be called dead letters (Fig. 70).[21] As though fallen to earth, these letters are immobile, even cumbersome. They lie about, waiting to be found. But these letters have none of the "fatal treasure" of earlier alphabets, for there's nothing very valuable or interesting about them. Once noticed, they're simply accounted for. They give the impression of detritus, something left over or left behind, lost baggage. It's as if the cultural imaginary, oversaturated with letters, is expelling them, sweating them out. These images convey a new reality: the letters are simply in the way.

FINIS

REFERENCE MATTER

NOTES

Prologue

1. George Plimpton reprinted this image in his article on the hornbook, finding in it a more elevated value put on the alphabet than I do: "Thus you see what an important part the hornbook played in education at the beginning of the sixteenth century,—that of the key to unlock all the treasures of learning" (265).

2. On the end of rhetoric, see, for example, John Bender and David Wellbery, eds., *The Ends of Rhetoric*, and Paul de Man's "The Rhetoric of Temporality." On alphabetization, see Jonathan Goldberg, *Writing Matters* (especially the final chapter), on Renaissance handwriting; and Friedrich Kittler's *Discourse Networks* for a description of the interpenetration of alphabetization and Romanticism in Europe around 1800. In their introductory essay to *The Ends of Rhetoric*, Bender and Wellbery cite shifts in scientific and political discourse and in the character of the state to explain rhetoric's collapse; in addition, "imaginative discourse became anchored in 'subjectivity'" and the "oratorical model of communication was replaced by print and publishing—Europe was alphabetized" (22).

3. The notion of a postrhetorical America may seem to run counter to certain assumptions about the American nineteenth century, for example that it was populated by orators and relied on traditions of rhetoric for popular education in lyceums and circuit speaking. I don't dispute this; in fact, the democratization of rhetoric, as Kenneth Cmiel has shown in *Democratic Eloquence*, contributes to its transformation and disappearance.

4. For example, T. W. Baldwin's work in English Renaissance pedagogy showed, among other things, how Erasmus's *De copia* provides the conditions for Shakespeare's particular kind of copious language.

5. See, for example, Foucault, *The Order of Things*; Kittler, *Discourse Networks*; Illich and Sanders, *ABC: The Alphabetization of the Popular Mind*.

Chapter 1   Alphabetical Order

1. In what remains the only book-length scholarship on *The New England Primer*, Paul Leicester Ford wrote in 1897 that an "over conservative claim for it is to estimate an annual average sale of twenty thousand copies during a period of one hundred and fifty years, or total sales of three million copies" (19). In 1915 Charles Heartman estimated six million copies between 1690 and 1830 (*New-England Primers*, xix). Heartman and Ford both note that, for example, the Philadelphia print shop of Benjamin Franklin and David Hall, one of the few eighteenth-century firms whose records are extant, printed some 37,000 copies of the *Primer* between 1749 and 1766. A new bibliography, a scholarly edition, and a printing history of the *Primer* are overdue. Renewed interest in the *Primer*—witness, for example, Jean Ferguson Carr's contribution to the *Heath Anthology of American Literature* (326–340) and the work of David Watters—promises renewal as well of such scholarship.

2. A full discussion of the structure of this alphabetic statement, an innovation of the eighteenth century, follows in Chapter 2.

3. The first primers were aids for the laity to the book of hours of the Blessed Virgin Mary. The name "primer" may refer to the first of the nine devotional hours (prime) or simply mean "liber primarius," first book, "either because it was in such constant service or, more likely, because it was useful in learning to read" (Butterworth, 3; see also Baldwin, 33–34).

4. "Apart from the *Orbis Pictus* of Amos Comenius . . . no book of this kind found its way into our hands" (Goethe's *Aus meinem Leben*, quoted in Keatinge's introduction to *The Great Didactic*, 79). The catalog to Wordsworth's library lists "Komensky, Jan Amos. Orbis Sensualium pictus . . . J. A. Commenius's [*sic*] visible world . . . translated into English by C[harles] Hoole. 12th ed. 1777" (ellipsis in original) and notes that the auction catalog for the contents of Rydal Mount in 1859 indicated the "late Laureate's Autograph" (Shaver and Shaver, 147–148).

5. As the editor's note points out, the first notion he adapts from Horace who recommends food as an enticement to learning (*Satires*, 1.1.25), the second from Quintilian (1.1.26).

6. On the manufacture of hornbooks, see Tuer, 90ff.; and Folmsbee, 14–24.

7. Variously the pattée or formée cross (Tuer, 330). Ségolène Le Men notes such alphabets in nineteenth-century French chapbooks, headed by the *"crois de Jesus,"* a maltese cross (117).

8. Anne Ferry finds it spelled also "crossrowe, crosrow, crosrowe, crosrew" (19).

9. See Yates, *Art of Memory*; the ancient sources for the memory art, as Yates points out, are Quintilian's *Institutio oratoria* XI, Cicero's *De oratore* II, and, most important, the pseudo-Cicero's *Ad Herennium* IV.

10. From *Hore beate marie virginis ad usum insignis ac preclare ecclesie Sarum* (published by Richard Pynson, 1514): "God be in myn heed / And in myn vnderstandynge / God be in myn eyen / And in my lokynge / God be in my mouthe / And in my spekynge / God be in my herte / And in my thynkynge / God be at myn ende / And my departynge" (Butterworth, 6).

11. For more oral rituals, see Tuer, 62–82. Plimpton also notes that the Exorcism ("In the name of the Father," etc.) often follows the ABCs on the hornbook (266).

12. Ferry points out that the cross lingers in the hornbook even after being routed from church services during the Reformation (130).

13. The significance of the cross's institutionalizing force was recognized by French revolutionary pedagogy; in at least one such primer, the cross's position is filled by the Liberty Cap (*Syllabaire républicain pour les enfants du premier âge*, Paris, Aubry An II) (the alphabet is reproduced in Le Men, 103).

14. I take the necessity of wholeness to holiness from Mary Douglas: "To be holy is to be whole, to be one; holiness is unity, integrity, perfection of the individual and of the kind" (68).

15. Le Men also attributes calligramlike visual force to such alphabets headed with the cross, which she describes as *carré[s] magique[s]*—magic squares (117, 119)—and reads these alphabets as straddling the image-text border.

16. "For the Greeks the letters had an atomistic and elemental character. The letters were indecomposable: there were no smaller, more significant, or more basic elements of the cosmic order. It was from these units that the material form of the universe, and the natural world, was constructed" (Drucker, *Alphabetic Labyrinth*, 56). According to the *OED*, *alphabētum* appears relatively late, first in Tertullian (c. 155–220 A.D.).

17. The Stations originated with veterans of the Crusades in the twelfth and thirteenth centuries as a replacement Via Dolorosa pilgrimage for those unable to make the real one. It has no set liturgy, and even the number of stations—now set at fourteen—varied widely. S.v. "Way of the Cross" in the *New Catholic Encyclopedia.*

18. *OED,* s.v. "Christ-Cross." One of the earliest citations is to Thomas Morley, *Plaine and Easie Introduction to Practicall Musicke* (1597), who uses this verse set to music to teach how to sing from a part-book (36–53).

19. See Butterworth, 178. Butterworth speculates that "est amen" comes from the *Ite missa est* closing to the mass. Perhaps the "est amen" also expresses the unity of the alphabet to keep it from breaking back into elements: *est,* not *sunt,* amen.

20. In reference to children's first encounter with alphabet rhymes, Roy Harris notes that "right at the alphabetic beginning we are plunged into ritual" (9).

21. For these and other origin myths of the alphabet, see Drucker, 22; Allen, passim; Senner, 10–16; Firmage, 8; Goldberg, 218–220.

22. For Comenius and New England, see Robert Fitzgibbon Young's *Comenius and the Indians of New England.* While Young is skeptical of the Harvard offer per se, he believes that Comenius must have received "an invitation of some kind to go to New England," based on evidence in Comenius's own writing, perhaps to "come to New England to organize the education of the children of the Indian converts" (4). The *Janua Reserata* was used in Massachusetts Bay curricula, according to Matthews, "perhaps in Harvard College . . . more probably in the Boston Latin School" ("Comenius," 180).

23. For what is still the best introduction in English to Comenius's life and works, see Keatinge; see also Bowen's introduction to the *Orbis Pictus.* Rood, Busek, and van Vliet and Vanderjagt provide fairly recent assessments. For Comenius in England, see Turnbull and Young. See Svetlana Alpers for a situating of Comenius within visual culture (91–98). Ségolène Le Men, who calls Comenius the "Gutenberg of the image alphabet," sees him in terms very close to my own, positioning him both within the tradition of the rhetorical memory art and as an important influence on the development of the alphabet text (172–183).

24. Bowen notes, citing H. S. Steinberg's *500 Years of Printing,* that

Gutenberg published twenty-four editions of Donatus's *Ars Minor* and that 40 percent of Wynken de Worde's publications were school grammars (25–26).

25. Alpers (252n.39), citing Kurt Pilz, ed., *Die Ausgaben des Orbis Sensualium Pictus*, Beiträge zur Geschichte und Kultur der Stadt Nürnberg, 14 (Nuremberg: Stadtbibliothek, 1967).

26. Mathew Carey publishes in 1787 *The Philadelphia Vocabulary, English and Latin: Put into a new method, proper to acquaint the Learner with Things as well as pure Latin Words. Adorned with twenty-six pictures. For the Use of Schools* by James Greenwood. The full Hoole Comenius is printed by T. & J. Swords in New York in 1810. In 1816, *The Philadelphia Vocabulary* becomes *The London and Paris Vocabulary, English Latin and French*, published by N. Faucon, in Cambridge. For the nursery set, Carey publishes, in 1810, a Comenian alphabet in *The Child's Guide to Spelling and Reading; or, an attempt to facilitate the progress of small children when first sent to school.* Carey publishes a similar primer in 1813 called *The American Primer; or, an easy introduction to spelling and reading*, using the Comenian pictures; but it's as if he looked at them for the first time and realized how odd they were: now the same picture of the Hare, in the *Orbis* accompanying "The Hare squeaketh vá W," is updated to the new alphabet synecdoche: "H is for Hare."

27. Other writers of the period begin to employ what Murray Cohen calls "visual mnemonics," but Comenius perhaps most thoroughly reflects and participates in the Baconian new science. In addition, perhaps because of his special sympathy for children and a kind of genius for presentation, his works have been the most enduring. See Cohen, 18–20.

28. "It went through numberless editions, and was bought by thousands of parents who knew little of Comenius, and cared less for his didactic principles. They found that children liked the pictures and picked up their alphabet, and a few words, easier in that way than in any other. . . . For years it remained unequalled" (Keatinge, 78–79).

29. All quotations from the *Orbis Pictus* are from the 1970 Scolar Press facsimile of the 1659 Hoole translation.

30. The *Orbis Pictus* has for models various illustrated books in manuscript and early print traditions, such as emblem books, dream visions, the *Biblia Pauperum*, William Caxton's illustrated Aesop, as well as earlier en-

cyclopedias, both illustrated, like Gregorius Reisch's *Margarita Philosophica* (see Fig. 1), and not illustrated, like Bartholemaeus's *All the Propyrties of Thyngs* and the *Encyclopedia* of Johann Heinrich Alsted, a follower of Petrus Ramus and a teacher of Comenius. See Bowen, 25–26. For discussions of early print illustration, see the essays in Hindman. For a discussion of Counter-Reformation pedagogy and illustration, especially in relation to girls, see also Larson.

31. Werner Jaeger's three-volume *Paideia: The Ideals of Greek Culture* offers the comprehensive account of this idea; for a definition of *enkyklios paideia*, see 3:3. For a description of Renaissance encyclopedism in the context of New World colonialism and literacy, see Mignolo, 186–216.

32. Animals in association with the alphabet, in both manuscript and print, precede Comenius, but they function very differently. A ninth-century Merovingian manuscript, for instance, uses birds and fish to form letters (Drucker, *Alphabetic Labyrinth*, 108), but this is not an alphabet text. In the alphabet of Jacobus Publicius in *Artes orandi, epistolandi, memoranda* (Venice, 1482), animals appear with letters for mnemonic purposes (Massin, 36). This and similar Renaissance alphabets are strictly "mnemotechnic" and not addressed to the pedagogy of small children or to literacy education. Other Reformation alphabets of the sixteenth century may more closely anticipate Comenius—for example, Peter Jordan's *Lay Book* (1533) and Valentin Ickelsamer's *German Grammar* (1533), both discussed by Kittler (39).

33. The story of the grapes of Zeuxis is the locus classicus for discussions of mimesis as a perfect replica of nature; Pliny, *Natural History*, 35:64–66, quoted in Bryson, *Vision*, 1; see also Bryson, *Vision*, 1–12; Bryson, *Tradition*, 8–9; Mitchell, *Iconology*, 17, 90; and Mitchell, *Picture Theory*, 335.

34. Petrus Ramus (1515–1572) influenced Comenius through the works and teachings of the German Ramist Johann Alsted. This influence is evident in Comenius's use of Ramist taxonomies and visual organizations of knowledge. In addition, Ramist rhetoric dispenses with the memory art altogether. According to Walter Ong, for Ramus memory "is everywhere, its 'places' or 'rooms' being the mental space which Ramus' arts all fill" (*Ramus*, 280).

35. For a Lacanian interpretation of how pleasurable visual experience works, with reference to cinema, see Mulvey, 14–26.

36. For a description of the *imagines agentes*, see Yates, 11.

37. Particularly in the Massachusetts Bay Colony where the *Primer* originates, literacy and schooling were not only culturally and religiously promoted but also legally fostered. The Boston Latin School was founded in 1635 to train boys for the ministry. In 1642 an ordinance required masters to teach reading and writing to their families and servants. In 1647, the colony declared that towns with more than fifty families were required to have a school and hire a teacher, and towns with more than 100 families had to have someone teaching Latin as well. By 1647 there were nine schools in Massachusetts. While Massachusetts is the emphatic example, literacy was valued and promoted in New Netherlands and Virginia as well in the seventeenth century. In addition, by the last quarter of the century, Sunday school had become a regular facet of worship for children, filling the time between the morning and evening services; these sessions were devoted to catechizing, rather than reading instruction per se. See Cremin, 1:176–191. See also Matthews, "Early Sunday Schools."

38. The date of the first *New England Primer* is not yet definitively known; suggestions have ranged widely from the first mention of the title in a 1683 advertisement to the earliest known copies of 1727. David Watters has argued prudently for considering these extant copies from 1727 as signifying the first edition, since evidence for earlier editions is circumstantial. But I tend to agree with Paul Leicester Ford's assessment a century ago, which points to Benjamin Harris as compiler and first printer of the *Primer* in 1690, a view supported as well by Worthington Chauncy Ford's work on Harris as printer, and by Gillian Avery's article on the *Primer*. In addition, references to Charles First (the "man of blood") and Second (see the discussion of the Royal Oak, below) in the image alphabet argue for a seventeenth-century origin; it strikes me that these references might seem very dated to a 1727 American audience if they hadn't already accrued a tradition.

39. See Watters on the crisis of authority and generational conflict at this period in relation to the *Primer*.

40. These newspapers included *The Domestick Intelligence; News from Country and City* (London, 1679–1680), the *Weekly Discoverer Strip'd Naked; or, Jest and Earnest Expos'd to Publick View, &c.* (London, 1681), the *Weekly Entertainment* (London, 1700), and *Publick Occurrences* (Boston, September 25, 1690), a one-issue run and the first bona fide newspaper in America, which was immediately suppressed by Governor Simon

Bradstreet. See W. C. Ford. For Harris in the context of the history of journalism, see Clark, 71–73, 79–80.

41. See W. C. Ford for Harris's publications. The last two items appear in Harris's printing of John Tulley's *Almanack for the Year of Our Lord, MDCXCIII* (probably, according to the American Antiquarian Society's catalog, printed in 1692).

42. The *Primer* contents vary somewhat over its long life, but always consist of these three kinds of texts. See Watters, 208–210, for a useful description of what a "normative" version of the *Primer* would contain.

43. Nine of the twenty-four letters in the 1727 edition are biblical: A, J, P, Q, R, S, U, X, and Z.

44. See Lievsay, 217.

45. In his 1899 reprint of the *Primer*, Paul Ford notes that Benjamin Harris published a chapbook entitled "The Fables of Young Aesop, with Their Morals," which includes images and rhymes closely linked to the cat and fiddle, the lion and lamb, and the nightingale images and rhymes of *The New England Primer*. The earliest known edition of these fables is a fourth edition in 1700, pointing to an originating date close to that of the primer; Ford reprints a picture of a fiddling cat from this edition, which is a close relation, even possibly an identical twin, of the primer cat (57).

46. A. S. Rosenbach remarks on the resemblance of this image to the folk rhyme, first published by John Newbery in London in about 1760 and by Isaiah Thomas in about 1785 in *Mother Goose's Melody*: "It provides us with the hope that the children's lives may not have been entirely black, but that they may have learned from their mothers the frivolous rhymes of their own girlhood" (see Rosenbach, xxxvii–xxxviii and 76).

47. Cats, playing fiddles, lutes, bagpipes, and in association with goats, pigs, and mice, appear on bench ends and misericords at Beverley Minster, Wells, and Fawsley Church, among others. The book of hours is Harleian MS. 6563 in the British Museum; see Sillar and Meyler, 37–49. See also Michael Camille's *Image on the Edge* on the "low" themes of misericords and on the relative freedom of execution of these carvings (93–97).

48. For the 1589 sign, see Larwood and Hotten, 438. In Jonathan Goldberg's discussion of David Browne's 1638 writing manual, *Introduction to the true understanding of the whole Arte of Expedition in teaching to write*, he quotes the author's self-advertisement for writing lessons: the teacher can

be found "most of the afternoone in the vacation, at the *Cat* and *Fiddle* in *Fleet-Street*" (Goldberg, 134–135). Richard Flecknoe, in *Aenigmatical Characters* (1665), remarks that shop signs "have pretty well begun their reformation already, changing the sign of the Salutation of Our Lady into the Souldier and Citizen, and the Catherine Wheel into the Cat and Wheel; such ridiculous work they make of this reformation, and so jealous they are against all mirth and jollity, as they would pluck down the Cat and Fiddle too, if it durst but play so loud as they might hear it" (quoted in Larwood and Hotten, 11–12).

49. See Opie and Opie, *Oxford Dictionary of Nursery Rhymes*, for a review of proposed etymologies of "cat and fiddle" (203–205).

50. See Partridge's *Dictionary of the Underworld* and *Dictionary of Slang*; Brewer's *Dictionary*; Henke's *Courtesans and Cuckolds*. Both cat and fiddle refer to female genitals; cat is slang for prostitute, "fiddle-bow" for penis, "fiddle," as a verb, for copulation. Cat refers as well to whipping, as the short form of cat-o'-nine-tails; to cat, or throw the cat, is to vomit. Fiddle is slang for sixpence and for a writ of arrest. The numerous catchphrases linking cats to other human behaviors—"it's enough to make a cat laugh" or "speak"; "a cat can look at a king"—may also be apposite, as well as the ancient association of cats and magic (sacred or black) arts. See also Sillar and Meyler, passim; Larwood and Hotten, 438; Briggs, passim, and 161 for cat and fiddle.

51. An illustration of Adam and Eve, tree, apple, and serpent was the sign of the fruiterers' company; this was also both a printer's sign and a tavern sign (Larwood and Hotten, 257). The Bible was a printer's sign, and in combination with *ball, crown, dove, dial*, appeared in tavern signs (ibid., 253). The Royal Oak is a Restoration sign, commemorating Charles II's escape at Boscopel (ibid., 49). The eagle is a common heraldic sign and inn sign, the half moon and the crescent moon as well as the man in the moon are inn signs; the "Heart in Bible" and the lion and lamb appear on trade tokens (ibid., 299). See also Delderfield, 22–27, 45, 65, 90. For an account of street signs from the late eighteenth century, see *Helps for Spiritual Meditation* (1775), which finds the sun, moon, lion, lamb, Cross, Bible, Adam and Eve, the eagle, the dog, and the tree all suspended over the streets of London.

52. For rhymes that often captioned tavern signs, see Larwood and Hotten, 18; and Field, esp. 89–92.

53. See, for example, Denise Schmandt-Besserat's *Before Writing*.

54. It may not go without saying that I do not mean to suggest that only capitalist economies can carry out thoroughgoing literacy programs; the examples of Sweden in the seventeenth century and Nicaragua in the twentieth clearly prove otherwise.

55. In "Origins and Predecessors of the *New England Primer*," Gillian Avery notes that a nearly identical image-alphabet appeared in London in *A Guide for Children and Youth* by "T. H." (52). Paul Leicester Ford cites Simon Wastell's *Microbiblion* (London, 1629), a rhyming Bible, as one precursor to the *Primer*. Rhyming Bibles were designed as mnemonics; the *Microbiblion*, for example, is subtitled *The Bible's epitome: In Verse. Digested according to the Alphabet, that the scriptures we reade may more happily be remembred, and things forgotten more easily recalled.* The *Microbiblion* redacts books of the Bible into quatrains, organized in alphabetical order. Like Benjamin Harris's own rhyming Bible, which shares several images with *The New England Primer*, such works are not addressed to children, but rather to the "Christian Reader." Harris's Bible in verse, which is not alphabetically arranged, is also explicitly promoted as "an excellent antidote against a weak Memory" (W. C. Ford, 286).

The Opies (in *Christmas Party Games*, 25) cite alphabet games as origins for rhyming alphabets, and notice that Samuel Pepys engages in one. His diary for March 4, 1669, notes that after dinner at the Duke of York's "there I did find the Duke of York and Duchess with all the great ladies sitting upon a carpet on the ground, there being no chairs, playing at 'I love my love with an A because he is so and so; and I hate him with an A because of this and that;' and some of them, but perticularly [*sic*] the Duchess herself and my Lady Castlemaine, were very witty" (469).

56. P. L. Ford mentions Edward Finch's alphabet, along with the *Microbiblion* and two other rhymed alphabets (*New-England Primer: A History*, 25). The Finch alphabet opens: "Adam our Father being the first man / Through Eve his wife the which vile sinne began: / But God of his mercie thought it very good, / We should be sau'd through Christ our Sauviors blood // Betimes in the morning when thou doest awake, / Vnto the Lord see thou thy Prayers make, / And after that then goe to thy Vocation, / This is a way that leadeth to saluation" (Finch, n.p.).

57. See Ambrose Heal's *English Writing Masters* for alphabet rhymes in copybooks.

58. This puts me at odds with the two previous literary readers of the *Primer* alphabet, David Watters and Elisa New, both of whom discover a consistent pattern in the image-rhyme alphabet. Watters's "'I spake as a child': Authority, Metaphor, and *The New-England Primer*" offers an interesting reading of the patterns of patriarchal authority in the *Primer* and provides an excellent bibliography of *New England Primer* scholarship. He assesses the *Primer* overall in the context of "how language acquisition contributed to the maintenance of authority structures" (193) and reads the alphabet as a narrative through which children might see reflected their own "conflicts with parental authority" and which "provides a historical context for [the] first image of the fatherhood of God" (200). Watters finds a "typological habit of interpretation . . . engendered" by such patterns in the rhymes as the tree in the opening image repeated in a salvific New Testament version at the end (201). The essay as a whole insightfully contextualizes the *Primer* in Puritan psychology and structures of authority. But the alphabet reading, while full of helpful observations, is necessarily somewhat forced. Much more problematic is Elisa New's essay on the poet Edward Taylor and the *Primer*; the essay reads an image-alphabet (without rhymes), which in all probability was only included in the *Primer* in the second half of the eighteenth century, as though it would have been available to the poet Edward Taylor (1642?–1729). New's reading of these images' festive aspects in fact places them firmly in the latter part of the century, and is in line with my reading of such later alphabet images, which I discuss in Chapter 2.

59. The Royal Oak refers to Charles II (see n. 51 above). "Man of Blood" is an epithet for Charles I. For a debate over the source of the expression (Numbers 35:33, 2 Samuel 16:7–8, Psalms 5:6 all use the phrase), see *Times Literary Supplement*, Letters, July 30 and August 6, 1993.

60. Two modern reprints of the *Primer* perhaps illustrate this point. In 1900, during the vogue of pedagogical nostalgia (Henry Ford was reprinting the McGuffey readers about the same time), the textbook publisher Ginn & Company choose to reprint a 1775 edition with the original alphabet. The conservative publisher of the only edition in print in the 1990s has opted for Christian over free-market values, reprinting an "evangelized" edition, whose text and images really are constrained to provide a pious narrative.

61. See Goldberg, *Writing Matters*.

62. *Helps for Spiritual Meditation* suggests that the existing "Signs in Town and Country are here endeavoured to be spiritualized, with an Intent, that when a Person walks along the streets . . . they may be able to think of something profitable. . . . Even the common Signs at the People's Doors . . . hold forth a large Field for Meditation" (2).

Chapter 2   The Republic of ABC

1. The Bill for the More General Diffusion of Knowledge, which would provide for elementary through university education, among other matters, was put forward by Jefferson in the Virginia legislature between 1778 and 1785; it was passed by the House but failed in the Senate. In 1796, a portion of the bill, much watered down and providing only for primary education, was passed. See Cremin, 2:106–121, for a discussion of Republican educational theories.

2. I am indebted to David Freedberg's *The Power of Images* and to W. J. T. Mitchell's *Iconology* for my thinking about images in this section.

On images in the rearing and education of children, see, for example, Giovanni Dominici's *Rule for the Management of Family Care* (1403): One should have "paintings in the house, of holy boys, or young virgins, in which your child when still in swaddling clothes may delight as being like himself, and may be seized upon by the like thing, with actions and signs attractive to infancy" (quoted in Freedberg, *Power*, 4).

See also two of Erasmus's influential treatises on child-rearing and pedagogy, the 1511 *On the Methods of Study* (671), and the 1528 *The Right Way of Speaking*, for a related means of visual stimulation involving inscribing expressions that one wishes to remember on everyday objects ("gateway, front door, window-frames, every pane of glass, the beams, the ceilings, the floor-tiles, the walls, and all the furniture too, blankets, kettles, curtains, tables, chairs, clothes, plates, tankards, ladles, spoons, basins, pots, chafing-dishes"; *Right Way*, 475).

3. From Burgh's *The Dignity of Human Nature* (1754), quoted in Fliegelman, *Prodigals*, 21.

4. See William Ivins's *Prints and Visual Communication* for a masterly discussion of the pervasive impact of the exactly repeated visual image.

5. Fliegelman calls *Some Thoughts* "perhaps the most significant text of the Anglo-American Enlightenment" (*Prodigals*, 5). Like all of Locke's

works, it was a frequently imported title, according to Edwin Wolf's study of eighteenth-century American book ownership, library holdings, and booksellers' catalogs, *The Book Culture of a Colonial American City* (9, 84, 85–86, 159–60).

6. Fénelon, though Catholic, is immensely influential in America through such works as the *Treatise on the Education of Daughters* (1687), which is reprinted, excerpted, and referred to with regularity in American pedagogy at least to the mid–nineteenth century, and through *Telemachus*, "the most popular book of French authorship in colonial America" (Wolf, 53).

7. Watters (209) credits Thomas Prince with the evangelizing of the *Primer* icon alphabet in the 1750s.

8. See, for example, the 1761 Boston edition.

9. Heartman, *The New-England Primers*, quoted in Watters, 211, who notes that this passage "underscores a belief in the danger of representational systems whose interpretation is not strictly controlled." Watters is concerned largely with the hermeneutics of metaphor and does not here make any distinction between verbal and visual images.

10. See Freedberg, "Iconoclasts and Their Motives," on the "dialectic of the relationship between image as material object and beholder" (12), especially in relation to twentieth-century attacks on works of art. See also Liza Mundy's report in *Lingua Franca* (Sept.–Oct. 1993) on campus struggles over pornographic and other images.

11. Isaac Watts expresses, in secular terms, both the utility and the fear of images (and of spectacle) in "On the Education of Youth": "I confess freely, that I would recommend the sight of uncommon things in nature or art, in government civil or military, to the curiosity of youth. If some strange wild beasts and birds are to be shown, if lions and eagles, ostriches and elephants, pelicans or rhinoceroses, are brought into our land . . . or some nice and admirable clockwork, engines, or moving pictures, &c. be made a spectacle to the ingenious; if a king be crowned . . . or when there is a public trial of criminals before a judge, I readily allow these sights are worthy of the attendance of the younger parts of mankind . . . that their minds may be furnished with useful ideas of the world. . . . But for children to haunt every public spectacle . . . suffering nothing to escape them that may please their senses . . . this is a vanity which ought to be restrained by those to whom God and nature hath committed the care of their instruc-

tion" (542–543). This warning appears under the subheading of "Appetite" in the "Self-Government" section of the discourse, underscoring the period's alignment of images with desire and the requirement for regulating both.

12. See Welch, xxi–xxiii. Harris's *The Holy Bible in Verse* is one of the few illustrated books of the period, with woodcuts identical to those in *The New England Primer*.

13. Welch describes *A Little Book for Little Children* as "a gruesome compilation containing some of the most harrowing stories taken from Foxe's *Book of Martyrs*" (475).

14. Ariès notes the existence of the child paragon in sixteenth- and seventeenth-century Catholic books (124–127). Janeway's *Token* is part of the continuing competition and emulation between the Catholic and Protestant Reformations.

15. *Corderius*, 17.

16. A concern for the physical well-being of the child in educational theory is as old as Plato's *Republic*. Against the backdrop of Reformation pedagogy's emphasis on the child's soul, however, Locke's interest in the body seems especially striking.

17. The 1787 *A Little Pretty Pocket-Book*, though written for children, opens, characteristically, with a Lockean preface addressed to parents: "The grand Design in the Nurture of Children, is to make them *Strong, Hardy, Healthy, Virtuous, Wise*, and *Happy*"(7; emphasis in original) and continues with recommendations on choosing a nurse, selecting the child's diet, and clothing him "thin" to encourage hardiness.

18. See, for example, *A Little Pretty Pocket-book* and Moody's *The School of Good Manners*.

19. An overt example of this phenomenon is the rhyme "The House That Jack Built," in, for example, *Nurse Truelove's New Year's Gift; or, The Book of Books for Children*, which opens with a picture of Jack's house, reminiscent of the ancient, medieval, and renaissance memory palaces described in Frances Yates's *Art of Memory*. The images throughout the rhyme all have striking details of the kind recommended for memorableness in the *Ad Herennium* and other memory treatises: "The cow with the crumpled horn," for example. The rhyme is followed by a short treatise on the training of the child's memory.

20. According to Fliegelman (citing Paul Michael Spurlin's *Rousseau in America, 1760–1809* [University of Alabama Press, 1969] and David Lundberg and Henry May's "The Enlightened Reader in America," *American Quarterly* 26 [1976]: 262–272), *Emile* was the book most often advertised by American booksellers and appeared in 38 percent of library holdings and booksellers' catalogs between 1777 and 1790. "It was available in English in Philadelphia . . . [in] 1763, in Williamsburg in 1765, and in New York City in 1773" (Spurlin, quoted in Fliegelman, *Prodigals*, 275n.52).

21. See von Mücke, 24–26, for a discussion of Rousseau's critique of fables as a critique of language as a symbolic code.

22. Oral dialogue is excluded from the curse put on representation; in fact, his tutor's posers to Emile help to save Emile from falling under the thrall of spectacle, images, and mere signs. For a further discussion of this issue, see Chapter 3 below.

23. An abridged *Crusoe* was an American bestseller in 1774 and 1775 under the title *The Wonderful Life, and Surprizing Adventures of That Renowned Hero, Robinson Crusoe: Who Lived Twenty-Eight Years on an Uninhabited Island, Which He Afterwards Colonized* and, in a variety of abridgments, appeared in 125 editions between 1774 and 1825 (see Fliegelman, *Prodigals*, 79–82).

24. See Margaret Spufford, *Small Books and Pleasant Histories*, on the chapbook in England; and for the American situation, see Victor Neuberg, "Chapbooks in America," and David Hall, "The Uses of Literacy" in *Worlds of Wonder*, 21–70. Rosenbach quotes a worried Cotton Mather's diary entry for September 27, 1713: "I am informed that the Minds and Manners of many people about the Countrey are much corrupted by foolish Songs and Ballads, which the Hawkers and Peddlars carry into all parts of the Countrey" (xxxix–xl).

25. See Welch, xxiv; Neuberg, passim; Darton, 1–7, 101–102, 122–140.

26. There is a separate and long tradition, which would seem to derive from the acrostic Psalms of the Bible, of acrostic moral dicta; such acrostics appear repeatedly in *The New England Primer* and other primers. For a discussion of these acrostics in relation to the Hebrew alphabetic tradition, see Demers, 78.

27. For example, in Shippie Townsend's *The History of the Mother and Child* (c. 1794):

Child. Please . . . if I can tell them all [the letters], may I have another lesson?

Mother. Well, you have told them all prettily. . . . (11)

28. *The A, B, C, in Verse,* 15.

29. According to Welch, *The Child's New Play-Thing* (no. 194.1), published by J. Draper and J. Edwards in Boston, reprints the 1743 English edition published by T. Cooper; Mary Cooper also printed an edition later in 1743. The Opies note that the rhyme is current as early as 1671, in a text which implies that it is already well established by then (*Three Centuries,* 9). In *Some Observations upon the Answer to an Enquiry into the Grounds and Occasions of the Contempt of the Clergy,* John Eachard "ridicules preachers who find meaning in every letter of a word, and would exhort their congregation to repent letter by letter: 'Repent, R. readily; Repent, E. earnestly; Repent, P. presently; Repent, E. effectually; Repent, N. nationally; Repent, T. throughly [*sic*]. . . . And also, why not,' he continues, 'A apple-pasty, B bak'd it, C cut it, D divided it, E eat it, F fought for it, G got it, &c.'"

30. "A Apple Pye's" "apple" may resonate for modern readers, not only because of *The New England Primer*'s fallen A, but because of these alphabets' heir, "A is for apple." But "pye," and "pie" as later versions spell it, has its own lettered genealogy, conflating food with books. "Pye" descends from the primer tradition and refers to a small ready-reckoner for calculating saints' days. The term has a similar secular bureaucratic function: "Pye Books" are lists of indictments in use as early as 1660. Etymologically, "pye" is linked as well to "pica," the type font, and "to pie" is to get your letters out of sort in the print shop (*OED* and Partridge, *Origins,* s.v. "pye" and "pie").

31. See Terry Castle's discussion of masquerade costume as a "kind of discourse" that can "reinscribe . . . a person's sex, rank, age, occupation" (55). The alphabet catalogs of types relied on some of the same "popular iconography" (70) as the masquerade costumers.

32. Welch dates this Boston edition, printed by A. Barclay, as 1764, noting, however, that it may be 1761 or 1762. This edition is signed by Isaiah Thomas "when A'prentice," which, as Rosenbach points out (33), is interesting in the light of Thomas's later career as a printer and publisher of so many children's books.

33. Opie and Opie, *Fairy Tales,* 36. The tale's first appearance, in a

London forty-page chapbook, is, according to the Opies, the first extant printing of a fairy tale in English, though Tom Thumb's name appears in print as early as 1579. In the tale a husband sends his barren wife to Merlin, whom she finds "mumbling spells of incantation, making Characters in sand." Merlin's oracle predicts the "abortive" birth of a "shapelesse child" who will be "No bigger then thy Husbands thumbe: / And as desire hath him begot, / He shall haue life, but substance not; / . . . / His shapelesse shadow shall be such, / You'l heare him speake, but not him touch" (42). The Opies note that Tom is classified as a "swallow" tale, which is to say that, like Red Riding Hood and other fairy-tale figures, he makes a snack for other creatures. By the mid–eighteenth century, according to the Opies, the name "Tom Thumb" primarily conveyed smallness, literally and figuratively. Tom's name gained some literary prestige with Henry Fielding's 1730 *Tom Thumb*.

34. The appropriation of folk motifs by the literary marketplace is a typical move in this period. In the *Little Pretty Pocket-Book*, "Jack the Giant-Killer," another character drawn from the folktale (Opie and Opie, *Fairy Tales*, 58–82), appears as an avuncular letter-writer to the children who stand in for the child-reader, "Master Tommy" and "Pretty Miss Polly." He bears no trace of his origins and is, rather, the type of the eighteenth-century gentleman.

35. Children younger than the age of four or five are exempt from the humane prohibition against corporal punishment ("Thoughts upon Amusements," 3), for they are too young to be reasoned with.

36. In her essay "Women on Top," Natalie Zemon Davis describes the occasional reigns, in fiction and carnival, of "disorderly" women. She argues that "comic and festive inversion could *undermine* as well as reinforce that assent [to entrusting power in legitimate social authorities] through its connections with everyday circumstances outside the privileged time of carnival and stage-play. . . . The image of the disorderly woman . . . was a multivalent image that could operate . . . to sanction riot and political disobedience for both men and women in a society that allowed the lower orders few formal means of protest" (131). While this may seem a far cry from the function of alphabetic images, this section will make some parallel claims for the way festiveness operates in alphabetic learning. Note, however, that when images of women enter the alphabetic field, they func-

tion to discipline "disorderly women" and children. See Chapter 3 below for a discussion of gender and the alphabet.

37. I rely here on Peter Stallybrass and Allon White's *The Politics and Poetics of Transgression*, particularly in its analysis of interconnections and interdependence between high and low discourses and their inevitable intersection in representations of the body as well as in living bodies.

38. These alphabet rhymes may have started life as folk forms. In any event, despite being in print—the medium of the unchanging, of the exactly repeatable—they behave like folklore, changing in small ways over the years: "Y was a Youth, / and did not love School. // Z was Zany, / and look't like a Fool" is how this one goes, for example, in *Tom Thumb's Play-Book* (Boston, 1764).

39. See Molinari; and Duchartre; for the etymology of *zanni* and descriptions of his characteristic behavior, see Castagno, 95–102.

40. See George Frow's history of English pantomime, *"Oh, Yes It Is!"* (29–30) for a description of a stock panto "school-room" scene, which originates in English in Edward Ravenscroft's *Scaramouch a Philosopher, Harlequin a Schoolboy, Bravo, Merchant and Magician* (1677), but derives from earlier Italian commedia. Here Harlequin goes to school:

> *Harlequin (reciting).* A, B, C, D, E, F, G, H, I, K, L, M, N, P . . .
> *Mistress.* N–P? What's the next letter to N?
> *Harlequin.* P.
> *Mistress.* P, again? Hold out your hand.
> *Harlequin.* My hand?
> *Mistress.* Hold it out to receive instruction thus. (*He holds his hand out.*) So, now look on the top of the house, and see what letter sticks on the ceiling. (*He looks up, and she hits his hand with the cane.*)
> *Harlequin (crying out).* O!
> *Mistress.* "O" then is the next letter! . . .

Frow also notes the 1843 panto *The Harlequin Grammar; or, Lindley Murray and A.E.I.O.U.* (129).

41. The first American edition of *The History of Little Goody Two-Shoes* is by the printer Hugh Gaine in New York, 1775. This citation is from an 1814 Hartford edition, which drops "little" from its title.

42. *The Alphabetical Tattoo; or, Assembly of the Great and Little Let-*

ters, at the Critic's Palace, in Hartford (Hartford, Conn.: Hale & Hosmer, 1813). The first American printing of the "Alphabetical Tattoo" occurs in *The Pretty Play-thing, for Children of All Denominations* (Philadelphia, 1794), based on Newbery's 1759 edition. (Welch lists a Hugh Gaine edition advertised in 1774, but this has never surfaced.) The "Tattoo" is reprinted as late as 1835 as *The Critic, or Lessons in Life* (Albany, between 1827 and 1835).

43. Roy Harris refers, similarly, to an "'internal' semiology" of the alphabet (115). He notes the alphabet characters' "equipollence" and their "free sequential combination."

44. The chapbooks are often quite small; the "snuffbox" or "waistcoat pocket" size (Rosenbach, 33) is about two by three inches. Some are even smaller than that, and in their gay dutch-paper covers look more like postage stamps or candy wafers than books. For a cardboard battledore, see Figure 35; for an image from an accordion format, see Figure 62.

45. See the further discussion of the "alphabet tattoo" below.

46. Voegelin describes the swallow story as a "type of folktale based on the extraordinary swallowing motif." The "extraordinary swallowings" motif, a subcategory of "Marvels," is Stith Thompson motif F910, with several subcategories.

47. See Robert Darnton's "Peasants Tell Tales" on the topic of hunger and fairy tales.

48. Like most pedagogical tropes, that of consumption has a classical provenance. See, for example, Horace's often-cited description of teachers who used cookies to entice reluctant abecedarians (*Satires*, 1.1.25–26). Rosenbach extends the trope to the fate of the books themselves, perhaps with good reason: "[Children] have always taken a strange delight in the flavor of printer's ink, have nibbled at the pages and sampled the bindings of the books provided for them" (xxvii).

49. Other editions make the festive traces even more emphatic in a downright cannibalistic title: "The Tragical Death of An Apple-Pye, Who was cut in Pieces, and Eat by Twenty-Five Gentlemen" (1803, 1814). See Welch, 1328.1, 1328.2, 438.

50. In *The Renowned History of Giles Gingerbread*: "Giles . . . sung the whole Cuzzes Chorus, which the sly Rogue had got out of Mr. *Newbery's* pretty Play-thing" (23). In this example, the American printers Mein and

Fleeming, while pirating the Newbery *Giles Gingerbread*, had neglected to update the promotional reference to Newbery in the text; perhaps these printers didn't have their own edition of the *Play-Thing*, and didn't care to advertise an American rival's, but it's a frequently encountered oversight.

51. William Gilmore captures this phenomenon in his history of this period in New Windsor, Connecticut, *Reading Becomes a Necessity of Life*. See also Kittler's discussion of reading's "hallucinatory sensuousness" (117) and the formation of subjectivity through literacy.

52. Originally printed in London by the prolific broadside printer Carington Bowles in 1782, this alphabet was a popular broadside in the colonies. It was reprinted in chapbook form in Philadelphia in 1814 (see Chapter 3 below). The Williamsburg Foundation has sponsored a new circulation of these images, on almost every conceivable surface; in addition to broadsides, they have printed it on address book covers, satchels, tea towels, coloring books, puzzles, and wallpaper.

53. See Massin, 46–133, for an exuberant catalog of body alphabets, from the sacral to the pornographic to the pedagogic.

54. Tory's *Champfleury*, 1529. See Drucker, *Alphabetic Labyrinth*, 162–165; and Massin, 31.

55. These citations are from the Hartford Hale & Hosmer 1813 version.

56. See Rebora and Staiti, 87, 176, 215, 257.

57. The phrase belongs to Guy Debord: "The spectacle is not a collection of images, but a social relation among people, mediated by images" (sec. 4, n.p.).

58. From *The A, B, C, in Verse* (New York, between 1825 and 1833), 15.

59. Some of the images accompanying this chapter illustrate these sentimental, midcentury alphabets; I take up the issues that these images raise in more detail in Chapter 3.

Chapter 3   "That Mother's Kiss"

1. In *Means and Ends, or Self-Training*, Catharine Maria Sedgwick calls Maria Edgeworth a "benefactress to the young and old of the reading world" (27).

2. James Webster may not have printed other pedagogical texts; this is his only publication listed in d'Alté Welch's bibliography of children's literature (which excludes schoolbooks). He was a publisher mainly of popular

and professional medical manuals, such as, interestingly enough in this context, *A Treatise on the Management of Female Complaints and of Children in Early Infancy* (1818).

3. There is a vast primary and secondary literature about girls' and women's literacy and women in education at this period. Here I will sketch some of the basic trends. First, secondary works that provide a good orientation to aspects of the subject: indispensable to the background of nineteenth-century literacy is Monaghan's "Literacy Instruction and Gender in Colonial New England"; for the nineteenth century, see Beatty, 31–37, on preschool and home education and Tyack and Hansot, 28–78, on girls in grammar school. On domestic ideology and women's education, see Ryan, *Empire of the Mother*; Kuhn, *The Mother's Role in Childhood Education*; Cott, 101–125; Ann Douglas, especially on "Feminine Disestablishment," 44–79. On conduct books, see Rose, "Conduct Books for Women"; and Nancy Armstrong's analysis of conduct books as a foundation of the domestic novel in *Desire and Domestic Fiction*. Important biographies are Kathryn Kish Sklar's on Catherine Beecher and Joan Hedrick's on Harriet Beecher Stowe, esp. 31–66. The central spokeswomen for female education in the period are Emma Willard (*An Address to the Public* and *Advancement of Female Education*), Willard's sister Almira Phelps (*Lectures to Young Ladies*), and Mary Lyon (*Female Education*), who prudently couch their progressivism in conventional terms; and Frances Wright, who doesn't (although her *Address to the People of Philadelphia* is tame enough). Key memoirs are Lucy Larcom's *New England Girlhood*, Lydia Huntley Sigourney's *Letters of Life*, the lesser-known Catherine Badger's *Teacher's Last Lesson*, and the little-known but immensely rich memoir of a Kentucky schoolteacher, Julia Tevis's *Sixty Years in a School-Room*. Central figures for maternal home education are Abigail Mott (*Observations*) and William Alcott, Lydia Sigourney, Lydia Child, and Catharine Sedgwick, whom I discuss below. I also discuss, later in this chapter and in Chapter 5, the elementary educators Mary Peabody Mann, Anna Lowell, and Elizabeth Palmer Peabody.

The men who support women's education tend to do so in floridly misogynist terms; important figures are Joseph Emerson (Mary Lyon's teacher), Charles Burroughs, James Garnett, Samuel Hall, Benjamin Rush (who belongs to an earlier period but remains influential), and Horace Mann.

4. Mother Bunch is a traditional figure, known as early as the sixteenth century, according to the Opies (*Oxford Dictionary of Nursery Rhymes*, 321). The hybrid cat-dog here might be owing to a conflation of Old Mother Hubbard's dog (1805) with Old Dame Trot's cat, an apparently traditional figure that first saw print in 1706 but was current in an English edition of 1803.

5. In *Discipline and Punish*, Michel Foucault describes the "spectacle of the scaffold" as a "triumph of the law" (49) and a manifestation of state (via kingly) power. The narrative produced by the images of *The Good Boy's and Girl's Alphabet*—with its butcher, parson, king, and queen—might be read as a full allegory of old-style disciplines embedded within the letters.

6. The link of this alphabet to domestic ideology is explicit in its subtitle's evocation of Lydia Huntley Sigourney, the "American Hemans" and poet-laureate of domesticity: "Being an Introduction to Mrs. Sigourney's Pictorial Reader." The *Pictorial Reader*, however, seems never to have been produced, though this may refer to her *Child's Book* (New York: Turner & Hayden, 1846) or *A Book for Girls, in Prose and Poetry* (New York: Turner & Hayden, 1843).

7. "Washington at Prayer" is based on the much-repeated Weems story of Washington at Valley Forge (181).

8. See Beatty, 9–13, for the influence of Pestalozzi (1746–1827) in America; and Hürlimann, 134, 250–253, for Pestalozzi's Comenian roots and European context. See also Elizabeth Palmer Peabody's *Kindergarten Guide* (1863), based in part on Pestalozzian principles (as well as on Friedrich Froebel).

9. Due, presumably, to Eleanor Fenn's influence, "Mrs. Teachwell" and "Mrs. Lovechild" become American children's literature brand-names; a number of texts are therefore incorrectly attributed to Eleanor Fenn in the National Union Catalog. Eleanor Fenn shares many of her techniques, including the dialogue form, with her contemporaries Maria Edgeworth and Anna Barbauld, both extremely popular in America; see Immel; Avery, 65–78; and Meigs et al., 96–107.

10. Boston, 1814; New Haven, 1820; the original was advertised in England in 1783. Fenn's *Cobwebs to Catch Flies* is also a central children's book in America, in print from its imported English edition of 1783 through several American editions until at least 1851.

11. The printer would have had these images to hand, since Sidney's Press published two editions of the Robinsoniade, in 1810 and 1814.

12. See Welch, no. 909, for a full description of the extant copies. I would revise Welch's translation of "Douceurs," which appears on the box lid; it means, simply, "sweets." According to Welch, Fenn drew the images herself.

13. "As soon as it is possible to convey instruction by toys, it is well to choose such as will be useful. The letters of the alphabet on pieces of bone are excellent for this purpose. . . . When they are playing with their letters, and you are at leisure, take pains to tell them the name of each one, as often as they ask" (Child, 53).

14. The West anecdote surfaces again and again. See William C. Brown's periodical *The Mother's Assistant and Young Lady's Friend* 1 (1841): 52; and *The Mother's Assistant* 12 (1848): 101; see also William Alcott's *The Young Woman's Guide to Excellence*: "A mother's kiss, in token of her approbation of some little pencil sketch, is believed by Benjamin West to have given the turn to his character—the character of a man who said, and justly, that he painted for eternity. 'That mother's kiss,' he observes, 'made me a painter'" (28). Nathaniel Hawthorne uses the incident as well in his West biography in his 1842 *Biographical Stories for Children*.

15. See, for example, "First Impressions" by Rev. A. Stevens in *The Mother's Assistant* 12 (1848): 127. Daphne S. Giles also offers a conventional version of the Byron's mother story in her 1849 *Religious and Political Influence of Educated and Uneducated Females*: "I took up the life of Byron in order to discover, if possible, the origin of those dark traits so prominent in his character, and so banefully diffused throughout his works. Byron was early left under the entire control of an unprincipled mother, who fostered the pride, and cherished the selfishness of her son, while she cruelly wounded his sensibility by unnatural remarks on his natural deformity of person" (137). This "begat in his sensitive bosom the feelings of an outcast. . . . Who can wonder at the waywardness of his mighty intellect, or that he has left behind him so imperishable monuments of unsanctified genius, and of cruel spoliations of maternal influence! Byron was what the mother made him" (138).

16. John S. C. Abbott combines the examples of Washington and Byron: "Had Byron and Washington exchanged cradles during their infancy, it is very certain that their characters would have been entirely changed;

and it is by no means improbable that Washington might have been the licentious profligate, and Byron the exemplar of virtue and the benefactor of nations" (4).

17. The mother's hand on the child's head is nearly as frequent an apparition as the mother's lips; John Abbott recounts that John Newton's "pious mother . . . often retired to her closet, and, placing her hand upon his youthful head, implored God's blessing upon her boy" (6). Newton nonetheless becomes "a wicked wanderer" who "went to the coast of Africa, and became even more degraded than the savages upon her dreary shores. But the soft hand of his mother was still upon his head" (6–7). These metonymized maternal body parts are typically broadcast across great distances; in Maria Cummins's *The Lamplighter*, a mother (in New York) dreams (later verified as a reality by her son) that she appears at her son's side in Paris "in a gorgeous hall, dazzlingly lit, filled with gayety and fashion" and at first "touched his shoulder" to draw him away from a Parisian siren and finally sweeps him up in her arms and flies off with him (172). This mother wishes for death so that she can be ever more efficient in watching over her son. See also Chapter 4 below on the metonymized mother after death.

18. I am relying throughout this section on Friedrich Kittler's identification of a shift in "discourse networks" around 1800, especially in "The Mother's Mouth" chapter of *Discourse Networks*, which links German pedagogical practice, circa 1800, to literary Romanticism. David Wellbery's gloss in his foreword lucidly captures Kittler's argument: "Kittler begins with the new pedagogy of the late eighteenth century, a discourse that addressed itself to mothers and thereby constituted the Mother as the agency of primary socialization. It is the Mother who manages the child's initiation in the cultural techniques of reading and writing, and in doing so invests this initiation with an aura of erotic pleasure. This pleasure clings especially to the maternal voice, a kind of aural envelope that binds the mother-child dyad in a pre-articulate unity. . . . Primary orality, the Mother, the self-presence of the origin . . . produce reality by linking bodies (e.g., the eyes and ears and hands of children) to the letter and to instances of power" (xxii). In Germany, these formations are explicitly linked to state systems. In the United States, institutions of state bureaucracy are subordinated to "voluntary" and private networks, largely based on print; but a democratic

state's need for literate citizens and for smooth transmission of power underwrites both pedagogy and literature in similar ways. My focus in this and the following chapter is on the demands placed on women in this reorganization of female subjectivity and on the consequences for both female and male authorship in this setting.

19. The *OED* notes that Old English contained only thirteen recorded instances of "self-" compounds; the prefix gained currency in the seventeenth century, "when many new words appeared in theological and philosophical writing." The examples here are gleaned from a survey of approximately one hundred conduct manuals, pedagogical treatises, and related periodicals between the 1790s and the 1840s.

20. For one example, in the afterword to *The Wide, Wide World*, Jane Tompkins compares the values of the novel—e.g., "self-sacrifice," "self-abnegation"—to current values of "self-determination," "self-actualization," "self-assertion" (S. Warner, 585). It strikes me that the scales of discipline may drop just as low under determine, actualize, and assert as under sacrifice and abnegate; a century has changed the vector of these operations, as the self gets pushed forward or upward rather than backward or downward, but the mechanism remains the same. This is a point with which Tompkins may well agree, for it is one of the reasons that late twentieth- and twenty-first-century women can still be proper readers of *The Wide, Wide World*.

21. See Kittler, 26; this monolithic definition of the feminine is exactly what Luce Irigaray attempts to counter in *This Sex Which Is Not One*.

22. See Kittler, 51.

23. Examples of a few of these will be noted here. The British linguist John Collier's *Alphabet for the Grown-Up Grammarians of Great-Britain* (1778), with which Mann might have been familiar, has some of the nearly parodic texture of Mann's essay. Mann shared Noah Webster's sense that "the sounds of our letters are more capricious and irregular than those of any alphabet with which we are acquainted" (*Grammatical Institute*, 5). William Burton recalls in his 1833 memoir of district schooling an alphabet very like Mann's—"twenty-six strangers" (72) who are "motionless and mute and uninteresting" and impossible to remember (73). Mann would likely have read William R. Weeks's "Essay on Learning to Read and Write the English Language," excerpted in the *American Annals of Education and Instruction, and Journal of Literary Institutions* 2 (Sept. 1832).

Notably taking the example of the word *phantom*, Weeks calculates that, given the variety of phonic values of each of the letters, a student "may pronounce it wrong in 3839 different ways" (440).

24. Mann calls Brownson a "Proteus of doctrine" (Mann to Samuel Gridley Howe, July 21, 1839, quoted in Messerli, 326). For a comprehensive description of the Whig position and its genealogy, see D. Howe.

25. An anonymous critique of *The Franklin Primer* in the *American Journal of Education* 1, no. 10 (1826), which, like Mann's essay, also argues for learning words before letters, asserts similarly that the "infant does not learn to recognise a *tree* as such by studying first the roots, then the trunk, then the twigs, then the bark, then the leaves. His eye and his mind grasp the whole object, and do not descend to particulars till afterwards: he does not analyse till compelled to do so" (639).

26. In Lecture 1, "Means and Objects of Common School Education," Mann, with a striking reluctance, writes that it "is too late to stop the art of printing, or to arrest the general circulation of books. Reading of some kind, the children will have" (*Lectures*, 33).

27. Mann's own prose—vivid, violent, muscular—would seem to support the desirability of the rhetorical memory-art approach to images, which would encourage precisely the bloody, violent, and shocking images most likely to stick in the memory. But his humane strictures—for he's in many ways an iconophobe—prevent him from sporting these as pedagogical tools. The twentieth-century educator Sylvia Ashton-Warner (1908–1984) developed her teaching method out of a similar perception of children's innate leaning toward primal emotions, but rather than suppressing these, she puts them to work in her "organic method": "*The Key vocabulary centers round the two main instincts, fear and sex*" (42). She describes a Maori student who had been struggling to learn to read; when she asked him what he was frightened of, student and teacher collaborated in making a list of words that he instantly learned; his chosen words are strikingly similar to Mann's list of prohibited ones: "police, butcher knife, kill, gaol, hand and fire engine" (43).

28. See Messerli, 12–15.

29. For descriptions of traditional school punishments that were only gradually being excised and whose traces lingered, see Ong, *Rhetoric*, 113–141; Ong, *Fighting*, 119–148; Stone, 116–117, 278–285.

30. See Brodhead, "Sparing the Rod," in *Cultures of Letters*, esp. 23–26.

31. See Sedgwick's chapter "Toward the Gothic: Terrorism and Homosexual Panic" in *Between Men*, 83–96. She notes the gothic tropes of the unspeakable and the illegible as forms of social control (94), which might help explain some of Mann's dismay at the alphabet's near invisibility.

32. Mann's near resistance to alphabetization and his panicked reaction also are akin to what Mark Seltzer sees later in the century; it is necessary, Seltzer argues, that naturalist discourse keep the "mechanics of writing" invisible "because the capacity to represent and reproduce that, by this account, makes up persons also makes visible the technology of writing. And such a becoming visible of the technology of writing in machine culture risks making visible the links between the materiality of writing and the making of persons, and thus the internal relations between persons and machines" (75–76).

33. Mary Tyler Peabody Mann published as "Mrs. Horace Mann," but these letters were written when she was still Mary Peabody. In this chapter, I will refer to her by her maiden name.

34. In 1841, the year of these letters, Mary Peabody published a *Primer of Reading and Drawing* in which an early lesson focuses on the words *nest, house, bird*; a full page is devoted to the large-type repetition of these three words in every possible juxtaposition to each other:

nest . . . house . . . bird
house . . . bird . . . nest
bird . . . nest . . . house

And so on (7). In his published spelling lecture, Horace Mann refers approvingly to this primer (36), which was published after the oral delivery of the lecture.

35. Charlotte Brontë seems to be participating in this same world of alphabetization. An interesting analogy to Horace Mann's and Mary Mann's descriptions of alphabetization occurs in *Jane Eyre*; Brontë calls her heroic schoolmistress "Miss Temple"—a maternal institution—and the sinister schoolmaster, Mr. Brocklehurst, is depicted as an "apparition" who is "buttoned up in a surtout, and looking longer, narrower and more rigid than ever" (64).

36. See Ong, *Orality*, 110–111, for a description of the oral, "agonistic

and formulaic" processes of rhetorical training. Ong notes that into "the nineteenth century most literary style throughout the west was formed by academic rhetoric, in one way or another, with one notable exception: the literary style of female authors."

Chapter 4   The Wide, Wide World's Web

1. W bears a special relation to Warner's contemporary, Nathaniel Hawthorne. Hawthorne redeemed the *w* in his family name when he was in his twenties and forming an identity for himself as a writer. Camille Paglia sees his inserted *w* as representing "Woman" (582). In addition, I believe it is Hawthorne's means of distinguishing himself from his father, Captain Hathorne, and a way of flying over the generation that was weighing him down as he was finding his vocation; see Crain, "Hawthorne." Georges Perec—who has captured more comprehensively and self-consciously than any other contemporary writer the aesthetics of alphabetization in such works as *La disparation* (written without the letter *e*) and *Life: A User's Manual*—entitles his allegorical memoir *W; or, The Memory of Childhood.*

W stands out in the alphabet as the widest of the letterforms, and is the only letter that draws on another letter for its form (on two other letters, actually, a vowel and a consonant—u and v). For the history of W, see Firmage, 240–248; and Humez and Humez, 226–228.

2. I am grateful to James Richardson for drawing my attention to this tale.

3. I would suggest that these are the implications of the letter embedded in the richly allegorical scene in which Jim Burden kills a snake—"he was lying in long loose waves, like a letter 'W'"—in Willa Cather's *My Ántonia*. I am grateful to Diana Fuss for bringing this scene to my attention. In claiming a homoeroticism for the letter W, I am responding in part to Jeffrey Masten's brilliant work on the letter Q, as the signifier of male homoeroticism, in his *Queer Philology*.

4. The paradigm for such coincidences is the television network that calls itself "ABC."

5. A German translation of *The Wide, Wide World* (published in Cincinnati in 1876) even inserts a "home" into the title: *Heimwärts: oder, Führung durch die Weite Welt* (Foster, 49).

6. Amariah Brigham's 1832 *Remarks on the Influence of Mental Culti-*

vation upon Health puts it this way: "It is fearful to contemplate the excited state of mind which every where prevails throughout this republic, and the vast amount of *machinery*, if I may so say, which is in operation, to increase and perpetuate it; and the little attention that has hitherto been given to the dangers it may produce." The catalog of "machinery" in Hartford that produced such menacing excitation includes schooling from ages three or four for six hours a day "for several years," home libraries that contain "books for children, besides newspapers and other periodicals," nine churches of six different denominations, filled two and three times on Sundays, twenty to thirty other religious meetings every week, two lyceums, each meeting once a week gratis, with weekly debates and lectures, plus seven weekly political newspapers, representing three parties, and five religious newspapers, "no two of which belong to the same sect" (75). Brigham's compulsive accounting seems an attempt to ward off some version of the mathematical sublime, which the sheer number of media in existence threaten him with, for no one person in Hartford would actually be able to encounter all of these stimulating experiences.

Similarly, Lydia Huntley Sigourney writes in *Letters to Mothers*: "This is emphatically the age of book-making and miscellaneous reading. Profound thought is becoming somewhat obsolete. The rapidity with which space is traversed, and wealth accumulated, the many exciting objects which arrest attention in our new, and wide country, indispose the mind to the old habits of patient investigation and solitary study.

"Would it not be better for us, if we read less? . . . The periodical publications . . . act as a stimulant to the mental appetite, provoking it beyond its capacity of digestion" (145).

7. In addition to the Emerson and Hawthorne epigraphs, following are examples from British literature: "He would have given me half his fortune, without demanding so much as a kiss in return, rather than I should have flung myself friendless on the wide world" (Brontë, *Jane Eyre*, 443); "and a sense of his loneliness in the great wide world sank into the child's heart for the first time" (Dickens, *Oliver Twist*, 53). Robert Burns's variation, in "Strathallan's Lament," provides a key to nineteenth-century usage: "The wide world is all before us— / But a world without a friend!" (1:350). As Carol McGuirk points out, Burns here makes explicit reference to the close of *Paradise Lost* (12:646): "The World was all before them." In the

epithet "wide," these writers seem to merge their sense of resignation to a nonsacred world with a longing for an Edenic home.

8. Susan Warner died in 1875, Anna Warner in 1915. Their father, Henry Whiting Warner, was also an author, of legal texts and patriotic treatises. The sisters often worked in tandem; Susan helped paint the images for *The Game of Natural History*, and Anna, according to Alice Jordan, suggested the title for *The Wide, Wide World* (83). Some of their works were more thoroughgoing collaborations. See Sanderson, 34–39; and Foster, 131.

9. See Wilson; Sanderson. The number of cards—twenty-four—is suggestive, but no set of cards has survived, and it is not known whether there was an explicitly alphabetic component to them.

10. See Kelley, 90–93; Foster, 17–24.

11. "The Story of Ellen Montgomery's Bookshelf," prefacing the first volume of the "Bookshelf" series, *Mr. Rutherford's Children*, explains that Ellen had her own bookshelf at the parsonage where her surrogate brother and sister, John and Alice Humphreys, live. One day, John, needing shelf space, begins pulling the books out, asking Alice what these children's books are doing on the bottom shelf. Alice explains, and John "put the books back again in due order." But Ellen can see "that somebody had been meddling with them" (6–7). According to Foster, these books are written by Anna Warner, except for *Carl Krinken*, an object narrative in which all the items in a Christmas stocking tell their stories (73–75).

12. The widely read and very well educated Susan Warner had, of course, read *Crusoe*, in her late teens (Weiss, 215–216), before her life had shifted permanently from New York to Constitution Island. She had also read *The Swiss Family Robinson* with pleasure in August 1834 and again in June 1835 (Weiss, 130, 132, 186).

13. "Ellen" also, of course, contains two "elles" (*l*'s) within itself. Learning French is one of many language disciplines Ellen enacts in the novel. Susan Warner studied French for many years, as well as Italian, and wrote her journal entries in French during the fall of 1839, after the family had moved to Constitution Island (Weiss, 229–242).

14. *Oliver Twist* is published in 1838; *Jane Eyre* not until 1847. It is certainly possible that Warner read *Jane Eyre* while writing *The Wide, Wide World*. Another plausible model is the 1819 *Mansfield Park* (Fanny,

like Ellen, stays young longer; John Humphreys is more Edmund than Rochester), published in America by Carey & Lea in 1832.

15. For example, Catherine Beecher's 1845 *Duty of American Women* asks: "What, then has saved our country from those wide-sweeping horrors that desolated France?" Her answer is that "there has been such a large body of educated citizens, who have had intelligence enough to understand how to administer the affairs of state, and a proper sense of the necessity of sustaining law and order who have had moral principle enough to subdue their own passions and to use their influence to control the excited minds of others" (31). This leads to her eventual argument that teaching is a proper profession for women (64).

16. Melville is the supreme counterexample. Melville's heroes are almost always youths, and the pressure Melville exerts on them is, among other things, the pressure of modernity.

17. In Maria Cummins's *The Lamplighter* (1854), for example, the child-hero's kitten gets boiled in front of her eyes by a sadistic guardian (11).

18. Jane Tompkins, afterword to *The Wide, Wide World*. By this she means that "instead of initiating her into society, the heroine's experience teaches her how to withdraw into the citadel of herself. . . . At the endpoint of the disciplinary process, the heroine does not exist for herself at all any more but only for others" (598).

19. As the plot moves geographically away from the contemporary New York setting of the opening, it also seems to move backward in time: to a country setting, at first crudely rural (with her guardian, Aunt Fortune Emerson) and then aristocratically pastoral (the minister's household, with the young adult siblings John and Alice Humphreys), as though in two fantasies of the Early Republic; the plot then jettisons Ellen out of America entirely to Edinburgh, into a family depicted as somewhat decadent and cosmopolitan European gentry.

20. If *The Wide, Wide World* is the first major example, *Little Women* and *Tom Sawyer* are others. *Huckleberry Finn* shows up the genre, as it shows up so much else: if Tom is a finely alphabetized figure (in a later entrepreneurial and corporate "good bad boy" line), Huck lights out for the territory in a last desperate hope to get unalphabetized.

21. Ellen's mother, against her own mother's wishes, married an American and moved to New York, following the trajectory of that earlier best-

seller *Charlotte Temple* (1794), whose heroine ran off with the similarly named Montraville. Mrs. Montgomery hates her husband; though she shares his bed, his only heavy breathing is slumberous, a sign of his maddening insensitivity. The woman who ran away with the Yankee soldier, thwarting her family, leaving her country, has been transformed into an invalid, whose still fiery passions are parceled out between her small daughter and Jesus Christ. Ellen replicates her mother's struggles, on a paler, smaller scale. What constitutes *her* rebellion? Only that she weeps when she discovers her parents are going to abandon her. Ellen's life is far less dramatic than her mother's because, although her actions are as broad in scale, they are necessarily, because she is a little girl, less *willed*. If, in Warner's scheme, an earlier American generation broke with mother and mother country in order to establish a new order, Ellen's generation has to cope with the parents' failures and lacks on a strictly psychological plane.

22. See Ivins on the exactly repeatable in print.

23. In "Language, Images, and the Postmodern Predicament," Godzich distinguishes the ways in which language as opposed to images can serve to master or cope with the velocity of modernity: "Language could slow down the world, thanks to its tremendous negative capability, but cannot slow down images, for they operate out of the very imaginary that language would have to be able to organize in the first place" (370).

24. In 1818, the *Report of the Trial of Charles N. Baldwin* was published, "The whole being taken down in short hand, at the trial, with great accuracy, by H. W. Warner, Esquire."

25. Goshgarian reads the novel as posing God's law against worldly law (86–87). In *Cultures of Letters*, Brodhead reads the lawsuit as representing a world "unavailable to [Warner's] literary knowing" and considers that "neither the book's characters nor the book itself can get access to the transprivate world in which they could know what the suit's occasion was" (30). But I think that Warner is posing the world of the novel as precisely an alternative to the world of the law; her exclusion of the law from the novel is strategic. Brodhead points out that Warner is creating a kind of institution, or participating in one, but considers her as already excluded rather than as creating an exclusion, or a resistance.

26. According to the preface to *Mr. Rutherford's Children*, even the

sainted John Humphreys doesn't know how to arrange Ellen's books on her shelf.

27. Anna Bartlett Warner reports that her sister liked "bright colors (especially red), which she was fond of wearing" (quoted in Tompkins's afterword, 588).

28. In *Carl Krinken*, Warner makes this relation more explicit by creating a text in which a series of objects narrates her (and their) story. Christopher Flint offers a brilliant analysis of how object narratives represent a new relationship of authors to the circulation of their texts in the eighteenth century. A contemporary review describes the circulation of *The Wide, Wide World*, which was "bought to be presented to nice little girls. . . . Elder sisters were soon found poring over the volumes, and it was very natural that mothers next should try the spell. . . . After this, papas were not very difficult to convert. . . . We are much mistaken if *The Wide, Wide World* [has] not been found under the pillow of sober bachelors. . . . They were found on everybody's table, and lent from house to house" (*North American Review*, Jan. 1853, quoted in Baym, *Novels, Readers, and Reviewers*, 49). It is notable that while the novel's distribution may bind people together via their relation to the book, the actual reading of the book is quite private and solitary—as solitary as the "sober bachelor's" sleep.

29. Warner's relation to property is in some ways closer to the "romantic property" that Mark Seltzer explicates in his reading of *The House of the Seven Gables* as a "rewriting of economics as erotics" (71).

30. As secretary of education in Massachusetts, Horace Mann has to contend with parental possessiveness and imagines parents saying: "Why all this interference? Why this obtrusion of the State in to the concerns of the individual? Are not our children . . . our own?" But Mann supposes that even "the monster-parent who wishes to sell his children to continuous labor . . . may cry out to the Legislature,—'By what right do you come between us and our offspring? By what right do you . . . pry into our domestic arrangements, and take from us our parental rights?'" If the worst parent treats the child as a commodity, Mann makes his argument for public schooling by reference to contracts for merchandise: if the goods "be valueless, or even materially defective . . . the law exonerate me from all obligation to receive it." But "when parents deliver over to the community" uneducated and corrupted children, the community has to accept them, like

so many bad pennies (Lecture 2, "Special Preparation, a Pre-requisite to Teaching" [1838], in *Lectures on Education*, 69–70).

31. In "Sparing the Rod" (*Cultures of Letters*, 13–47), Brodhead describes the antebellum alternative to older modes of corporal punishment: "The cultural assertion embodied in disciplinary intimacy generates on one front an animus against corporal punishment; on another front a normative model of character formation; on another, a particular configuration of training institutions designed to support that character-building plan; and on yet another, a new place for literary reading in cultural life" (18).

32. See, for example, *The Lady's Pocket Library* (1797), which contains, along with Hannah More, Dr. Gregory, and Lady Pennington, the misogynist screeds of Swift's "Letter to a Young Lady Newly Married" and Moore's "Fables for the Female Sex"; Lyman Gale's *The Ladies' Companion* (1824), which also reprints the Moore and Swift, next to Fénelon and Hannah More; and James Garnett's Pestalozzian *Lectures on Female Education* (1825), which concludes with the scurrilous "Gossip's Manual."

33. On sentimental transparency, see Halttunen, 57–59.

34. A catalog of this work would include, at the very least, apple-paring, butter-churning, cake-mixing, candle-making, cheese-making, cow-milking, dancing, dishwashing, drawing, dusting, egg-scrambling, French speaking, gravy-stirring, horseback riding, hymn-singing, ironing, knitting, laundering, letter-writing, mending, milk-skimming, nursing, ox-herding, painting, pie-baking, pork-frying, porridge-cooking, reading, scrubbing, sewing, spinning, stew-cooking, sweeping, table setting, tea- and toast-making.

35. Lisa Gitelman reads the history of shorthand in America in the context of changing patterns of authority and authorship: "At stake in the fractious history of shorthand were the constructed authority of legal and legislative process, the nature of evidence and of fact, as well as the regulation of the writer's body as a kind of valve between orality and literacy."

36. See John Irwin's *American Hieroglyphics* for a discussion of the influence of Champollion's discovery and interpretation of Egyptian hieroglyphs, esp. 3–20 on Emerson's and Thoreau's language theories.

37. When Ellen tells the pragmatic Mr. Van Brunt that John noticed one of her faults, Van Brunt drily notes: "'He must have mighty sharp eyes, then'" (414).

38. John's strictures, by 1850, are beginning to seem out of date; on the

whole John conducts himself like an arbiter of the previous generation, and probably Warner models him on her father. Many of John's decrees echo the conduct books that were imported from England around 1800 (though many were still being printed in America into the forties and fifties), which took the form of anthologies such as *The Lady's Pocket Library* (1797). Here, in "The Rudiments of Taste, by the countess of Carlisle," are all of John's rules: "For my own part, I had rather see a girl wholly ignorant of the alphabet, than attached to that species of writing [i.e., novels]; for I am convinced that infinitely more have erred in the conduct of life from that cause, than from any other. The sentiments and ideas they impress, are fatal illusions to mislead the poor reader" (186); furthermore, "Just as well may a traveller think to make the tour of Europe by a chart of Asia" (187). The orientalist notion of novels as a kind of Asia of sensibility perfectly captures John's anxieties; as he is the keeper of Oriental language—hieroglyphs and oracles—he is also the keeper of Oriental sensuality.

Other important conduct books, which convey similar precepts, are John Bennett's *Strictures*; Thomas Gisborne's *Enquiry into the Duties of the Female Sex* (British, but reprinted in Philadelphia in 1798), which is pirated nearly verbatim by Charles Butler as his 1836 *The American Lady*; the widely reprinted Rousseauist Aimé-Martin's *The Education of Mothers* (1843); and Harvey Newcomb's *The Young Lady's Guide* (1840).

39. On the novel's use of typology, see Goshgarian, 112–113.

40. Goshgarian makes a similar observation about John's authority in the text, but reads it differently, as part of the novel's typological drive: "Warner authorizes herself to create *The Wide, Wide World* by *de-authorizing* herself. *John* writes in imitation of God's way of writing; his putative author trails after time's rider." This is how Goshgarian also reads John's writing on Ellen: "He forms her into the *typos* she was born to become" (115). What Goshgarian's account can consequently make no room for is the significance of the long nontypological passages in the text.

41. "I shall try you"—this is the expression he uses as well about Ellen's poor little horse. Following the novel's only scene of explicit sadism (beyond the perhaps implicit sadism of various family circles), in which both Ellen and her horse are physically menaced, John takes the pony out to jump fences: "'I have been trying him. . . . I wished to make sure in the first place that he knew his lesson'" (404–405). He wants the horse to be

"fit to be trusted" with Ellen, just as, in "trying" Ellen, he will see whether she is "fit" for him.

42. Tompkins is talking about the way both novels link eroticism with punishment and submission. There are other parallels, as well, which have more to do with the network of exchange into which the heroines are placed; for example, John's transaction with Lindsay, which guarantees Ellen's continued accessibility to John, is like the contract among the members of the Roissy club in *Story of O*.

43. "The coupling of reading oneself and satisfying oneself became unbreakable" (Kittler, 95).

Chapter 5   The Story of A

1. Evert A. Duyckinck, *Literary World*, March 30, 1850, reprinted in Scharnhorst, ed., *The Critical Response*, 22.

2. See E. H. Miller, 49.

3. See Tharp, 213–216. For Kraitsir's language theory and his influence on Thoreau, see Gura, 126–137.

4. See David Leverenz's "Mrs. Hawthorne's Headache: Reading *The Scarlet Letter*," 259–278 in *Manhood and the American Renaissance*. "When Hawthorne read the end of *The Scarlet Letter* to his wife, it 'broke her heart and sent her to bed with a grievous headache—which I look upon as a triumphant success!'" (259). The quotation is from Hawthorne's letter to Horatio Bridge, Feb. 4, 1850; reprinted in *Hawthorne: The Critical Heritage*, ed. J. Donald Crowley (New York: Barnes & Noble, 1970), 151, cited by Leverenz, 350n.1.

5. I am indebted to Renee Burgland, who first brought this entry to my attention. Just following this entry is one that, as many scholars have seen, muses on a theme of surveillance central to the novel: "The strange sensation of a person who feels himself an object of deep interest, and close observation, and various construction of all his actions, by another person" (*American Notebooks*, 183).

6. Following is a schematic layout of the relationship between Hawthorne's letter-men semiology and that of Barthes. The first three columns represent Hawthorne's system: in the first column, the distance of the viewer or reader from the letter-men; in the second, the object of perception; and in the third, Hawthorne's description of the kind of meaning that

arises from each set. In the final column is how Barthes describes the same phenomena; in parentheses is the "consciousness" Barthes ascribes to each set, along with the "axis" along which meaning is charted.

Distance	Object	Term	Barthes's semiotics
close	men	positive	signifier-signified (symbolic/internal)
middle	letters	relative	sign to reservoir-of-signs (paradigmatic/vertical)
distant	words	composite	sign to discourse (syntagmatic/horizontal)

7. Hawthorne's fictive world is strikingly anatomized, with people and objects suffering the fate of the images in an alphabet array, seeming to exist without natural ligatures to one another. In his tales previous to *The Scarlet Letter*, Hawthorne drew his images and his characters in high relief by isolating them from their surroundings. "The Snow-Image," "The Gentle-Boy," "The Antique Ring," "Rappacini's Daughter," "The Birth-Mark"—these are some of the tales in which the singularity of an image or a character drives the plot. In "The Minister's Black Veil" an image bonds, as though symbiotically, to a character. "Wakefield" builds upon the hero's shift from his usual place, at home with his wife, to the next street. This (from one point of view) slight relocation radically dislocates Wakefield, reducing every other event in his life to an insignificant blur.

8. Hawthorne knew all the Peabodys well. Mary Tyler Peabody, the purported beauty of the family, married at age thirty-seven—late, like Hawthorne (they married in the same year)—after a courtship with Horace Mann as prolonged as Hawthorne and Sophia Peabody's. Hawthorne accompanied Mary Peabody to lectures in 1838, and she reported to Horace Mann that the writer was "deeply interested in such things as interest my mind" (E. H. Miller, 139).

9. Though written in 1841, the letters were not published until 1863; it is possible that Mary Peabody Mann or Elizabeth Peabody edited them for publication.

10. Quoted in the Centenary Edition of *The Scarlet Letter*, xx. All citations to *The Scarlet Letter* are to this edition, unless otherwise noted.

11. All references to Hawthorne's tales are to the Library of America edition of *Tales and Sketches*.

12. Originally titled "The Mermaid: A Reverie," the tale was first published in a gift annual of 1835, and was reprinted in the 1842 *Twice-Told Tales* as "The Village Uncle."

13. Elsewhere in "The "Custom-House" Hawthorne identifies with the position of the child. In mock-submission to his ancestors he describes his vocation in nursery terms: "A writer of story-books" (10). An officeholder is as a child to Uncle Sam: "While he leans on the mighty arm of the Republic, his own proper strength departs from him. He loses . . . the capability of self-support" (38).

14. See Laqueur, esp. 218–222.

15. For a comprehensive discussion of reading as a menacing source of masturbatory fantasy for nineteenth-century American men, see Barker-Benfield, esp. 163–188.

16. See Chapter 4, note 6, page 254–55.

17. For a pertinent Lacanian reading of *The Scarlet Letter*, see Dolis, 174–195. Of the discovery of the letter he writes: "Within the register of the symbolic, the Letter is itself the very 'cutting edge' of the (Oedipal) Law: the 'cut' in Hawthorne's discourse, the eradication (erasure) of the phallus, which allows it to (re)emerge as the signifier of desire. It is this wounded, this 'fallen' signifier which dis(inter)upts the discourse of the manuscript (history) and confers upon Hawthorne the responsibility of authorship (fatherhood) for his story" (174).

18. See Delaney, Lupton, and Toth, 205–211.

19. Jerome Loving suggests in *Lost in the Customhouse* that this figure may be Hawthorne's mother: "We might imagine that this is Elizabeth Hawthorne come back from her fresh grave to call her son back to himself in the present as the father of Una instead of Pearl" (29).

20. The story of Bellerophon is the only reference to writing in Homer (*Iliad* 6:160ff.). The beautiful and brave Bellerophon snubs the seducing Anteia, wife of Proitos, Argive king. In revenge, Anteia accuses Bellerophon of attempted rape, whereupon Proitos banishes him to Lycia, with "baneful tokens, graving in a folded tablet many signs and deadly, and bade him show these to his own wife's father, that he might be slain." Roy Harris suggests that in this story "writing stands between the individual and an understanding of his own fate" (16). See also Stroud for the context of the Bellerophon story. Hawthorne picks up the Bellerophon tale at a later point

in *The Wonder Tales*, where the hero tames Pegasus and vanquishes the chimaera.

21. See Tschichold, 20: "The upper and lower case letters received their present form in the Renaissance. The serifs of the capitals, or upper case letters, were adapted to those of the lower case alphabet. The capitals are based on an incised or chiseled letter; the lower case characters are based on a pen-written calligraphic form."

22. Here I am following up the suggestion of Jonathan Arac's 1979 review article in *Diacritics*, where he proposes that we think of Hawthorne with *Origins of German Tragic Drama* in mind: "Even to mention some motifs of [Benjamin's] analysis suggests its relevance. Allegory is fundamentally related to the nature of writing: indeed its 'philosophic basis' is the relation 'between spoken language and script' (think of Hester's letter and Dimmesdale's sermon, or Dimmesdale's sermon and his hidden letter). The development of seventeenth-century allegory is illuminated by the new use of the capital letter and the function of the monogram. Allegory reveals not a moment of totality, fusing time and space, but the inexorable movement of time over a life, the fragments that betoken the absence of a whole, the ruin (recall the tattered A in the attic). . . . If Christian allegory functioned as an exorcism of the pagan deities, is Hawthorne's an exorcism of the Calvinist tradition that it brings back while hollowing out?" (50).

23. See van Gennep, esp. 120–121 and 190–192.

24. See Cross, 78.

25. From the Apocrypha's additions to the Book of Esther (14:16). Queen Esther (whose rise to the throne, notably, depended on her predecessor Vashti's antipatriarchal rebellion) has a history, as well, in the annals of alphabetization. *The New England Primer*'s rhyme for Q reads: "Queen Esther comes in Royal State / To Save the Jews from dismal Fate" (1727 ed.). In addition, King Ahasuerus, to whom Esther petitions, is none other than Xerxes I, the salvation of ABC-book composers ("Xerxes the great did die / And so must you & I" (1727 ed.). Moreover, Esther is one of the books of the Bible most concerned with writing, particularly in its death-dealing potentiality.

26. The Marvell editor Hugh MacDonald sends the reader to Otto van Veen's *Amorum Emblemata* (Antwerp, 1608), but Marvell exceeds his sources, for nothing in van Veen quite matches the imaginative range or in-

tensity of love's tortures in the poem. Herewith the full text (Marvell, 132–135):

The Unfortunate Lover

Alas, how pleasant are their dayes
With whom the Infant Love yet playes!
Sorted by pairs, they still are seen
By Fountains cool, and Shadows green.
But soon these Flames do lose their light,
Like Meteors of a Summers night:
Nor can they to that Region climb,
To make impression upon Time.

'Twas in a Shipwrack, when the Seas
Rul'd, and the Winds did what they please,
That my poor Lover floting lay,
And, e're brought forth, was cast away:
Till at the last the master-Wave
Upon the Rock his Mother drave;
And there she split against the Stone,
In a *Cesarian Section*.

The Sea him lent these bitter Tears,
Which at his Eyes he alwaies bears.
And from the Winds the Sighs he bore,
Which through his surging Breast do roar.
No Day he saw but that which breaks,
Through frighted Clouds in forked streaks.
While round the ratling Thunder hurl'd,
As at the Fun'ral of the World.

While Nature to his Birth presents
This masque of quarreling Elements;
A num'rous fleet of Corm'rants black,
That sail'd unstulting o're the Wrack,
Receiv'd into their cruel Care,
Th'unfortunate and abject Heir:
Guardians most fit to entertain
The Orphan of the *Hurricane*.

They fed him up with Hopes and Air,
Which soon digested to Despair.
And as one Corm'rant fed him, still
Another on his Heart did bill.
Thus while they famish him, and feast,
He both consumed, and increast:
And languished with doubtful Breath,
Th'*Amphibium* of Life and Death.

And now, when angry Heaven wou'd
Behold a spectacle of Blood,
Fortune and He are call'd to play
At sharp before it all the day:
And Tyrant Love his brest does ply
With all his wing'd Artillery.
Whilst he, betwixt the Flames and Waves,
Like *Ajax*, the mad Tempest braves.

See how he nak'd and fierce does stand,
Cuffing the Thunder with one hand;
While with the other he does lock,
And grapple, with the stubborn Rock:
From which he with each Wave rebounds,
Torn into Flames, and ragg'd with Wounds.
And all he saies, a Lover drest
In his own Blood does relish best.

This is the only *Banneret*
That ever Love created yet:
Who though, by the Malignant Starrs,
Forced to live in Storms and Warrs;
Yet dying leaves a Perfume here,
And Musick within every Ear;
And he in Story only rules,
In a Field *Sable* a Lover *Gules*.

27. See Ticknor, 13–29.

28. See especially Tompkins, "Masterpiece Theater." In this discussion
I follow Pierre Bourdieu's definition of rites of institution in *Language and*

Symbolic Power, 117–126. Bourdieu extends van Gennep's notion of the rite of passage to institutional performances. The rite of institution is an "act of communication" that *"signifies* to someone what his identity is" (121). While elementary literacy training bears the characteristics of the classic rite of passage, advanced literacy training, agonistic and identity-shaping, might be seen as a rite of institution, inducting readers through "performative magic" into the realm—or the institution—of literature.

Epilogue

1. The commission resulted in a series of lunettes (installed in 1988) containing unrelated letters and words (*if, but, when,* and so on) along with a rotunda inscribed with Claudius's "Words without thoughts never to heaven go" (*Hamlet* 3.3). Even in a library setting, which presumes both public-spiritedness and fluid literacy, Ruscha is more interested in failure and bad faith (I don't mean *his* bad faith). In his project proposal he suggests that he will choose "words referring back to language itself" and "all reflecting their duty to the nature of linguistics and the English language" (133); along with single letters, his word choices are in the main conjunctions and interrogatives, words signifying contingency, the subjunctive, the conditional. *F House* is one of the paintings that emerged during, but remained separate from, Ruscha's work on the Miami-Dade project. The more or less pious attitude toward literacy required by the catalog for the library commission leads its writers to gloss the most emphatically iconoclastic aspects of Ruscha's pranksterish career, such as his book *Royal Road Test* (1967), which documents Ruscha's tossing his typewriter out the window of his 1963 Le Sabre and then photographing the wreckage of the writing machine (see Wakefield).

F House echoes the similarly named *Villa R* (1919) by Paul Klee and Robert Rauschenberg's *Factum 1* (1957), which appears to directly quote the Klee painting. Although these two works also foreground an isolated red capital letter and refer to houses, they are crowded, bustling, collage-like images. Ruscha's contrastingly letter-centric picture seems to have a different project in sight.

2. "Imagetext" designates "composite, synthetic works (or concepts) that combine image and text" (Mitchell, *Picture Theory,* 89n). Aside from *Picture Theory,* other works that I've found useful on this topic are Mitch-

ell's *Iconology*; Joanna Drucker's *Theorizing Modernism*; Jerome McGann's *Black Riders*; and Roland Barthes's "Rhetoric of the Image." Only those who are interested in letterforms per se seem to have made the connection between pedagogical alphabets and modern art objects; the principal and most exuberant example is Massin's *Letter and Image*.

3. The error does work in the other direction: so irresistible is the alphabetic statement that one online bibliography misprints the title as *H House*.

4. I am indebted to the art historian Erin Blake for explaining color stereoscopy to me ("Re-Mapping the City").

5. I am grateful to Lucy Rinehart, Patrick Horrigan, and Paul Gehl for conversations about this painting. The narratives that the image seems to evoke, having to do with notions of "home" and of F-for-failure, carry the texture of childhood memory.

6. Cited in the *OED*, s.v. "F": "1551 Act 5–6 Ed. VI, c. 4. To be . . . burned in the cheeke with an hot yron, hauing the letter F. whereby . . . they may be knowne . . . for fraymakers and fighters. 1809 Tomlins Law Dict., F. is a letter wherewith felons &c. are branded and marked with a hot iron, on their being admitted to the benefit of clergy."

7. Given the current hysteria over standards and grading, it is remarkable that so little work has been done on the history of grades. See Smallwood; Presley; and Bradford. General histories of nineteenth-century education provide the context from which grading emerged. See Cremin, vol. 2; Schultz; Katz, *Irony* and *Class, Bureaucracy, and Schools*; and Berman.

8. Michel de Certeau has articulated the potential for a special pleasure in this position as well: "The act of suffering oneself to be written by the group's law is oddly accompanied by a pleasure, that of being recognized . . . , of becoming an identifiable and legible word in a social language, of being changed into a fragment within an anonymous text, of being inscribed in a symbolic order that has neither owner nor author" (140).

9. Foucault has characterized this gesture, in reference especially to the examination, as "the entry of the individual . . . into the field of knowledge" at the end of the eighteenth century in Europe; previously, the individual had been "below the threshold of description," and written chronicle belonged only to the great. But now "this description [was] a means of control and a method of domination" and "is no longer a monument for future memory, but a document for possible use" (*Discipline*, 190–191).

10. In a numeric system, only o (zero) can carry anything like the semantic gravity of F. F is more mobile than o and permits the teacher—requires the teacher—to define sufficiency.

11. I've been on both sides of "F" exchanges, as student and teacher. From both sides tears accompanied the transaction and precipitated heated contact between teacher and student. The fall into language represented by the F is also a fall into feelings.

12. Show 2615, March 28, 1989.

13. *Sesame Street* and the books and videos that the Children's Television Workshop produces use a full range of alphabetic devices, inherited from previous alphabets: body alphabets, synecdoche, tropes of consumption, alphabet tableaux. I'm interested here in the innovations in the alphabet that *Sesame Street* promotes.

14. Prime mover of *Sesame Street*, Joan Ganz Cooney conceived the show, which first aired on November 10, 1969, to "promote the intellectual and cultural growth of preschoolers, particularly disadvantaged preschoolers" ("Television for Preschool Children: a Proposal," Children's Television Workshop, February 19, 1968, quoted in Cook et al., 7). The show was "considered . . . as a national resource" (22) by its founders and financial backers, and was meant as a living-room "Head Start" program, to "narrow the academic achievement gap" (30). See also Polsky, *Getting to Sesame Street*, and Lesser, *Children and Television*, for the show's history.

15. At the same time, the condescension shown toward its "target" audience is similarly an artifact of late nineteenth-century social work; the first show contains several lessons about personal hygiene and a segment, perhaps aimed at parents, devoted to the benefits of drinking milk.

16. In this case Ernie might love E because it's his initial, but in subsequent shows Ernie falls for other letters and numbers.

17. Aside from right-wing political attacks on *Sesame Street*, this is the main criticism of the show, often adduced by educators. See, for example, Mates and Strommen.

18. Of course tropes of consumption linger on *Sesame Street*, since the show often simply imitates earlier alphabets. But not all consumption is the same as internalization. For example, when Cookie Monster devours letters, he gives the impression of dispensing with them, *doing* them in, rather than internalizing them and bringing them in.

19. June 4, 1999, episode 3800. The theme is "V-Day," the meaning of which is never mentioned, though a kind of martial music is played whenever the letter V is on the scene.

20. The phrase is from the Hawthorne tale "The Christmas Banquet" (*Tales and Sketches*, 867) and describes a character who has passed his life in a state of utter disengagement and of whom another character concludes "nothing wearies the soul more than an attempt to comprehend [such people] with its grasp" (867). J. Hillis Miller has noted the force of this "extraordinary phrase" and observes that "someone who is really 'outside of everything' is also outside of language" (57).

21. The *Sesame Street* video *Learning about Letters* exemplifies this technique. Here the letters are variously piled up randomly, like dirty laundry, or posted on objects. As Big Bird points out, "You can find letters almost everywhere."

BIBLIOGRAPHY

Primary Sources

The A, B, C, in Verse. New York: Mahlon Day, [1825–1833].

"A was an archer and shot at a frog"! The Old Alphabet with New Explanations, for the Tommy Thumbs of Yankeedom. Boston: N. Dearborn, 1846.

A Was an Archer, or A New Amusing Alphabet, for Children. Newark, N.J.: Benjamin Olds, 1836.

Abbott, John S. C. *The Mother at Home; or, The Principles of Maternal Duty Familiarly Illustrated*. Revised and corrected by Daniel Walton. London, 1834. Reprint New York: Arno, 1972.

Addison, Joseph. "The Adventures of a Shilling." In *Addison and Steele, Selections from "The Tatler" and "The Spectator,"* ed. Robert J. Allen, 90–94. New York: Holt, 1970.

Aimé-Martin, L. *The Education of Mothers; or, The Civilization of Mankind by Women*. Trans. Edwin Lee. Philadelphia: Lea & Blanchard, 1843.

Alcott, William A. *The Young Woman's Guide to Excellence*. 9th ed. Boston: George W. Light, 1845.

The Alphabet Ladder, or Gift for the Nursery; Interspersed with a Number of Pretty Plates, to Please and Instruct the Infant Mind. New York: Solomon King, c. 1822.

The Alphabetical Tattoo; or, Assembly of the Great and Little Letters, at the Critic's Palace, in Hartford. Hartford, Conn.: Hale & Hosmer, 1813.

The American Primer; or, An Easy Introduction to Spelling and Reading. Philadelphia: Mathew Carey, 1813.

Austen, Jane. *Mansfield Park* (1819). London: Oxford University Press, 1975.

———. *Northanger Abbey* (1818). London: Oxford University Press, 1975.

Badger, Catherine. *Teacher's Last Lesson: A Memoir of Martha Whiting*. Boston: Gould & Lincoln, 1855.

Beecher, Catherine. *The Duty of American Women to Their Country.* New York: Harper, 1845.

———. *Suggestions on Education, Published at the Request of the Hartford Female Seminary.* Hartford, Conn.: Packard & Butler, 1829.

Bennett, John. *Strictures on Female Education; Chiefly as It Relates to the Culture of the Heart, in Four Essays.* Philadelphia: W. Spotswood and H. & P. Rice, 1793.

Brigham, Amariah. *Remarks on the Influence of Mental Cultivation upon Health.* Hartford, Conn.: F. J. Huntington, 1832.

Brontë, Charlotte. *Jane Eyre* (1847). New York: Signet, 1960.

Burns, Robert. *Poems and Songs of Robert Burns.* 3 vols. Ed. James Kinsley. Oxford: Clarendon, 1968.

Burroughs, Charles. *An Address on Female Education Delivered in Portsmouth, New-Hampshire, October 26, 1827.* Portsmouth, N.H.: Childs & March, 1827.

Burton, William. *The District School As It Was* (1833). Boston: Phillips, Samson & Co., 1850.

Butler, Charles. *The American Lady.* Philadelphia: Hogan & Thompson, 1836.

Cather, Willa. *My Ántonia* (1918). New York: Bantam, 1994.

Child, Lydia Maria. *The Mother's Book.* Boston: Carter & Hendee, 1831. Reprint New York: Arno, 1972.

The Child's First Primer; or, A New and Easy Guide to the Invaluable Science of A, B, C. Philadelphia: W. Jones, 1800.

The Child's Guide to Spelling and Reading; or, An Attempt to Facilitate the Progress of Small Children When First Sent to School. Philadelphia: Mathew Carey, 1810.

The Child's New Play-Thing: Being a Spelling-Book Intended to Make the Learning to Read a Diversion Instead of a Task. Boston: J. Draper, J. Edwards, 1750.

The Child's Picture Book, of ABC. Concord, N.H.: Rufus Merrill, 1847.

Children's Story Cards. N.p.: n.p., [1835–1850?].

Christmas ABC. Philadelphia: Turner & Fisher, [1835–1840].

Cicero. *Ad Herennium.* Trans. Harry Caplan. Cambridge, Mass.: Harvard University Press, 1954.

Collier, John. *An Alphabet for the Grown-up Grammarians of Great-Britain.* N.p., 1778.

Comenius, Johann Amos. *Janua Linguarum Reserata.* London: James Young, 1647.

———. *Orbis Sensualium Pictus* (1659). Trans. Charles Hoole. Menston, Eng.: Scolar Press, 1970.

———. *Orbis Sensualium Pictus* (1659). Trans. Charles Hoole. New York: T. & J. Swords, 1810.

———. *Orbis Sensualium Pictus* (1672). [Trans. Charles Hoole.] Introduction by James Bowen. Sydney: Sydney University Press, 1967.

The Comical Hotch-Potch, or the Alphabet Turn'd Posture-Master. London: Carington Bowles, 1782.

The Comical Hotch Potch, or the Alphabet Turn'd Posture Master. Philadelphia: J. Webster, [1814].

The Critic, or Lessons in Life. Albany: G. J. Loomis, [1827–1835].

Cummins, Maria. *The Lamplighter* (1854). Ed. Nina Baym. New Brunswick, N.J.: Rutgers University Press, 1988.

Davy, Charles. *Conjectural Observations on the Origin and Progress of Alphabetic Writing.* London, 1772.

Defoe, Daniel. *Robinson Crusoe* (1719). New York: Bantam, 1981.

———. *The Wonderful Life, and Surprizing Adventures of that Renowned Hero, Robinson Crusoe: Who Lived Twenty-Eight Years on an Uninhabited Island, Which He Afterwards Colonized.* New York: Hugh Gaine, 1774.

Dickens, Charles. *Oliver Twist* (1837–1839). New York: Penguin, 1966.

Edwards, Jonathan. *Images and Shadows of Divine Things.* Ed. Perry Miller. New Haven: Yale University Press, 1948.

Emerson, Joseph. *Female Education: A Discourse.* Boston: Samuel T. Armstrong and Crocker & Brewster, 1822.

The Entertaining History of Tommy Gingerbread: A Little Boy, Who Lived upon Learning. New York: James Oram, 1796.

Erasmus, Desiderius. *On the Method of Study. De ratione studii ac legendi interpretandique auctores* (1511). Trans. Brian McGregor. In *Literary and Educational Writings,* vol. 24 of *Collected Works of Erasmus,* 661–692. Toronto: University of Toronto Press, 1978.

———. *The Right Way of Speaking Latin and Greek: A Dialogue. De recta latini graecique sermonis pronuntiatione* (1528). Trans. Maurice Pope. In *Literary and Educational Writings*, vol. 26 of *Collected Works of Erasmus*, 347–475. Toronto: University of Toronto Press, 1985.

Family Pastime, or Homes Made Happy. New York: Bunce & Brother, 1855.

Fénelon, François de Salignac. "The Education of Girls." In *Fénelon on Education*, trans. and ed. H. C. Barnard, 1–96. Cambridge: Cambridge University Press, 1966.

[Fenn, Eleanor]. *The Mother's Remarks on a Set of Cuts for Children*. Philadelphia: Jacob Johnson, 1803.

—— [Mrs. Lovechild]. *Rational Sports, in Dialogues Passing among the Children of a Family: Designed as a Hint to Mothers How They May Inform the Minds of Their Little People respecting the Objects with Which They Are Surrounded*. Boston: Cummings & Hilliard, 1814.

[Finch, Edward.] *Finch His Alphabet, or a Godly Direction, Fit to Be Perused of Each True Christian*. London, 1630. In *Fugitive Tracts Written in Verse Which Illustrate the Condition of Religious and Political Feeling in England and the State of Society There during Two Centuries*, 2d ser., 1600–1700. London, 1875.

Fisher, Samuel. *Female Education: An Address Delivered at the Dedication of the Ohio Female College*. Cincinnati: Ben Franklin Book & Job Rooms, 1849.

Fugitive Tracts Written in Verse Which Illustrate the Condition of Religious and Political Feeling in England and the State of Society There during Two Centuries. 2d ser., 1600–1700. London, 1875.

Gale, Lyman. *The Ladies' Companion, Containing Politeness of Manners and Behaviour from the French of the Abbé de Bellegarde. Second, Fenelon on Education—Third, Miss More's Essays—Fourth, Dean Swift's Letters to a Young Lady Newly Married—Fifth, Moore's Fables for the Female Sex. Carefully Selected and Revised by a Lady*. Worcester, Mass., 1824.

Garnett, James M. *Lectures on Female Education. Comprising the First and Second Series of a Course Delivered to Mrs. Garnett's Pupils, at Elm-wood, Essex County, Virginia. To Which Is Annexed, The Gossip's Manual*. Richmond, Va: Thomas W. White, 1825.

Giles, Daphne S. *The Religious and Political Influence of Educated and Uneducated Females.* Boston: J. Howe, 1849.

Gisborne, Thomas. *An Enquiry into the Duties of the Female Sex.* Philadelphia: James Humphreys, 1798.

The Good Boy's and Girl's Alphabet. Philadelphia: B. Bramell, [1841–1851?].

Goodrich, Samuel. *Peter Parley's Primer, with Engravings.* Philadelphia: Henry F. Annres, 1840.

Greenwood, James. *The London and Paris Vocabulary, English Latin and French.* Cambridge, Mass.: N. Faucon, 1816.

———. *The Philadelphia Vocabulary, English and Latin: Put into a New Method, Proper to Acquaint the Learner with Things as Well as Pure Latin Words. Adorned with Twenty-Six Pictures. For the Use of Schools.* Philadelphia: Mathew Carey, 1787.

Hall, Samuel R. *Lectures to Female Teachers on School-Keeping.* Boston: Richardson, Lord & Holbrook, 1832.

Hawthorne, Nathaniel. *The American Notebooks.* Ed. Claude M. Simpson. Vol. 8 of the Centenary Edition of the Works of Nathaniel Hawthorne. Columbus: Ohio State University Press, 1972.

———. *Biographical Stories for Children.* In *True Stories from History and Biography*, vol. 6 of the Centenary Edition of the Works of Nathaniel Hawthorne, 211–284. Columbus: Ohio State University Press, 1962.

———. *The Scarlet Letter.* Vol. 1 of the Centenary Edition of the Works of Nathaniel Hawthorne. Columbus: Ohio State University Press, 1962.

———. *The Scarlet Letter.* In *The Norton Anthology of American Literature*, ed. Nina Baym et al., 3d ed., 1:1162–1302. New York: Norton, 1989.

———. *Tales and Sketches.* New York: Library of America, 1982.

Helps for Spiritual Meditation; Earnestly Recommended to the Perusal of All Those Who Desire to Have Their Hearts Much with God. Wolverhampton: J. Smart, c. 1775.

The History of an Apple Pie. Dunigan's edition. New York: Dunigan, [1843–1848].

The History of an Apple Pie; Written by Z. New York: Evans & Dickerson, [c. 1850s].

The History of Goody Two-Shoes, to Which Is Added The Rhyming

Alphabet, or Tom Thumb's Delight. Hartford, Conn.: Hale & Hosmer, 1814.

Homer. *The Iliad*. Trans. A. T. Murray. Cambridge, Mass.: Loeb, 1988.

Horace. *Satires, Epistles, and Ars Poetica*. Trans. H. Rushton Fairclough. Cambridge, Mass.: Loeb, 1978.

The Illuminated American Primer, Being an Introduction to Mrs. Sigourney's Pictorial Reader. New York: Turner, 1844.

The Infant's Cabinet. New York: S. Wood, 1814.

James, Henry. *Hawthorne* (1879). In *Henry James: Literary Criticism. Essays in Literature, American Writers, English Writers*. New York: Library of America, 1984.

Johnson, A[lexander] B[ryan]. *A Treatise on Language; or, The Relation Which Words Bear to Things, in Four Parts*. New York: Harper & Brothers, 1836.

Johnstone, Charles. *Chrysal; or, The Adventures of a Guinea . . . by an Adept*. London: T. Becket, 1765–1766.

[Jones, Giles.] *Lilliputian Masquerade*. Worcester, Mass.: Isaiah Thomas, 1787.

Kraitsir, Charles. *The Significance of the Alphabet*. Boston: E. P. Peabody, 1846.

The Lady's Pocket Library. Containing, 1. Miss More's Essays. 2. Dr. Gregory's Legacy to His Daughters. 3. Lady Pennington's Unfortunate Mother's Advice to Her Daughters. 4. Rudiments of Taste, by the Countess of Carlisle. 5. Mrs. Chapone's Letter on the Government of the Temper. 6. Swift's Letter to a Young Lady Newly Married. 7. Moore's Fables for the Female Sex. 3d American ed. Philadelphia: Mathew Carey, 1797.

Larcom, Lucy. *A New England Girlhood Outlined from Memory* (1889). Boston: Northeastern University Press, 1986.

A Little Lottery Book for Children: Containing a New Method of Playing Them into a Knowledge of the Letters, Figures, &c. Worcester, Mass.: Isaiah Thomas, 1788.

A Little Pretty Pocket-Book, Intended for the Instruction and Amusement of Little Master Tommy and Pretty Miss Polly. Worcester, Mass.: Isaiah Thomas, 1787.

Locke, John. *An Essay Concerning Human Understanding*. Ed. P. H. Nidditch. New York: Oxford University Press, 1975

————. *Some Thoughts Concerning Education* (1693). Ed. Yolton & Yolton. Oxford: Clarendon, 1989.

Lovechild, Miss. *The Ladder to Learning.* Albany: Gray, Sprague, [1851 or 1852?].

Lovechild, Mrs. *The Mother's Own Primer.* New York: John Levison, 1840.

Lovechild, Nurse. *Tommy Thumb's Song Book, for All Little Masters and Misses, to Be Sung to Them by Their Nurses, Until They Can Sing Themselves. To Which Is Added, a Letter from a Lady on Nursing.* Worcester, Mass.: Isaiah Thomas, 1788.

Lowell, Anna. *Theory of Teaching, with a Few Practical Illustrations.* Boston: E. P. Peabody, 1841.

Lyon, Mary. *Female Education: Tendencies of the Principles Embraced, and the System Adopted in the Mount Holyoke Female Seminary.* South Hadley, Mass., 1839.

Mann, Horace. *A Lecture on the Best Mode of Preparing and Using Spelling-Books Delivered before the American Institute of Instruction, August, 1841.* Boston: William D. Ticknor, 1841.

————. *Lectures on Education.* Boston: W. B. Fowle & N. Capen, 1845.

Mann, [Mary Tyler Peabody], and Elizabeth P. Peabody. *Moral Culture of Infancy, and Kindergarten Guide, with Music for the Plays.* Boston: T. O. H. P. Burnham, 1863.

————. *Primer of Reading and Drawing.* Boston: E. P. Peabody, 1841.

Marvell, Andrew. *The Complete Works in Verse and Prose of Andrew Marvell.* Ed. Alexander Grosart. Vol. 1. London, 1872.

Mather, Cotton. *Corderius Americanus: An Essay upon the Good Education of Children.* John Allen: Boston, 1708.

————. "Mather on Catechising." Preface to *The Man of God Furnished.* In *The New-England Primer: A History of Its Origin and Development,* ed. Paul Leicester Ford, app. 3, 261–273. New York: Dodd, Mead, 1897.

The Men among the Letters. Boston: Munroe & Francis, 1824, 1831.

[Moody, Eleazar]. *The School of Good Manners. Composed for the Help of Parents in Teaching Their Children How to Carry It in Their Places during Their Minority.* Boston: T & J. Fleet, 1772.

Morley, Thomas. *A Plaine and Easie Introduction to Practicall Musicke, Set Down in Forme of a Dialogue.* London, 1597. Reprinted in

Shakespeare Association Facsimiles, no. 14. London: Oxford University Press, 1937.

The Mother's Assistant and Young Lady's Friend. Ed. William C. Brown. Boston: 1841, 1848.

Mott, Abigail. *Observations on the Importance of Female Education, and Maternal Instruction, with Their Beneficial Influence on Society.* New York: Mahlon Day, 1825.

The New-England Primer, Enlarged. For the More Easy Attaining the True Reading of English. To Which Is Added, the Assembly of Divines Catechism. [Boston: S. Kneeland & T. Green, 1727].

The New-England Primer Enlarged; or, An Easy and Pleasant Guide to the Art of Reading, Adorn'd with Cuts, to Which Are Added, The Assembly of Divines, and Mr. Cotton's Catechism, &c. Boston: E. Draper, c. 1785–1790. Reprint New York: Ginn & Co., 1900.

The New-England Primer Improved. For the More Easy Attaining the True Reading of English, to Which Is Added, The Assembly of Divines, and Mr. Cotton's Catechism. Boston: D. & J. Kneeland, 1761.

The New-England Primer. Improved for the More Easy Attaining the True Reading of English, To Which Is Added The Assembly of Divines, and Mr. Cotton's Catechism. Boston: E. Draper, 1777. Reprint Aledo, Texas: Wallbuilder Press, 1991.

Newcomb, Harvey. *The Young Lady's Guide to the Harmonious Developement [sic] of Christian Character.* Boston: James B. Dow, 1840.

Nurse Truelove's New Year's Gift; or, The Book of Books for Children. Worcester, Mass.: Isaiah Thomas, 1800.

Peabody, Elizabeth P., ed. *Aesthetic Papers* (1849). Facsimile reprint Gainesville, Fla.: Scholars' Facsimiles and Reprints, 1957.

———. *Kindergarten Guide.* See M. Mann and E. Peabody, *Moral Culture of Infancy.*

Pepys, Samuel. *The Diary of Samuel Pepys.* Vol. 9, *1668–1669.* Ed. Robert Latham and William Matthews. Berkeley: University of California Press, 1976.

Perrault, Charles. *Histories, or Tales of Past Times.* London: J. Pote & R. Montague, 1729.

Phelps, Almira H. *Lectures to Young Ladies, Comprising Outlines and*

Applications of the Different Branches of Female Education, for the Use of Female Schools, and Private Libraries, Delivered to the Pupils of Troy Female Seminary. Boston: Carter & Hendee & Allen & Ticknor, 1833.

Pictured A, B, C. Philadelphia: Fisher & Brother, [c. 1850].

The Pretty Play-thing, for Children of All Denominations. Philadelphia: Benjamin Johnson, 1794.

The Renowned History of Giles Gingerbread: A Little Boy Who Lived upon Learning. Boston: Mein & Fleeming, 1768.

Robbins, Chandler. *Remarks on the Disorders of Literary Men, or an Inquiry into the Means of Preventing the Evils Usually Incident to Sedentary and Studious Habits.* Boston: Cumming, Hilliard & Co., 1825.

Rousseau, Jean-Jacques. *Emile, or On Education.* Trans. Allan Bloom. New York: Basic Books, 1979.

The Royal Alphabet; or, Child's Best Instructor. To Which Is Added, The History of a Little Boy Found under a Haycock. Worcester, Mass.: Isaiah Thomas, 1787.

The Royal Primer; or, An Easy and Pleasant Guide to the Art of Reading. Boston: Samuel Hall, 1796

Rush, Benjamin. *A Plan for the Establishment of Public Schools and the Diffusion of Knowledge in Pennsylvania; to Which Are Added Thoughts upon the Mode of Education, Proper in a Republic. Addressed to the Legislature and Citizens of the State.* Philadelphia: Thomas Dobson, 1786.

———. "Thoughts upon the Amusements and Punishments Which Are Proper for Schools. Addressed to George Clymer, Esq." N.p., 1790.

———. *Thoughts upon Female Education, Accommodated to the Present State of Society, Manners and Government, in the United States of America. Addressed to the Visitors of the Young Ladies' Academy in Philadelphia, 28 July, 1787, at the Close of the Quarterly Examination . . .* Philadelphia: Prichard & Hall, 1787.

Sedgwick, Catharine Maria. *Means and Ends, or Self-Training.* New York: Harper, 1842.

Sigourney, Lydia Huntley. *Letters of Life.* New York: D. Appleton, 1866.

———. *Letters to Mothers.* Hartford: Hudson & Skinner, 1838.

Stennett, R. *Aldiborontiphoskyphorniostikos, a Round Game for Merry Parties*. New York: Solomon King, 1829.

Tevis, Julia. *Sixty Years in a School-Room: An Autobiography of Mrs. Juila A. Tevis, Principal of Science Hill Female Academy. To Which Is Prefixed an Autobiographical Sketch of Rev. John Tevis*. Cincinnati: Western Methodist Book Concern, 1878.

Tom Thumb's Play-Book; to Teach Children Their Letters as Soon as They Can Speak. Being a New and Pleasant Method to Allure Little Ones in the First Principles of Learning. Boston: A. Barclay, [1764].

Tory, Geoffrey. *Champfleury*. Trans. George B. Ives. New York: Grolier Club, 1927.

Townsend, Shippie. *The History of the Mother and Child. A New Primer, Attempting an Early, Entertaining, and Effectual Method of Teaching Young Children the Alphabet, So As to Lay a Foundation for Making Them Good Readers;— Who Have Need of Milk, and Not of Strong Meat. To Which Is Annexed, the Young Child's Catechism*. Boston: S. Hall, [c. 1794].

The Uncle's Present, a New Battledoor. Philadelphia: Jacob Johnson, [c. 1809].

Warner, Anna Bartlett. *Mr. Rutherford's Children*. Ellen Montgomery's Bookshelf. 2 vols. New York: Putnam, 1853.

———. *Robinson Crusoe's Farmyard*. New York: Putnam, 1849.

Warner, Henry Whiting (transcriber). *Report of the Trial of Charles N. Baldwin, for a Libel, in Publishing, in the "Republican Chronicle," Certain Charges of Fraud and Swindling, in the Management of Lotteries, in the State of New-York*. New York: C. N. Baldwin, 1818.

Warner, Susan. "'Many things take my time': The Journals of Susan Warner." Ed. Jane Weiss. Diss., City University of New York, 1995.

———. *The Wide, Wide World* (1850). Afterword by Jane Tompkins. 1892; reprint New York: Feminist Press, 1987.

Watts, Isaac. *The Art of Reading and Writing English* (1721). Menston, Eng.: Scolar Press, 1972.

———. "A Discourse on the Education of Children and Youth." In *The Works of the Rev. Isaac Watts, D.D.*, 7:527–590. Leeds, Eng.: Edward Baines, 1813.

————. "The Improvement of the Mind." In *The Works of the Rev. Isaac Watts, D.D.*, 8: 2–216. Leeds, Eng.: Edward Baines, 1813.

————. "Logic." In *The Works of the Rev. Isaac Watts, D.D.*, 7: 312–526. Leeds, Eng.: Edward Baines, 1813.

Webster, Noah. *A Grammatical Institute of the English Language, Comprising an Easy, Concise and Systematic Method of Education.* Hartford, Conn.: Hudson & Goodwin, n.d.

————. "On the Education of Youth in America." In *Essays on Education in the Early Republic*, ed. Frederick Rudolph. Cambridge, Mass.: Harvard University Press, 1965.

Weeks, William R. "Essay on Learning to Read and Write the English Language." *American Annals of Education and Instruction, and Journal of Literary Institutions* 2 (Sept. 1832).

Weems, Mason L. *The Life of Washington* (1809). Ed. Marcus Cunliffe. Cambridge, Mass.: Harvard University Press, 1962.

Willard, Emma. *An Address to the Public, Particularly to the Members of the Legislature of New-York, Proposing a Plan for Improving Female Education.* Middlebury, Vt.: J. W. Copeland, 1819.

————. *Advancement of Female Education: or, A Series of Addresses in Favor of Establishing at Athens, in Greece, a Female Seminary Especially Designed to Instruct Female Teachers.* Troy, N.Y.: Norman Tuttle for the Troy Society, 1833.

Wilkins, John. *An Essay towards a Real Character and a Philosophical Language.* London, 1668.

Wise, Daniel, ed. *The Ladies' Pearl, and Literary Gleaner: A Collection of Tales, Sketches, Essays, Anecdotes, and Historical Incidents; Embellished with Engravings and Music.* Lowell, Mass.: E. A. Rice, 1841.

Wordsworth, William. "Essay upon Epitaphs." In *The Prose Works of William Wordsworth*, ed. W. J. B. Owen and Jane Worthington Smyser, 2:45–119. Oxford: Clarendon Press, 1974.

Wright, Frances. *Address to the People of Philadelphia* (4th of July Address). New York: George Evans, 1829.

"Youths' Battledoor." *Giddy Gertrude; a Story for Little Girls.* Northhampton: E. Turner, [c. 1828].

Secondary Sources

Ahlstrom, Sydney F. *A Religious History of the American People*. New Haven: Yale University Press, 1972.

Allen, Arthur B. *The Romance of the Alphabet*. London: Warne, 1937.

Alpers, Svetlana. *The Art of Describing: Dutch Art in the Seventeenth Century*. Chicago: University of Chicago Press, 1983.

Arac, Jonathan. "Reading the Letter." *Diacritics* 9 (1979): 42–52.

Ariès, Philippe. *Centuries of Childhood: A Social History of Family Life*. Trans. Robert Baldick. New York: Vintage, 1962.

Armstrong, Nancy. *Desire and Domestic Fiction*. New York: Oxford University Press, 1987.

Ashton-Warner, Sylvia. *Teacher*. New York: Simon & Schuster, [1963] 1986.

Avery, Gillian. *Behold the Child: American Children and Their Books, 1621–1922*. Baltimore: Johns Hopkins University Press, 1994.

———. "Origins of *The New England Primer*." *Proceedings of the American Antiquarian Society* vol. 113, part 1, 1999: 33–61.

Axtell, James. *The School upon a Hill: Education and Society in Colonial New England*. New Haven: Yale University Press, 1974.

Bakhtin, Mikhail. "The *Bildungsroman* and Its Significance in the History of Realism (Toward a Historical Typology of the Novel)." In *Speech Genres and Other Late Essays*, ed. Caryl Emerson and Michael Holquist, trans. Vern W. McGee, 10–59. Austin: University of Texas Press, 1986.

———. *The Dialogic Imagination: Four Essays*. Ed. Michael Holquist, trans. Caryl Emerson and Michael Holquist. Austin: University of Texas Press, 1981.

———. *Problems of Dostoevsky's Poetics*. Trans. Caryl Emerson. Theory and History of Literature 8. Minneapolis: University of Minnesota Press, 1984.

———. *Rabelais and His World*. Trans. Hélène Iswolsky. Bloomington: Indiana University Press, 1984.

Baldwin, T. W. *William Shakspere's Petty School*. Urbana: University of Illinois Press, 1943.

Barker-Benfield, G. J. *The Horrors of the Half-Known Life*. New York: Harper, 1976.

Barthes, Roland. "The Imagination of the Sign." In *A Barthes Reader*, trans. Richard Howard, 211–217. New York: Hill & Wang.

——. "The Reality Effect." In *The Rustle of Language*, trans. Richard Howard, 141–148. New York: Hill & Wang, 1986.

——. "The Rhetoric of the Image." In *The Responsibility of Forms: Critical Essays on Music, Art, and Representations*, trans. Richard Howard, 21–40. Berkeley: University of California Press, [1985] 1991.

——. "The World as Object." In *Critical Essays*, trans. Richard Howard, 3–12. Evanston: Northwestern University Press, 1972.

Baym, Nina. *Novels, Readers, and Reviewers: Responses to Fiction in Antebellum America*. Ithaca, N.Y.: Cornell University Press, 1984.

——. *The Scarlet Letter: A Reading*. Twayne's Masterwork Studies 1. Boston: Twayne, 1986.

——. *Women's Fiction: A Guide to Novels by and about Women in America, 1820–1970*. Ithaca, N.Y.: Cornell University Press, 1978.

Beatty, Barbara. *Preschool Education in America: The Culture of Young Children from the Colonial Era to the Present*. New Haven: Yale University Press, 1995.

Bender, John, and David Wellbery, eds. *The Ends of Rhetoric: History, Theory, Practice*. Stanford: Stanford University Press, 1990.

Benjamin, Walter. *The Origins of German Tragic Drama*. Trans. John Osborne. London: New Left Books, 1977.

——. "The Work of Art in the Age of Mechanical Reproduction." In *Illuminations*, ed. Hannah Arendt, trans. Harry Zohn, 217–251. New York: Schocken, 1969.

Bercovitch, Sacvan. *The Office of the Scarlet Letter*. Baltimore: Johns Hopkins University Press, 1991.

Berman, Barbara Ann. "The Impenetrable Fortress: A Study of Nineteenth-Century American Social Values Inherent in United States Elementary and Secondary Public School Disciplinary Literature, 1830–1890." Ph.D. diss., University of Rochester, 1971.

Billington, Sandra. *A Social History of the Fool*. Sussex, Eng.: Harvester Press; New York: St. Martin's, 1984.

Blake, Erin. "Re-Mapping the City: Perspective Views, Polite Society, and Virtual Reality in Eighteenth-Century Britain." One-Day Seminar in the History of Cartography, Newberry Library, Chicago, April 29, 1999.

Bonner, Stanley F. *Education in Ancient Rome*. Berkeley: University of California Press, 1977.

Bourdieu, Pierre. *Language and Symbolic Power*. Ed. John B. Thompson; trans. Gino Raymond and Matthew Adamson. Cambridge, Mass.: Harvard University Press, 1991.

———. *Outline of a Theory of Practice*. Trans. Richard Nice. Cambridge: Cambridge University Press, 1977.

Bowen, James. Introduction to *Orbis Sensualium Pictus*, by Johann Amos Comenius (1672). Sydney: Sydney University Press, 1967.

Boyarin, Jonathan, ed. *The Ethnography of Reading*. Berkeley: University of California Press, 1993.

Bradford, John. "Policing the Movement of Modern Education." Paper presented at the 37th annual meeting of the Midwest Sociological Society, St. Louis, Mo., April 21–24, 1976.

Brewer, E. Cobham. *The Dictionary of Phrase and Fable* (1870). New York: Avenel, 1978.

Briggs, Katharine M. *Nine Lives: The Folklore of Cats*. New York: Pantheon, 1980.

Brodhead, Richard H. *Cultures of Letters: Scenes of Reading and Writing in Nineteenth-Century America*. Chicago: University of Chicago Press, 1993.

———. *The School of Hawthorne*. New York: Oxford University Press, 1986.

Brown, Gillian. *Domestic Individualism: Imagining Self in Nineteenth-Century America*. Berkeley: University of California Press, 1990.

Bryson, Norman. *Tradition and Desire: From David to Delacroix*. Cambridge: Cambridge University Press, 1984.

———. *Vision and Painting: The Logic of the Gaze*. New Haven: Yale University Press, 1983.

Burke, Kenneth. *A Grammar of Motives*. Berkeley: University of California Press, 1969.

Busek, Vratislav, ed. *Comenius*. Trans. Kaca Polackova. New York: Czechoslovak Society of Arts and Sciences of America, 1972.

Butterworth, Charles C. *The English Primers, 1529–1545*. New York: Octagon, 1971.

Camille, Michael. *Image on the Edge: The Margins of Medieval Art*. Cambridge, Mass.: Harvard University Press, 1992.

————. "Reading the Printed Image: Illuminations and Woodcuts of the *Pèlerinage de la vie humaine* in the Fifteenth Century." In *Printing the Written Word: The Social History of Books, 1450–1520,* ed. Sandra Hindman, 259–291. Ithaca, N.Y.: Cornell University Press, 1991.

Carr, Jean Ferguson. "The Bay Psalm Book (1640); *The New England Primer* (1683?)." In *The Heath Anthology of American Literature,* ed. Paul Lauter, 1:326–328. Lexington, Mass.: D. C. Heath, 1994.

Castagno, Paul C. *The Early Commedia dell'Arte (1550–1621): The Mannerist Context.* New York: Lang, 1994.

Castle, Terry. *Masquerade and Civilization: The Carnivalesque in Eighteenth-Century English Culture and Fiction.* Stanford: Stanford University Press, 1986.

Chase, Richard. *The American Novel and Its Tradition.* New York: Doubleday, 1957.

Children's Television Workshop. *Learning about Letters.* Video. New York: CTW, 1986.

Clark, Charles. *The Public Prints: The Newspaper in Anglo-American Culture, 1665–1740.* New York: Oxford University Press, 1994.

Cmiel, Kenneth. *Democratic Eloquence: The Fight over Popular Speech in Nineteenth-Century America.* Berkeley: University of California Press, 1990.

Cohen, Murray. *Sensible Words: Linguistic Practice in England, 1640–1785.* Baltimore: Johns Hopkins University Press, 1977.

Cook, Thomas D., et al. *"Sesame Street" Revisited.* New York: Russell Sage Foundation, 1975.

Cott, Nancy. *The Bonds of Womanhood: "Women's Sphere" in New England, 1780–1835.* New Haven: Yale University Press, 1977.

Crain, Patricia. "Hawthorne." In *Encyclopedia of American Poetry: The Nineteenth Century,* ed. Eric. L. Haralson, 196–199. Chicago: Fitzroy Dearborn, 1998.

Cremin, Lawrence A. *American Education.* 2 vols. New York: Harper, 1980.

Cross, Frank Moore. "The Invention and Development of the Alphabet." In *The Origins of Writing,* ed. Wayne M. Senner, 77–90. Lincoln: University of Nebraska Press, 1989.

Darnton, Robert. "First Steps towards a History of Reading." In *The Kiss of Lamourette,* 154–187. New York: Norton, 1990.

————. "Peasants Tell Tales: The Meaning of Mother Goose." In *The Great Cat Massacre and Other Episodes in French Cultural History*, 9–72. New York: Basic Books, 1984.

————. "Readers Respond to Rousseau: The Fabrication of Romantic Sensitivity." In *The Great Cat Massacre and Other Episodes in French Cultural History*, 215–263. New York: Basic Books, 1984.

Darton, F. J. Harvey. *Children's Books in England.* 2d ed. Cambridge: Cambridge University Press, [1958] 1970.

Davidson, Cathy, ed. *Reading in America.* Baltimore: Johns Hopkins University Press, 1989.

————. *Revolution and the Word: The Rise of the Novel in America.* New York: Oxford University Press, 1986.

Davis, Natalie Zemon. "Women on Top." In *Society and Culture in Early Modern France*, 124–151. Stanford: Stanford University Press, 1975.

Debord, Guy. *Society of the Spectacle.* Detroit: Black & Red, 1983.

de Certeau, Michel. *The Practice of Everyday Life.* Trans. Steven Rendall. Berkeley: University of California Press, 1984.

Delaney, Janice, Mary Jane Lupton, and Emily Toth. *The Curse: A Cultural History of Menstruation.* New York: NAL, 1977.

Delderfield, Eric R. *British Inn Signs and Their Stories.* Newton Abbot, Devon: David & Charles, 1972.

de Man, Paul. "The Rhetoric of Temporality." In *Blindness and Insight: Essays in the Rhetoric of Contemporary Criticism*, 2d ed., 187–228. Minneapolis: University of Minnesota Press, 1983.

Demers, Patricia. *Heaven upon Earth: The Form of Moral and Religious Children's Literature, to 1850.* Knoxville: University of Tennessee Press, 1993.

Diringer, D. *The Alphabet: A Key to the History of Mankind.* New York: Funk & Wagnall, 1968.

Dolis, John. *The Style of Hawthorne's Gaze.* Tuscaloosa: University of Alabama Press, 1993.

Douglas, Ann. *The Feminization of American Culture.* New York: Doubleday, [1977] 1988.

Douglas, Mary. *Purity and Danger: An Analysis of Concepts of Pollution and Taboo.* Harmondsworth, Middlesex: Penguin, [1966] 1970.

Drucker, Johanna. *The Alphabetic Labyrinth: The Letters in History and Imagination.* London: Thames & Hudson, 1995.

———. *Theorizing Modernism: Visual Art and the Critical Tradition.* New York: Columbia University Press, 1996.

Duchartre, Pierre Louis. *The Italian Comedy: The Improvisation, Scenarios, Lives, Attributes, Portraits, and Masks of the Illustrious Characters of the Commedia dell'Arte* (1929). Trans. Randolph T. Weaver. New York: Dover, 1966.

Eisenstein, Elizabeth. *The Printing Press as an Agent of Change: Communications and Cultural Transformations in Early-Modern Europe.* 2 vols. Cambridge: Cambridge University Press, 1979.

Eliade, Mircea. *The Sacred and the Profane: The Nature of Religion.* Trans. Willard R. Trask. New York: Harper, 1961.

Ferry, Anne. *The Art of Naming.* Chicago: University of Chicago Press, 1988.

Field, Edward. *The Colonial Tavern: A Glimpse of New England Town Life in the Seventeenth and Eighteenth Centuries* (1897). Facsimile reprint Bowie, Md.: Heritage Books, 1989.

Firmage, Richard A. *The Alphabet Abecedarium: Some Notes on Letters.* Boston: Godine, 1993.

Fletcher, Angus. *Allegory: The Theory of a Symbolic Mode.* Ithaca: Cornell University Press, 1964.

Fliegelman, Jay. *Declaring Independence: Jefferson, Natural Language, and the Culture of Performance.* Stanford: Stanford University Press, 1993.

———. *Prodigals and Pilgrims: The American Revolution Against Patriarchal Authority, 1750–1800.* New York: Cambridge University Press, 1982.

Flint, Christopher. "Speaking Objects: The Circulation of Stories in Eighteenth-Century Prose Fiction." *PMLA* 113, no. 2 (Mar. 1998): 212–226.

Folmsbee, Beulah. *A Little History of the Horn-Book.* Boston: Horn Book, 1942.

Ford, Paul Leicester, ed. *The New-England Primer: A History of Its Origin and Development.* New York: Dodd, Mead, 1897.

———. *The New-England Primer: A Reprint of the Earliest Known Edition.* New York: Dodd, Mead, 1899.

Ford, Worthington Chauncey. "Benjamin Harris, Printer and Bookseller." *Proceedings of the Massachusetts Historical Society* 57 (1923): 34–68.

Foster, Edward Halsey. *Susan and Anna Warner*. Boston: Twayne, n.d.

Foucault, Michel. *Discipline and Punish: The Birth of the Prison*. Trans. Alan Sheridan. New York: Random House, 1979.

———. *The Order of Things: An Archeology of the Human Sciences*. New York: Random House, 1971.

Freedberg, David. "Iconoclasts and Their Motives." *Public*, no. 8 (1993): 10–47.

———. *The Power of Images: Studies in the History and Theory of Response*. Chicago: University of Chicago Press, 1989.

Freud, Sigmund. *Totem and Taboo* (1918). Trans. A. A. Brill. New York: Random House, 1946.

Frow, George. *"Oh, Yes It Is!" A History of Pantomime*. London: BBC, 1985.

Gilmore, William. *Reading Becomes a Necessity of Life: Material and Cultural Life in Rural New England, 1780–1835*. Knoxville: University of Tennessee Press, 1989.

Gitelman, Lisa. "Phonography and Orality: Shorthand in the Articulation of American Authority." Paper presented at Society for the History of Authorship, Reading, and Publishing conference, "Alphabets as Technology," Worcester, Mass., July 20, 1996.

Godzich, Wlad. "Language, Images, and the Postmodern Predicament." In *Materialities of Communication*, ed. Hans Ulrich Gumbrecht and K. Ludwig Pfeiffer, trans. William Whobrey, 355–370. Stanford: Stanford University Press, 1994.

Goldberg, Jonathan. *Writing Matters: From the Hands of the English Renaissance*. Stanford: Stanford University Press, 1990.

Goshgarian, G. M. *To Kiss the Chastening Rod: Domestic Fiction and Sexual Ideology in the American Renaissance*. Ithaca, N.Y.: Cornell University Press, 1992.

Gottlieb, Gerald. *Early Children's Books and Their Illustration*. New York: Pierpont Morgan Library; Boston: Godine, 1975.

Gura, Philip E. *The Wisdom of Words: Language, Theology, and Literature in the New England Renaissance*. Middletown, Conn.: Wesleyan University Press, 1981.

Hall, David. *Cultures of Print: Essays in the History of the Book.* Amherst: University of Massachusetts Press, 1996.

———. *Worlds of Wonder, Days of Judgment: Popular Religious Belief in Early New England.* New York: Knopf, 1989.

Halttunen, Karen. *Confidence Men and Painted Women: A Study of Middle-Class Culture in America, 1830–1870.* New Haven: Yale University Press, 1982.

Harris, Roy. *The Origin of Writing.* La Salle, Ill.: Open Court, 1986.

Haviland, Virginia, and Margaret N. Coughlan. *Yankee Doodle's Literary Sampler of Prose, Poetry, and Pictures.* New York: Crowell, 1974.

Heal, Ambrose. *The English Writing Masters, 1570–1800: A Biographical Dictionary and a Bibliography.* London, 1931. Reprint Hildesheim, Ger.: Georg Olms, 1962.

Heartman, Charles. *American Primers, Indian Primers, Royal Primers & Thirty-Seven Other Types of Non-New-England Primers Issued prior to 1830.* Highland Park, N.J.: Weiss, 1935.

———. *The New-England Primers Printed in America prior to 1830.* New York, 1915.

Hedrick, Joan. *Harriet Beecher Stowe: A Life.* New York: Oxford University Press, 1994.

Hench, John, David Hall, and William Joyce. *Printing and Society in Early America.* Worcester, Mass.: American Antiquarian Society, 1983.

Henke, James T. *Courtesans and Cuckolds: A Glossary of Renaissance Dramatic Bawdy.* New York: Garland, 1979.

Hindman, Sandra, ed. *Printing the Written Word: The Social History of Books, 1450–1520.* Ithaca, N.Y.: Cornell University Press, 1991.

Hobbs, Catherine, ed. *Nineteenth-Century Women Learn to Write.* Charlottesville: University of Virginia Press, 1995.

Howe, Daniel Walker. *The Political Culture of American Whigs.* Chicago: University of Chicago Press, 1979.

Humez, Alexander, and Nicholas Humez. *ABC et Cetera: The Life and Times of the Roman Alphabet.* Boston: Godine, 1985.

Hürlimann, Bettina. *Three Centuries of Children's Books in Europe.* Trans. Brian W. Alderson. Cleveland: World, 1959.

Illich, Ivan, and Barry Sanders. *ABC: The Alphabetization of the Popular Mind.* New York: Vintage Books, 1989.

Immel, Andrea. "'Mistress of Infantine Language': Lady Ellenor Fenn, Her Set of Toys, and the 'Education of Each Moment.'" *Children's Literature* 25 (1997): 215–228.

Irigaray, Luce. *This Sex Which Is Not One*. Trans. Catherine Porter. Ithaca, N.Y.: Cornell University Press, 1985.

Irwin, John. *American Hieroglyphics: The Symbol of the Egyptian Hieroglyphics in the American Renaissance*. New Haven: Yale University Press, 1980.

Ivins, William. *Prints and Visual Communication*. New York: Da Capo, [1953] 1969.

Jaeger, Werner W. *Paideia: The Ideals of Greek Culture*. Trans. Gilbert Highet. 2d ed. 3 vols. New York: Oxford University Press, 1986.

Jakobson, Roman. *Language in Literature*. Ed. Krystyna Pomorska and Stephen Rudy. Cambridge, Mass.: Harvard University Press, 1987.

Jordan, Alice M. *From Rollo to Tom Sawyer and Other Papers*. Boston: Horn Book, 1948.

Katz, Michael. *The Irony of Early School Reform: Educational Innovation in Mid-Nineteenth-Century Massachusetts*. Boston: Beacon Press, 1970.

———, ed. *Class, Bureaucracy, and Schools: The Illusion of Educational Change in America*. New York: Praeger, 1975.

Keatinge, M. W. Introduction to *The Great Didactic* (1910), by Johann Amos Comenius, 1–169. New York: Russell & Russell, 1967.

Kelley, Mary. *Private Woman, Public Stage: Literary Domesticity in Nineteenth-Century America*. New York: Oxford University Press, 1984.

Kesserling, Marion L. *Hawthorne's Reading, 1828–1850: A Transcription and Identification of Titles Recorded in the Charge-Books of the Salem Athenaeum*. New York: New York Public Library, 1949.

Kittler, Friedrich. *Discourse Networks*. Trans. Michael Metteer, with Chris Cullens. Stanford: Stanford University Press, 1990.

Kuhn, Anne. *The Mother's Role in Childhood Education: New England Concepts*. New Haven: Yale University Press, 1947.

Laqueur, Thomas. *Making Sex: Body and Gender from the Greeks to Freud*. Cambridge, Mass.: Harvard University Press, 1990.

Larson, Ruth. "Women, Books, Sex and Education in Seventeenth-Century French Literature." Ph.D. diss., Yale University, 1991.

Larwood, Jacob (pseud.), and John Camden Hotten. *The History of Signboards, from the Earliest Times to the Present Day*. London: Chatto & Windus, 1908.

Le Men, Ségolène. *Les abécédaires français illustrés du XIXe siècle*. Paris: Promodis, 1984.

Lesser, Gerald S. *Children and Television: Lessons from Sesame Street*. New York: Random House, 1974.

Leverenz, David. *Manhood and the American Renaissance*. Ithaca, N.Y.: Cornell University Press, 1989.

Lievsay, John L. "Emblem." In *Princeton Encyclopedia of Poetry and Poetics*, ed. Alex Preminger. Princeton: Princeton University Press, 1965.

Looby, Christopher. *Voicing America: Language, Literary Form, and the Origins of the United States*. Chicago: University of Chicago Press, 1996.

Loving, Jerome. *Lost in the Customhouse: Authorship in the American Renaissance*. Iowa City: University of Iowa Press, 1993.

Lyotard, Jean-François. *The Postmodern Condition: A Report on Knowledge*. Trans. Geoff Bennington and Brian Massumi. Theory and History of Literature 10. Minneapolis: University of Minnesota Press, 1985.

MacDonald, Hugh, ed. *The Poems of Andrew Marvell*. Cambridge, Mass.: Muse's Library, Harvard University Press, 1963.

Male, Roy R. "Hawthorne's Literal Figures." In *Ruined Eden of the Present: Hawthorne, Melville, and Poe—Critical Essays in Honor of Darrel Abel*, ed. G. R. Thompson and Virgil L. Lokke, 71–92. West Lafayette, Ind.: Purdue University Press, 1981.

Marrou, H. I. *A History of Education in Antiquity*. Trans. George Lamb. Madison: University of Wisconsin Press, 1982.

Marx, Karl. *Capital: A Critique of Political Economy*. Vol. 1. Trans. Ben Fowkes. New York: Vintage Books, 1977.

Massin. *Letter and Image*. Trans. Caroline Hillier and Vivienne Menkes. New York: Van Nostrand Reinhold, 1970.

Masten, Jeffrey. *Spelling Shakespeare, and Other Essays in Queer Philology*. Forthcoming.

Mates, Barbara Fowles, and Linda Strommen. "Why Ernie Can't Read: *Sesame Street* and Literacy." *Reading Teacher* 49, no. 4 (Dec. 1995): 300–306.

Matthews, Albert. "Comenius and Harvard College." *Colonial Society of Massachusetts, Transactions* 21 (1919): 146–190.

———. "Early Sunday Schools in Boston." *Colonial Society of Massachusetts, Transactions* 21 (1919): 259–285.

Matthiessen, F. O. *American Renaissance: Art and Expression in the Age of Emerson and Whitman.* New York: Oxford University Press, 1941.

McConachie, Bruce. *Melodramatic Formations: American Theatre and Society, 1820–1870.* Iowa City: University of Iowa Press, 1992.

McGann, Jerome. *Black Riders: The Visible Language of Modernism.* Princeton: Princeton University Press, 1993.

McGuirk, Carol. "Loose Canons: Milton and Burns, Art Song and Folk Song." In *Love and Liberty: Proceedings of the International Burns Bicentenary Conference.* Edinburgh: Tuckwell, 1996: 315–26.

McKeon, Michael. *The Origins of the English Novel, 1600–1740.* Baltimore: Johns Hopkins University Press, 1987.

McLuhan, Marshall. *Understanding Media: The Extensions of Man.* New York: McGraw-Hill, 1964.

Meigs, Cornelia, Anne Eaton, Elizabeth Nesbitt, and Ruth Hill Viguers. *A Critical History of Children's Literature: A Survey of Children's Books in English from the Earliest Times to the Present.* New York: Macmillan, 1953.

Messerli, Jonathan. *Horace Mann: A Biography.* New York: Knopf, 1972.

Mignolo, Walter D. *The Darker Side of the Renaissance: Literacy, Territoriality, and Colonization.* Ann Arbor: University of Michigan Press, 1995.

Miller, Edwin Haviland. *Salem Is My Dwelling Place: A Life of Nathaniel Hawthorne.* Iowa City: University of Iowa Press, 1991.

Miller, J. Hillis. *Hawthorne and History: Defacing It.* Cambridge, Mass.: Basil Blackwell, 1991.

Miller, Perry. Introduction to *Images and Shadows of Divine Things,* by Jonathan Edwards, 1–41. New Haven: Yale University Press, 1948.

————. *The New England Mind: From Colony to Province*. Cambridge, Mass.: Harvard University Press, 1953.

————. *The New England Mind: The Seventeenth Century*. Cambridge, Mass.: Harvard University Press, 1939.

Mitchell, W. J. T. *Iconology: Image, Text, Ideology*. Chicago: University of Chicago Press, 1986.

————. *Picture Theory: Essays on Verbal and Visual Representation*. Chicago: University of Chicago Press, 1995.

————, ed. *The Language of Images*. Chicago: University of Chicago Press, 1980.

Molinari, Cesare. *La commedia dell'arte*. Milan: Mondadori, 1985.

Monaghan, E. Jennifer. *A Common Heritage: Noah Webster's Blue Back Speller*. Hamden, Conn.: Archon Books, 1983.

————. "Literacy Instruction and Gender in Colonial New England." In *Reading in America*, ed. Cathy Davidson, 53–80. Baltimore: Johns Hopkins University Press, 1989.

Moretti, Franco. *The Way of the World: The Bildungsroman in European Culture*. London: Verso, 1987.

Mulvey, Laura. *Visual and Other Pleasures*. Bloomington: University of Indiana Press, 1988.

Mundy, Liza. "The New Critics." *Lingua Franca*, Sept.–Oct. 1993, 26–33.

Neuberg, Victor. "Chapbooks in America: Reconstructing the Popular Reading of Early America." In *Reading in America*, ed. Cathy Davidson, 81–113. Baltimore: Johns Hopkins University Press, 1989.

New, Elisa. "'Both Great and Small': Adult Proportion and Divine Scale in Edward Taylor's 'Preface' and *The New England Primer*." *Early American Literature* 28, no. 2 (1993): 120–132.

New Catholic Encyclopedia. New York: McGraw-Hill, 1967.

Ong, Walter J. *Fighting for Life: Contest, Sexuality, and Consciousness*. Ithaca, N.Y.: Cornell University Press, 1981.

————. *Orality and Literacy: The Technologizing of the Word*. London: Methuen, [1982] 1988.

————. *The Presence of the Word: Some Prolegomena for Cultural and Religious History*. Minneapolis: University of Minnesota Press, [1967] 1981.

———. *Ramus: Method and the Decay of Dialogue*. Cambridge, Mass.: Harvard University Press, [1958] 1983.

———. *Rhetoric, Romance, and Technology*. Ithaca, N.Y.: Cornell University Press, 1971.

Opie, Iona, and Peter Opie. *Christmas Party Games*. New York: Oxford University Press, 1957.

———, eds. *The Classic Fairy Tales*. London: Oxford University Press, 1974.

———, eds. *The Oxford Dictionary of Nursery Rhymes*. Oxford: Oxford University Press, [1951] 1977.

———. *Three Centuries of Nursery Rhymes and Poetry for Children*. London: Oxford University Press, 1973.

Paglia, Camille. *Sexual Personae: Art and Decadence from Nefertiti to Emily Dickinson*. New Haven: Yale University Press, 1990.

Parker, Patricia. *Literary Fat Ladies: Rhetoric, Gender, Property*. New York: Methuen, 1987.

Partridge, Eric. *A Dictionary of Slang and Unconventional English*. New York: Macmillan, 1950.

———. *A Dictionary of the Underworld*. 3d ed. London: Routledge, 1968.

———. *Origins: A Short Etymological Dictionary of Modern English*. 4th ed. New York: Macmillan, 1966.

Perec, Georges. *W; or, The Memory of Childhood*. Trans. David Bellos. Boston: Godine, 1988.

Plimpton, George. "The Hornbook and Its Uses in America." *Proceedings of the American Antiquarian Society*, Oct. 1916, 264–272.

Plumb, J. H. "The First Flourishing of Children's Books." In *Early Children's Books and Their Illustration*, by Gerald Gottlieb, xvii–xxx. New York: Pierpont Morgan Library; Boston: Godine, 1975.

Polsky, Richard. *Getting to Sesame Street: Origins of the Children's Television Workshop*. New York: Praeger, 1974.

Pratt, Mary Louise. *Imperial Eyes: Travel Writing and Transculturation*. New York: Routledge, 1992.

Praz, Mario. *Studies in Seventeenth-Century Imagery*. 2 vols. London: Warburg Institute, 1939.

Presley, John. "What Does Grading Mean, Anyway?" Paper presented at the 16th Annual Meeting of the Southeastern Conference on English in the Two-Year College, Biloxi, Miss., Feb. 19–21, 1981.

Propp, Vladimir. *Morphology of the Folktale.* 2d ed. Rev. and ed. Louis A. Wagner, trans. Laurence Scott. American Folklore Society Bibliographical and Special Series, vol. 9; Indiana University Research Center in Anthropology, Folklore, and Linguistics, Publication 10. Austin: University of Texas Press, 1968.

Réage, Pauline. *Story of O.* Trans. Sabine d'Estrée. New York: Ballantine, 1965.

Rebora, Carrie, and Paul Staiti. *John Singleton Copley in America.* New York: Metropolitan Museum of Art, 1995.

Richardson, Robert D., Jr. *Emerson: The Mind on Fire.* Berkeley: University of California Press, 1995.

Rood, Wilhelmus. *Comenius and the Low Countries: Some Aspects of Life and Work of a Czech Exile in the Seventeenth Century.* Amsterdam: Van Gendt, 1970.

Rose, Jane. "Conduct Books for Women." In *Nineteenth-Century Women Learn to Write,* ed. Catherine Hobbs, 37–58. Charlottesville: University of Virginia Press, 1995.

Rosenbach, A. S. W. *Early American Children's Books.* New York: Kraus Reprint Corporation, 1966.

Ruscha, Edward. *Words without Thoughts Never to Heaven Go.* New York: Abrams, 1988.

Ryan, Mary Patricia. *The Empire of the Mother: American Writing about Domesticity, 1830–1865.* New York: Haworth, 1982.

Sadler, John Edward. *J. A. Comenius and the Concept of Universal Education.* London: Allen & Unwin, 1966.

Samuels, Shirley, ed. *The Culture of Sentiment.* New York: Oxford University Press, 1992.

Sanderson, Dorothy Hurlbut. *They Wrote for a Living: A Bibliography of the Works of Susan Bogert Warner and Anna Bartlett Warner.* West Point, N.Y.: Constitution Island Association, 1976.

Scharnhorst, Gary, ed. *The Critical Response to Nathaniel Hawthorne's "The Scarlet Letter."* New York: Greenwood Press, 1992

Schmandt-Besserat, Denise. *Before Writing.* Vol. 1: *From Counting to Cuneiform.* Austin: University of Texas Press, 1992.

Schultz, Stanley K. *The Culture Factory: Boston Public Schools, 1789–1860.* New York: Oxford University Press, 1973.

Sedgwick, Eve Kosofsky. *Between Men: English Literature and Male Homosocial Desire.* New York: Columbia University Press, 1985.

Seltzer, Mark. *Bodies and Machines.* New York: Routledge, 1992.

Senner, Wayne M., ed. *The Origins of Writing.* Lincoln: University of Nebraska Press, 1989.

Shaver, Alice, and Chester Shaver. *Wordsworth's Library: A Catalogue.* New York: Garland, 1979.

Shesgreen, Sean. *The Criers and Hawkers of London: Engravings and Drawings by Marcellus Laroon.* Aldershot, Hants., Eng.: Scolar Press, 1990.

Shields, David. *Civil Tongues and Polite Letters in British America.* Chapel Hill: University of North Carolina Press, 1997.

Sillar, Frederick Cameron, and Ruth Mary Meyler. *Cats Ancient and Modern.* London: Studio Vista, 1966.

Simpson, David. *Fetishism and Imagination: Dickens, Melville, Conrad.* Baltimore: Johns Hopkins University Press, 1982.

———. *The Politics of American English, 1776–1850.* New York: Oxford University Press, 1986.

Sklar, Kathryn Kish. *Catherine Beecher: A Study in American Domesticity.* New York: Norton, n.d.

Smallwood, Mary Lovett. *An Historical Study of Examinations and Grading Systems in Early American Universities.* Cambridge, Mass.: Harvard University Press, 1935.

Soltow, Lee, and Edward Stevens. *The Rise of Literacy and the Common School in the United States: A Socioeconomic Analysis to 1870.* Chicago: University of Chicago Press, 1981.

Spufford, Margaret. "First Steps in Literacy: The Reading and Writing Experiences of the Humblest Seventeenth-Century Spiritual Autobiographers." *Social History,* 4th ser., 3 (Oct. 1979): 407–435.

———. *Small Books and Pleasant Histories: Popular Fiction and Its Readership in Seventeenth-Century England.* Athens: University of Georgia Press, 1981.

Stallybrass, Peter, and Allon White. *The Politics and Poetics of Transgression.* London: Methuen, 1986.

Stone, Lawrence. *The Family, Sex, and Marriage in England, 1500–1800.* Abridged ed. New York: Harper, 1979.

Strong, Roy. *Art and Power: Renaissance Festivals, 1450–1650.* Woodbridge, Suffolk, Eng.: Boydall Press, 1984.

Stroud, Ronald. "Writing in Ancient Greece." In *The Origins of Writing,* ed. Wayne M. Senner, 103–119. Lincoln: University of Nebraska Press, 1989.

Tharp, Louise Hall. *The Peabody Sisters of Salem.* Boston: Little, Brown, 1950.

Thompson, Stith. *Motif-Index of Folk Literature.* 6 vols. Bloomington: Indiana University Press, 1966.

Ticknor, Caroline. *Hawthorne and His Publisher.* Boston: Houghton Mifflin, 1913.

Tompkins, Jane. "Masterpiece Theater: The Politics of Hawthorne's Literary Reputation." In *Sensational Designs: The Cultural Work of American Fiction, 1790–1860,* 13–39. New York: Oxford University Press, 1985.

Tschichold, Jan. *Treasury of Alphabets and Lettering.* Trans. Wolf von Eckardt. New York: Design Books, 1992.

Tuer, Andrew. *History of the Horn Book* (1897). New York: Benjamin Blom, 1968.

Turnbull, G. H. *Hartlib, Dury, and Comenius: Gleanings from Hartlib's Papers.* London: Hodder & Stoughton, 1947.

Tyack, David, and Elisabeth Hansot. *Learning Together: A History of Coeducation in American Schools.* New Haven: Yale University Press; New York: Russell Sage Foundation, 1990.

van Gennep, Arnold. *The Rites of Passage.* Trans. Monika P. Vizedom and Gabrielle L. Caffee. Chicago: University of Chicago Press, 1960.

van Vliet, P., and A. J. Vanderjagt, eds. *Johannes Amos Comenius (1592–1670).* Amsterdam: Royal Netherlands Academy of Arts and Sciences, 1994.

Voegelin, Erminie W. "Swallow Stories." In *Standard Dictionary of Folklore, Mythology, and Legend,* ed. Maria Leach, 2:1091. New York: Funk & Wagnall, 1950.

von Mücke, Dorothea. *Virtue and the Veil of Illusion: Generic Innovation*

and the Pedagogical Project in Eighteenth-Century Literature.
Stanford: Stanford University Press, 1991.

Wakefield, Neville. "Ed Ruscha: Material Fictions and Highway Codes."
In *Ed Ruscha: New Paintings and a Retrospective of Works on Paper*,
23–31. London: Anthony d'Offay, 1998.

Warner, Michael. *Letters of the Republic: Publication and the Public
Sphere in Eighteenth-Century America.* Cambridge, Mass.: Harvard
University Press, 1990.

Watters, David. "'I spake as a child': Authority, Metaphor, and *The New-
England Primer.*" *Early American Literature* 20, no. 3 (1985–1986):
193–213.

Weiss, Jane. *See* Susan Warner, "'Many things take my time.'"

Welch, d'Alté. *A Bibliography of American Children's Books Printed
Prior to 1821.* Worcester, Mass.: American Antiquarian Society, 1972.

Wilson, Erika. "*Robinson Crusoe's Farmyard* and *The Wide, Wide World*:
How a Card Game Led to the Publication of a Victorian Best-Seller."
Game Researcher's Notes, Aug. 1992, n.p.

Wishy, Bernard. *The Child and the Republic: The Dawn of Modern
American Child Nurture.* Philadelphia: University of Pennsylvania
Press, 1968.

Wolf II, Edwin. *The Book Culture of a Colonial American City:
Philadelphia Books, Bookmen, and Booksellers.* Oxford: Clarendon,
1988.

Yates, Frances. *The Art of Memory.* Chicago: University of Chicago Press,
1966.

Young, Robert Fitzgibbon. *Comenius and the Indians of New England.*
London: School of Slavonic and East European Studies in the
University of London, King's College, 1929.

Zboray, Ronald J. *A Fictive People: Antebellum Economic Development
and the American Reading Public.* New York: Oxford University Press,
1993.

INDEX

In this index an "f" after a number indicates a separate reference on the next page, and an "ff" indicates separate references on the next two pages. A continuous discussion over two or more pages is indicated by a span of page numbers, e.g., "57–59." *Passim* is used for a cluster of references in close but not consecutive sequence. Illustrations are indicated by page numbers in italics.

alphabet blocks, 19

alphabet games, 236n55

alphabetic realism, 10, 166–71

alphabetization, 8–9, 11; conformation and, 191–92; mother-child relationship and, 10–11; *New England Primer* and, 15–16; poetics of, 96–101, 188; religious conventions for, 15f; role of women in, 9–10; *Scarlet Letter* as allegory of, 191–98; secular conventions for, 16, 18; socialization and, 5, 100–101, 103; as term, 4, 6–7

The Alphabet Ladder (1822), 1, 3, 3–4, 75

"The Alphabet Tattoo" (narrative alphabet), 90–91, 97

The Alphabet Turn'd Posture-Master, see The Comical Hotch-Potch, or the Alphabet Turn'd Posture-Master

Alsted, Johann, 232n34

American Spelling Book (Webster), 132

anchoring, 49, 139

animals: Borges's typology of, 92; Comenian phonology and, 33–38, 43; Comenian taxonomy and, 29–33; distinction between children and, 103f; festive discipline mode and, 76; in *New England Primer*, 45; prior to Comenius, 232n32. *See also* Cat and Fiddle image

anthropomorphism, 132–34

Apple Pie image: *Child's New Play-Thing* and, 65, 66, 68; *Dunigan's History of an Apple Pie* (1843–1848), 69; *The History of an Apple Pie* (by Z), 70; internalization and, 85; *Tom Thumb's Play-Book* and, 68

Arac, Jonathan, 265n22

arbitrary arrangement, *see* ordering

Archer image: *Child's New Play-Thing* and, 65, 67, 68; encyclopedic alphabets and, 95; *The old alphabet with new explanations, for the Tommy Thumbs of Yankeedom* (1846), 72; tableau format and, 111–12; *Tom Thumb's Play-Book* and, 68, 71–72

architectural space, 1, 2, 26–27, 111–19

Ariès, Philippe, 61

Aristotle, 29

art of reading, 8, 41–42. *See also* reading

Ashton-Warner, Sylvia, 252n27

autoeroticism, 171, 187, 262n43, 264n15

Bakhtin, Mikhail, 5–6, 85–86, 147–48, 149

Barthes, Roland, 48–49, 95, 109, 123, 178, 262n6; reality effect and, 167–68

battledore, *see* hornbook

Baym, Nina, 173

Beecher, Catherine: *Duty of American Women*, 257n15

tural Observations on the Origin and Progress of Alphabetic Writing, 205
Debord, Guy, 246n57
de Certeau, Michel, 269n8
Defoe, Daniel: *Robinson Crusoe*, 63f, 121, 121, 145–47, 167, 256n12
de Saussure, Ferdinand, 178
Dimmesdale (character), 189, 203–6
Dionysius of Halicarnassus, 203
disconnection, 144, 153
"discourse networks," 250n18
disorderly woman image, 243n36
Dolis, John, 264n17
domestic ideology, 9–10, 113–18, 179–81, 248n6. *See also* maternal, the
Dominici, Giovanni, 238n2
Douglas, Mary, 229n14
Dunce image, 75f. *See also* Zany image
Dunigan's History of an Apple Pie (1843–1848), 69
Dutch painting, 95, 109

E (letter), 220
Eachard, John, 242n29
eating, *see* consumption; hunger; internalization
education: corporal punishment and, 260n31; grading systems and, 216–19; Mann's opposition to the alphabet in, 131–37; maternal influence and, 126–31;

memory art and, 5, 62, 240n19, 252n27; mother-child model and, 104; power of visual image in, 57–60, 62; priority of alphabet in, 31–33; public schooling and, 55, 259n30; Reformation and, 26–27; republican discourse and, 55–57, 72–74; roles of women in, 105–6; shift in views of learning and, 1–3; of women, 127–28, 130–31, 247n3. *See also* literacy; maternal, the; religious pedagogy
Edwards, Jonathan, 58
Eliade, Mircea, 25
"Ellen Montgomery's Bookshelf" (series), 146, 256n11
emblems, 44, 96f, 113, 124, 265n26; Ellen Montgomery character and, 147, 149–50, 160–66; *F House* and, 211ff; *The Scarlet Letter* and, 198–203
Emile (Rousseau), 62–64, 119–21, 241n20
"empire of things," 95, 109
encyclopedic alphabets, 95–96
encyclopedism, 28–31, 91, 232n31
The Entertaining History of Tommy Gingerbread: A Little Boy, Who Lived upon Learning (1796), 86–87
Erasmus, 19, 238n2
erotics of the alphabet: in *The Scarlet Letter*, 185–89, 191, 198–206; in *The Wide, Wide,*

grading systems, 11, 216–19

Grammatica emblem, 2, 106, 115, 197

Greenwood, James: *London and Paris Vocabulary*, 27

Gules, as term, 199f, 201–2

gutturals, 201–3

Hanged man image, *116*

Harlequin, 77, 132, 244n40. *See also* Zany image

Harris, Benjamin, 233n38; "The Fables of Young Aesop, with Their Morals," 234n45; *The Holy Bible in Verse*, 61, 236n55, 240n12; print culture and, 39f. *See also The New England Primer*

Harris, Roy, 230n20, 245n43, 264n20

Hartlib, Samuel, 26

Harvard College, 26, 207, 230n22

Hawthorne, Julian, 176

Hawthorne, Nathaniel: *The American Notebooks*, 176–79; anatomized imagery and, 263n7; autobiography of "The Custom-House" and, 181, 182–91; letter-men and, 176–81, 188–89, 262n6; letter W and, 254n1; "The New Adam and Eve," 206–8; "The Village Uncle," 182–83, 207; West biography and, 249n14. *See also The Scarlet Letter*

Hawthorne, Sophia Peabody (Mrs. Nathaniel Hawthorne), 187, 263n8

Hawthorne, Una, 176

Heartman, Charles, 228n1

The History of an Apple Pie (by Z), 70

The History of Little Goody Two-Shoes (1775), 83f

Homer, 264n20

homoeroticism, 137–38, 253n31 254n3

Horace, 245n48

hornbook, 1, 19–20, 20, 23, 80, 84, 227n1

"The House That Jack Built" (rhyme), 240n19

Huckleberry Finn (Twain), 257n20

hunger, 245n47. *See also* consumption; internalization

"hybrid formation," 51

iconography: Catholic, 20–26; Hawthorne and, 198–202; icon-alphabet in the *Primer*, 42–43; movement from orality to literacy and, 100

The Illuminated A, B, C (c. 1850), *112*

The Illuminated American Primer (1844), 113–18, *117*, *118*

The Illustrated Primer (1847), 104

"imagetext," 211–12, 215. *See also F House*

image-text relation: Comenian alphabet and, 27–38; encyclope-

pire of things" and, 95; Fenn's *Mother's Remarks* and, 121–26; letters as, 126, 134, 182–91, 222–23; maternal narrative and, 138–40; "object lesson" and, 119–20, 122; synecdoche and, 99–100, 184; vs. signs of things, 63–64; Warner's *Wide, Wide, World* and, 152–57, 259n28. *See also* alphabet array

Ong, Walter, 30, 109, 253n36

Opie, Iona, 86, 242n33, 243n29

Opie, Peter, 86, 242n33, 243n29

oral practice: "book of cries" and, 80; Catholic iconography and, 23–24; Comenian alphabet and, 38–39; link between literacy and, 68, 71, 100; *New England Primer* and, 40–41, 48, 68; transmission of knowledge and, 4–5; visual image and, 37–38. *See also* consumption; internalization; rhetoric

Orbis Sensualium Pictus (Comenius), 19, 27–38; alphabet phonology from, 33, 34–35, 36; "Arts Belonging to the Speech," 32; comparisons between *New England Primer* and, 38–39; defining epigraphs in, 29–33; "God" and, 30, 33; "The Invitation," 28–29, 29; "Temperance," 31; "The Tormenting of Malefactors," 30, 115

ordering: alphabet array and, 91–96; as alphabetic function, 84; consistent sequencing of alphabet and, 83; gender and, 111; narrative and, 121; synecdoche and, 97, 98–100

Paglia, Camille, 254n1

paideia, 28, 74, 232n31

paintings, 11–12, 93–95, 109, 211–16. *See also* Ruscha, Edward

Parker, Patricia, 194

Peabody, Elizabeth Palmer, 175

Peabody, Mary Tyler, 137–40, 160, 179–81, 263n8; *Primer of Reading and Drawing*, 253n34

Peabody, Sophia, *see* Hawthorne, Sophia Peabody

Pearl (character), 196–98

pedagogical alphabet, as genre, 9

Pepys, Samuel, 236n55

Perrault, Charles: *Histories, or Tales of Past Time*, 64

personification, *see* prosopopoeia

Pestalozzi, Johann Heinrich, 248n8

phonetic instability, 132–34

Pictured A, B, C (c. 1850), 90

pleasure: books as source of, 152; education and, 134–35

Plimpton, George, 227n1

Poe, Edgar Allan: "The Purloined Letter," 174; "William Wilson," 143

popular culture, 213

postmodernism, 11, 215–16. *See*

also grading systems; painting; *Sesame Street*

posture-master, 88–89. *See also The Comical Hotch-Potch, or the Alphabet Turn'd Posture-Master* (1782, 1814)

Pratt, Mary Louise, 96

A Pretty Pocket-Book (1787), 87

primer, origin of, 19, 228n3. *See also The New England Primer*

print culture: Benjamin Harris and, 39f; Comenian alphabet and, 27–28, 40; early alphabetic representation in, 19–26

property, children as, 73, 155–57

Propp, Vladimir, 51, 84

prosopopoeia, 96, 97–99, 106–8, 188. *See also* Apple Pie image; Archer image

Proteus, 132, 252n24

Prynne, Hester (character), 193–95, 201

public-private distinction, 191f, 200. *See also* commerce

Puritanism, 43, 51, 60

pye, as term, 242n30

Q (letter), 254n3, 265n25

Quack-doctor image, 76, 79, 80

Ramus, Petrus, 4–5, 232n34

Rational Sports (Fenn), 121, 121

Rauschenberg, Robert: *Factum I*, 268n1

reading: alphabetic functions and, 84; excitation and, 165–66, 187–88, 254n6, 264n15; hallucination and, 180, 189, 199, 246n51. *See also* art of reading

"The Reality Effect" (Barthes), 167–68

Reformation, 57. *See also* Catholic iconography; *Orbis Sensualium Pictus*; Puritanism

Reisch, Gregorius: *Margarita Philosophica*, 1, 2

religious pedagogy: Anglican "Scripture Catechism" and, 68, 71; Catholic iconography and, 20–26; power of images and, 57–58; street signs and, 52

The Renowned History of Giles Gingerbread (1768), 84, 87, 88, 245n50

repetition, 24–26, 41, 186

replication, maternal, 147–50f, 157–60, 161ff, 181

representation: as alphabetic function, 84; body alphabets and, 88–91; emblem and, 96, 97; gender and, 111; maternal voice and, 104; *Sesame Street* and, 221; synecdoche and, 98

rhetoric, 4–5, 38–39, 227nn2, 3, 253n36. *See also* memory; oral practice

rhyming Bibles, 61, 236n55, 240n12

ritual, 19–26, 58

Robbins, Chandler: *Remarks on the Disorders of Literary Men*, 188

Robinson Crusoe (Defoe), 63f,
121, 121, 145–47, 167, 256n12
Robinson Crusoe's Farmyard
(Warner and Warner), 146, 167
Rogers, John, 41
romantic pedagogy, 72–74
Rosenbach, A. S., 234n46,
241n24, 245n48
Rousseau, Jean-Jacques: Emile,
62–64, 121, 241n20
Rowson, Susanna: Charlotte
Temple, 257n21
The Royal Alphabet; or, Child's
Best Instructor (1787), 81
Royal Oak image, 50, 51, 235n51
The Royal Primer (1796), 82
Ruscha, Edward, 211–16, 268n1
Rush, Benjamin, 61, 72–74, 156

The Scarlet Letter (Hawthorne), 6,
11; as allegory of alphabetization, 191–98; erotics of alphabetization and, 185–89, 191,
198–206; Hawthorne's own
alphabetization and, 175–81;
letter A in, 11, 173–74, 177,
182–83, 193; as rite of institution, 206–9; stages of narrator's
relation to A in, 182–91; tombstone epitaph in, 198–202,
206
Seltzer, Mark, 253n32, 259n29
semiotics: Hawthorne and,
177–81, 188–89, 262n6; Mary
Mann and, 179–81
"sentimental possession," 155–56

Sesame Street (television show),
11–12, 219–23; Learning about
Letters video, 271n21
sexuality: resistant narratives and,
133–34, 137–41; The Scarlet
Letter and, 185–91, 196, 201–2.
See also autoeroticism; erotics of
the alphabet; homoeroticism;
mother's lips
Shakespeare, William: Timon of
Athens, 201
shop signs, 48–49, 234n48,
235n51
shorthand, 164, 260n35
signs, see semiotics
Sigourney, Lydia Huntley, 103,
248n6; Letters to Mothers,
255n6
sound image, 33–37, 43f
spelling books, 132–38
Staiti, Paul, 94
Stallybrass, Peter, 244n37
Stations of the Cross, 24, 230n17
Stennett, R., 82
stereotypes, 95–96
Story of O (Réage), 170
storytelling, and the alphabet,
64–72
Stowe, Harriet Beecher, 155
street signs, 235n51. See also
advertising; commerce; shop
signs
Sunday school, 233n37
surveillance theme, in The Scarlet
Letter, 262n5
swallow alphabets, 85–88

Watts, Isaac, 59; "On the Education of Youth," 239n11
Webster, James, 105, 108, 246n2. *See also The Comical Hotch-Potch, or the Alphabet Turn'd Posture-Master*
Webster, Noah, 55, 72, 73; *American Spelling Book*, 132
Weeks, William R., 251n23
West, Benjamin, 94, 127–28, 249n14
Whig ideology, 132–33, 252n24
White, Allon, 244n37
The Wide, Wide, World (Warner), 10, 143–71; alphabetic realism and, 166–71; erotics of alphabetization and, 170–71; feminine transparency and, 157–60; maternal affect and, 151–55; narrative authority and, 166–71; objects and, 152–57, 259n28; parallel with *Robinson Crusoe*, 145–47; plot of, 257n19; replication and, 147–50f, 157–60, 161ff; "self" values and, 251n20; textual network in, 150–52, 155; "wide world" as term and, 144–45, 255n7; woman as emblem of literacy and, 160–66
Wilkins, John, 175, 203; *Essay towards a Real Character and a Philosophical Language*, 204
women: education of, 247n3;

representation of, 106; transmission of the alphabet and, 103; transparency and, 58, 159–60; work of, 162–63, 260n34. *See also* disorderly woman image; maternal, the
Worcester, Joseph Emerson, 175
words: men as, 177, 179; as substitute for letters, 134–36, 138–40; unlinked from language, 215–16
Wordsworth, William: "Essay upon Epitaphs," 200
worldly alphabet, *see* alphabet array
World Wide Web, 144
writing: in the Bible, 265n25; development of allegory and, 265n22; in Homer, 264n20; in Warner's *Wide, Wide, World*, 163–66

X (letter), 90
Xerxes, 50, 265n25

Y (letter), 144
youth: symbolic function of, 148
Youth image, *75f*, 75–76, 78
"Youth's Battledoor" (c. 1828), 93

Zany image, 74–81 *passim*, 75–76f, 115
Zavery, G. J., 77